Ben Nimmo

was born in Kendal in 1972 and grew up in Wolverhampton, where he still lives. He attended Gonville and Caius College, Cambridge. As a musician he has played in a brass band in New Zealand, recorded a CD with his University Swing Band and played in the Albert Hall. He has spent time helping to rebuild a twelfth century castle in France and teaching scuba diving in Egypt and Belize. He now travels and writes full time.

BEN NIMMO

Pilgrim Snail

Busking to Santiago

Flamingo
An Imprint of HarperCollinsPublishers

f l a m i n g o	**The term 'Original' signifies publication direct into paperback with no preceding British hardback edition.**
O R I G I N A L	**The Flamingo Original series publishes fine writing at an affordable price at the point of first publication.**

Flamingo
An Imprint of HarperCollins*Publishers*
77–85 Fulham Palace Road,
Hammersmith, London W6 8JB

www.fireandwater.com

First published in Great Britain by Flamingo 2001
9 8 7 6 5 4 3 2 1

Author photograph by Tom Battye

A catalogue record for this book is
available from the British Library

ISBN 0 00 710473 1

Set in Sabon by
Rowland Phototypesetting Ltd,
Bury St Edmunds, Suffolk

Printed and bound in Great Britain by
Omnia Books Limited, Glasgow

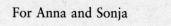

For Anna and Sonja

ACKNOWLEDGEMENTS

None of this would have been possible without the help of hundreds of friends and strangers. I'd particularly like to thank: Freda Lightfoot and Lucinda McNeile, for advice and support; Jeremy Atiyah, for good lessons; Sarah Barrell, for being on the end of the phone when I needed it; Mandy Noble at Jessop's, and the Birmingham University branch of Endsleigh Insurance, for service above and beyond the call of duty; Sam and Martin Rich, for endless hospitality; Ian Holden and Bernard Trafford, for music; David Iddon and Charles Martin, who drummed an education into me when I wanted to be tromboning.

Above all, thanks to all those on the way who saw a madman with a trombone and thought he was doing something worthwhile.

CONTENTS

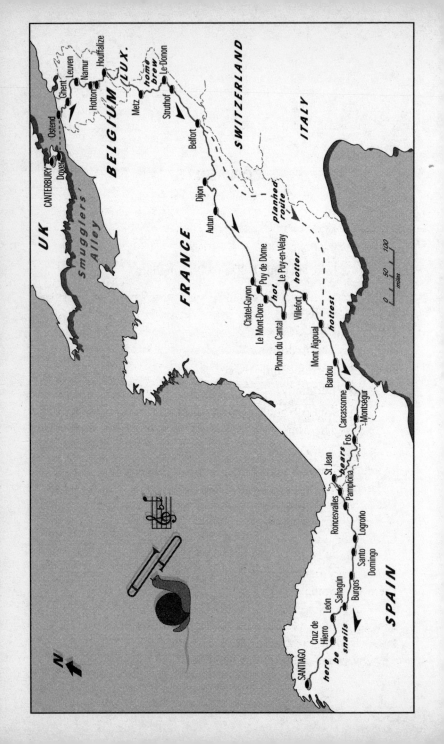

PROLOGUE

I was standing in the Cathedral staring at chickens when I heard the music.

Four chickens, perched above the altar in the south transept, glaring in beady-eyed insanity at the tomb of Santo Domingo de la Calzada. Two were painted in loving detail on the side panels of a fifteenth-century cage. The other two, in the cage, were real. A steady stream of worshippers walked up to them, genuflected, took photos and walked off. Occasionally one of the birds would crow and shake its head imperiously, precipitating a barrage of flashes from the faithful. Cameras apart, the cathedral was dark and empty. Piped Gregorian chants drifted around the pillars, mingling with a murmur of voices and footsteps. Only the crowing splintered the reverent hush. I watched in delight. I'd walked two thousand miles to get here and I thought I'd seen it all, but chicken worship was a new one.

The background music was halfway through a four-part Gloria when someone started playing *Tequila* outside.

You're not generally supposed to jump up and shout 'Yee-haa!' in Spanish cathedrals, otherwise I would have taken off like a champagne cork. Something about high-powered salsa blows every fuse in my brain, and whoever was playing out there was doing it with enough adrenaline for a battalion of Bond films. Not even the chickens could compete. Before I had time to think I was back in the ticket-office pulling my trombone from my rucksack.

'¿Qué pasa?' asked the receptionist, as I flung the instrument together with a crash of brass. 'What's happening?': a reasonable question under the circumstances.

'¡No sé!' I replied breathlessly, and bolted.

I'd barely set foot outside when a pretty girl pounced on me. This practically never happens, especially not outside provincial Spanish cathedrals on a wet Saturday lunchtime: I was still reeling when she shoved a straw hat at me and shouted '¡Dinero!' over the noise of the band. She had to shout. Three trumpets, three trombones and three saxes can make a hell of a noise when they want to.

'¿Qué?' I yelled back with my usual alertness. Her eyes flashed. My wit had aroused her passion.

'¡Dinero! Money!' she shouted, 'stupid foreigner' ringing in every syllable. '¡Fiestaaa!'

I gaped.

'Hey, trombone!' someone yelled. We both spun round and came eye to eye with a grinning drummer, young, bald, inundated with sweat. He had a snare drum hanging round his neck and a bongo strapped to each hip, and he was laying into them like Mike Tyson. Behind him the band were pushing the instruments so hard you could hear their ribs crack. The street was full of dancers, young, smartly dressed and incandescently drunk.

'Come and play!'

The band swung in around me. Adrenaline boiled through my veins, two thousand miles' worth of aches and weariness vanished in A flat, and I swung the trombone up onto my shoulder and took off for the stratosphere. The drummer threw his head back and whooped.

'Let's march!' he yelled, and we marched.

Santo Domingo's a small place. In British terms it would be a rural market town, quiet, comfortable and completely left behind by the new towns all around, but there aren't any new towns in northern Spain. We marched along narrow medieval streets with the dancers streaming ahead of us accosting all comers. Someone was letting off thunder flashes. Every time one detonated the dancers cheered. The noise shook the walls. Up ahead, whistles were blowing. We followed them into the main shopping street, all concrete and plate glass. Two death-defying teenagers had stopped the traffic, and the dancers cheered again and went waltzing from car to car demanding beer money. Half a dozen middle-aged Spanish matrons emerged from a dress shop to watch, smiling nostalgically. Two policemen exchanged jokes with the revellers. Nobody seemed disturbed by our merry mob. We flooded into a bar. The patrons flung the doors wide, then got out fast. They were laughing. What was going on? This wouldn't happen in Britain. Our lead trumpet launched into *When the Saints* and I stopped worrying. Mere urban anarchy can't hope to compete with Dixieland jazz.

Curiosity revived three pubs later. 'What's happening?' I shouted over the sound of the Spice Girls, as the band took a breather and a drink. The revellers were dancing on the tables and singing along karaoke style ('Eef you wanna be my loverrrr . . .'), which is something you don't often get the chance to appreciate at two in the afternoon.

'Birthday!' replied the lead sax: thick black hair, hawk nose, a grin so cool he could advertise toothpaste.

'Whose?'

He swept his arm around. 'Everyone!'

Twins? Times fifty? I was so bemused I missed the drummer's question.

'Pardon?'

'What are you doing here?' he shouted again.

I told him, but he didn't believe me, so I told him again.

'Serious?'

'Serious!'

He turned and shouted something to the others. They went into a huddle. Occasionally a head popped up to stare at me. I picked up the odd word through the din: 'Inglaterra', 'trombon', '¡loco!', which pretty well summed it up. Then the drummer came back, grinning.

'Want to play a solo?' he yelled. This is not the kind of invitation you can refuse.

'Right!' He shoved his way to the PA system and grabbed the microphone. A hideous burst of feedback shook every glass in the room. The singing tailed off into a bewildered buzz.

'Senores y senoritas, we have a surprise guest star with us!' Every eye that could still focus turned on me, and I fought down the urge to crawl inside the trombone and hide. 'This is Ben, who's just walked here from England – for charity.'

It was so quiet you could have heard a cigarette drop.

'Want to hear him play?'

It wasn't quiet.

They were still shouting as I took off into *Scotland the Brave*. After four bars the band kicked in behind me. Someone recognized the tune and started dancing, and then they were all at it, fifty drunken teenagers in a smoke-wreathed bar in Spain listening to a salsa band and dancing the Highland Fling, in a town where they keep chickens in the cathedral. It was turning into a good day.

INTRODUCTION

Belize to Birmingham

'Though this be madness, yet there is method in't . . .' (*Hamlet* II, ii, 211)

Practically nobody walks into northern Spain with a trombone and a rucksack by accident, and I'm not about to improve the figures. I'd been aiming to get there for seven months, and there I was, bang on time. It's pretty remarkable. My career up to that date had taken me through a flirtation with professional tromboning, a degree in medieval heroic literature, summer jobs as a bricklayer in a medieval castle, and two years as a scuba diving instructor. If you can spot the well-planned route, you're a better reader than I am.

It all went pear-shaped in 1998, just before my twenty-sixth birthday. At the time I was working as a diver and trainer for Raleigh International, a youth development charity, in Belize. I was part of a thirty-strong staff team leading a hundred young volunteers in projects as diverse as coral reef mapping, wildlife population studies and the construction of school-houses. It was my second expedition with Raleigh, and I'd already volunteered to do two more in Chile. I believed in the organization and what it achieves. I still do.

One of the staff was a girl called Anna, team leader on one of the school-building projects. We met at Field Base during the staff induction fortnight: thirty of us in an old colonial house by the Belize River, trying to get nine projects off the ground. It was intense. Friendships grew quickly. Within a week we were spending all our free time together. She taught me backgammon. We practised four-handed juggling together, played basketball, went canoeing up the river. By the end of the fortnight I was as close to falling for her as I ever have been with anyone: a buoyant, grinning whirlwind in a deep-red bush shirt, with short-cropped red-gold hair. She was less sure of me. I told myself to wait and hope. I wasn't in a hurry, and she was worth waiting for.

When the volunteers arrived we took them into the jungle for initial training. It was like being a parent to fifteen teenagers at once: we hardly saw one another. After jungle camp we barely managed a couple of hours together before we were deployed out to site for the first three-week phase. She was nervous. Could she run a building-site? Could she manage her team? The future was full of doubt. There was nothing I could say. We sat with our arms around each other for a while. Then it was time to go.

I didn't hear from her at all during phase one. We'd planned a group get-together halfway through, but a storm blew up and pinned my group to our island. Radio communications were erratic, post non-existent: we relied on rumour to keep track of each other. It wasn't until we met at Field Base to swap our groups around that I saw her, harried, but grinning. It had been hard, but she'd managed. The school was on track. Her volunteers loved her. I could see it in their faces when they stood up to tell the rest about their project. She shone with pride as they talked. Three weeks, and all her doubts were gone.

We shared a bus to return to our sites for Second Phase. For the first time, we had time to relax and chat. We barely stopped to breathe. She was alight with ideas. I'd never seen her so happy. She was in the right place, with the right people, doing what was important. Her school was going to be the best in

Central America. It was impossible not to be fired with her enthusiasm. I'd already been toying with the idea of heading overland to Chile, rather than flying home. One look at her and my mind was made up. You couldn't be prosaic when Anna was there. She laughed when I told her my decision – then asked if I wanted to spend some time travelling with her. That wasn't hard to decide either. When my crew left the bus we touched fists Belizean style and said simply, 'See you later'. I was glowing when I reached the island. Even my volunteers noticed.

Two weeks later we heard by radio that she'd disappeared. Three days later she was found murdered.

Raleigh gave us the option: pull out or stay. As an expedition, we decided to stay. The killing wasn't Raleigh's fault, it wasn't Anna's fault, it was only the fault of the two thugs who did the deed. Anna had believed in what we were doing. To end things would have been a betrayal. Her school was put on hold until the killers were caught, but the other sites kept running. We needed each other. Coming home would have put us among strangers.

We kept each other going for a month. Then, in due time, we came home.

It was a hard homecoming. I'd been working in the tropics for two yeas, and the cold and the grey of the British October sank into my heart. After a months' homelessness I moved in with an expedition friend: Emma, who'd been Field Base radio operator during the search for Anna. We'd grown very close in that final month. She was working as an art teacher in Birmingham. She had a spare room. I didn't know what I wanted to do, except that it wasn't diving. I needed a room. Bingo.

Thoughts burned me. Anna was special, but I'd never said goodbye. She'd inspired me, and I'd never said so. She'd cared about the school, and never seen it completed. (British Army engineers finished it a month after we left.) I wanted to do something for her. I didn't know what. Then Raleigh opened a fund in her memory, to provide her school with books.

Illumination came in a sleet-storm on the Welsh marches. I'd gone west of Shrewsbury for a day's walking with another expedition friend. We were talking about jazz. I started wondering if I could still play the trombone. I hadn't touched it since I became a diver, it's hard to combine the two. Then the sky clouded over and the sleet hit. As I ducked I found myself thinking, 'I've got to get out of this country.' Something clicked in my mind. I turned to Aidie and said, 'I'm going to walk to Gibraltar with the trombone in honour of Anna.'

He looked at me with a lopsided grin.

'Where from?'

'Here.'

'Great idea. Go for it.'

And that was that.

It's not actually difficult to plan a two thousand mile charity walk. Everyone knows you'd have to be crazy to do it, so I was just fine. The secret is to be crazy in the right way. You need to combine completely unrealistic goals that no sane person would consider for an instant (well, would you think of taking a trombone for a walk across a continent?) with the mind-numbing pedantry of an Army quartermaster. Imagine an accountant serenading his lady-love with 'Fly me to the moon, and this is how much fuel you'll need.' In my deepest soul, I am that accountant. Having decided to build my own personal stairway to Heaven, I did the mental equivalent of shopping around for two-by-four and nails.

For four months, my life was ruled by lists: kit lists, training lists, lists of sponsors, lists of pieces to play, lists of lists. I lived in a paper jungle, only emerging to court exhaustion in the hills. This must be how Sir Ranulph Fiennes feels all the time, I thought, my tongue furry with licking stamps for begging letters. An encouraging idea. I spent enough on stamps to keep the local post office in business, bought enough trekking gear for a guerrilla army, invested in a battered old trombone to replace my beloved six-kilo monster and fell in love with it at first blow. I changed my travel plan on four successive whims: Gibraltar looked boring, central Spain looked flat, there was a long-range footpath running from Ostend to the Mediterranean which looked too good to miss, I wanted to see some medieval sights. More by luck than by judgement I ended up with an itinerary that started in Canterbury, crossed the Channel from Dover to Ostend, wound down across the Alps, through Provence and Languedoc and over the Pyrenees, and finally followed the traditional pilgrim route to Santiago de Compostela, about which I knew absolutely nothing, except that it has been a place of pilgrimage for 1000 years. I'm not a Christian, but somehow that seemed an appropriate destination for a memorial walk. Knowing that I knew nothing, I spent an inordinate amount of time reading up on the history of the lands I was going to cross. Reading up on current events might have made more sense, but I used to be a medievalist. The passion lingers.

I discovered that the most important attribute any wannabe explorer can have is a housemate like Emma. It takes a very special kind of person to come home from a hard day's teaching to find the house strewn with papers, six messages on the answerphone and a trombonistic din shaking the upstairs windows, and not call for the police. Em was a star. She didn't mind sitting and listening as I hammered my lip and my repertoire back into shape. She didn't mind the flood of letters that jammed the doorstep when my sponsors' replies started rolling in. She didn't mind the constant stream of journalists who turned the front room into a photographic studio. She didn't even mind when I got more phone calls than she did. Greater love hath no house-mate than this . . .

The year turned almost unnoticed. January and February went by, and the suburban deserts of Birmingham began to tingle with the coming of spring. The shops turned red with

Valentine's Day marketing, then yellow with pre-Easter desperation. Emma flew into a horticultural frenzy in our three square inches of garden. I spent hours staring longingly at maps. Spring always gives me itchy feet, and this year was no exception. D-Day, 28 March, seemed a lifetime away. I spent all the time I could out in the fresh air, walking round local businesses asking for sponsorship, and began to rediscover my faith in human nature. Birmingham may not be the crown jewel of British architecture, but the people are brilliant. Their generosity left me lost for words. I made more and more trips to the hills, culminating in an ascent of Snowdon through thigh-deep drifts, and discovered how truly mountain-mad the British are: despite winds straight from the Pole, there must have been twenty people on the summit, so I proved how mountain-mad I am and serenaded them with *Summertime* and *Hot Toddy*. By the time I got back to Birmingham again it was raining, and spring might have been an Ice Age away.

I changed the plan once more before I set off. I'd gone to London to update Raleigh on proceedings, and while I was there I caught up with my two best friends, Samantha and Martin, both veterans of my student days. They had bad news. Martin's mother Edwina had just been diagnosed as having multiple sclerosis (MS). She's been a second mother to all Martin's friends. That she should have a disease as cruel as MS was so unfair it took my breath away. On the spot I decided to share my fundraising efforts between Anna's fund and the MS Society. Anna wouldn't have minded.

I got away to the hills once more before I left for good. I wanted to reassure myself that my fitness and map-reading skills were up to scratch, so I enrolled on a mountain leadership course in the Lake District, and together with a wonderful variety of other hopefuls spent a happy week swinging off high cliffs, fording freezing rivers, navigating across trackless quagmires and generally learning how to do all the things I hoped I'd avoid on the walk. I carried my full expedition rucksack with me, a thirty-kilo penance which was promptly dubbed the 'Pack From Hell'. It almost destroyed my knees before one of the instructors took pity on me and lent me two walking-poles, saving my joints from nine months' misery. With the camaraderie of suffering we developed the concept of the 'Bad Sack Day', which is like a bad hair day but heavier. Shivering in our sleeping-bags after the river-crossing afternoon, we swore to give our instructors a Bad Sack Day of their own before we finished – then fell asleep, too exhausted even to plot.

The course culminated in an overnight expedition assessing our pinpoint map-reading skills. We bivouacked in an abandoned bothy, and when it was dark made one last sortie into a sleet-storm to practise really blind navigation. Back in the shelter, cosily lit by candles, head-torches and a couple of camping stoves, my trombone and I were solemnly invited to entertain the masses. As I played, one of the team set up a rhythm section on three tin pots and a Sigg water-bottle, two of the others sang along, the wind wailed outside, the stone walls rang with music. None of us wanted to go to bed. Some evenings should last for ever . . . When we finally did crash out my head was buzzing with dreams. There couldn't have been a better omen for the walk.

The next day, as we left the centre for the last time, one of the others came up to me: a girl my age, with glorious wild black hair and the most bewitching eyes I'd ever seen. She put her hand on my arm, stared deeply into my eyes and said, 'I just wanted to tell you. You were wonderful last night,' – and drove away. Bad Sack Day.

And finally it was time to go. On the desk lay a pile of lists, two-thirds of the items crossed off. A file bulged with official letters. Maps and history books careered along the mantelpiece; the last book, half-finished, was in my rucksack for the train journey south. There were a million things I hadn't done, but I didn't care. At least and at last, the paperwork was over.

Em and I shared a last, silent cup of tea. The mad months wouldn't have been possible without her, it hurt to say goodbye. One hug, and she was out of the door in her usual chaos of flying papers, and gone. I went back upstairs, showered, shaved, dressed in my walking gear with ceremonious care, stared at myself in the mirror. Was I really doing this? My rucksack lay ready by the bed. It looked monstrous. I had to be crazy. Didn't I? I looked at myself again. How would I look in a few months' time? There was only one way to find out. I heaved the rucksack onto my back. Ye Gods, it was heavy! For some reason the Blues Brothers came into my head, and I found myself muttering as I shut the bedroom door behind me. *It's a hundred and six miles to Chicago.* I fought my way down the stairs. The rucksack was so wide I had to turn sideways. *We've got a full tank of gas.* One last look at the office. *Half a packet of cigarettes.* A last paranoid run through my own checklist. *It's dark, and we're wearing sunglasses.*

I stepped out of the door, slammed it behind me, posted my keys back through the letter-box, turned, and grinned at an imaginary audience.

Hit it.

It was show time.

PART 1

England

'I will arise an' get 'ence . . .' (Kipling, *Chant-Pagan*)

The show kicked off in Canterbury's Long Market, one of those delightful red-brick precincts which are England's answer to the jewel-decked bazaars of the *Arabian Nights*. It was a brilliant Saturday morning, the shops were overflowing with Easter merchandise and Easter shoppers, all nature seemed to smile and even the *Big Issue* salesmen looked cheerful. In fact, I was probably the only unhappy person within a ten-mile radius. This was the moment of truth. Did I really have the balls to stand up in front of a street full of strangers and trombone them into generosity? Could I remember any of my tunes? Did I even know which end of the instrument was which? I walked down the street in a daze, trying to ignore the stares and desperately looking for the perfect place to set up. My decision-making faculties were melting in a flood of terror. If I didn't get a move on I was going to dissolve on the pavement.

I stopped by a combined bench/litter bin/shrubbery, some urban planner's little piece of immortality. It seemed to have everything: sunshine, visibility, a constant stream of shoppers. Admittedly it also had Canterbury's entire public transport department roaring by twenty feet away, but at least it meant

I could make a quick getaway if it all got too much. I set up my stall for the very first time. Collecting boxes, one for each charity, not too near me, not too far. Emblazoned rucksack on the bench, the magic words coming true at last: 'Canterbury to Santiago de Compostela for Charity'. Water-bottle. My mouth was dry. I took a deep, deep breath and turned to the trombone

I've lost count of the number of times I've been introduced with the words 'This is Ben, he plays the trumpet', so I'd like to take this opportunity to explain that the trombone is the thing which looks like a cross between a paper-clip and a shower attachment beloved of Glenn Miller, *not* the short stumpy thing with valves played by Louis Armstrong. It consists of three parts: mouthpiece, bell, and slide. The mouthpiece is, astonishingly, the round silver bit that sits on your lip. Trumpets and French horns have small ones, trombones and tubas large ones, or at least that's what we always claim. The bell is the business end of the instrument, magnifying the ludicrous raspberry of the mouthpiece into a mellifluous torrent of sound, and it's a very good idea not to get too close to one. Trombones are *loud*. Linking the two is the slide, subject to more innuendoes than the rest of the orchestra put together. The longer it gets, the deeper you go. A thorough lubrication does it no end of good ... it's all true. The slide consists of two fixed inner legs and a mobile outer 'stocking,' which together form a standing column of air. Buzzing air into the mouthpiece oscillates the column and produces a note. Changing the frequency of the lip vibration changes the note in a strict harmonic series: the *Last Post* is a classic example of lip-only playing. Pushing the slide out lengthens the air column and lowers the note. Expert trombonists recognize seven positions on the slide which produce a perfectly pitched note, each a semitone lower than the last. (Unfortunately, inexpert trombonists usually discover about seventy more, all out of tune, and until you've heard a choir of beginners hacking their

2

way through *Swing Low, Sweet Chariot* in four-part harmony
and seventeen-part discord, you've never known the meaning
of pain.) Coordinate lip changes and slide movements and you
have an instrument capable of hitting any note in a three-octave
range, and – far more importantly – sliding between them in
the musical equivalent of pouring glue. Which is the whole
point of being a trombonist.

Clear?

As I screwed the instrument together with a rattle of brass,
a passing tourist looked at me curiously, and I fought down
the mad desire to crawl into my rucksack and hide. Stage fright
may be bad, but compared to street fright it barely nudges the
neurones ... I stuffed my hand up the bell and blew very
quietly, warming my lip up by hopping up and down the harmonics. Everything seemed to be working. My mind ran
around like a frightened squirrel looking for excuses to post-
pone the inevitable. There weren't any. The crunch had come.

I took a deep breath and launched into my overture, a piece
heard in back-stage warm-ups wherever the anarchists of the
brass section congregate to make musical mayhem:

'It's time to play the music, it's time to light the lights.

It's time to meet the Muppets on the Muppet Show
tonight ...'

I was on my way.

The street-fright lasted halfway into the first phrase. Then
my brain worked out that it wasn't the first time I'd picked up
an instrument, my ears stopped roaring and told me that it
sounded okay, my heartbeat dropped back from snare-drum
speeds, my breathing loosened, I realized that I was finally
living the dream, and delight blossomed inside me. I would
have laughed, but it's bad for the embouchure, so I settled for
bumping everything up an octave. Imagine the Muppets theme
sung by the Smurfs and you'll get the idea. Not musical, but
fun.

I went straight from the Muppets into a D minor blues, led

into a funkily swung version of *From Russia With Love*, and discovered that Canterbury likes trombonists. A middle-aged lady with a maternal smile read my rucksack, hesitated over my cash-boxes, dropped a handful of change exactly between the two, said 'Well done' and walked off. A younger woman with a push-chair stopped to watch: her baby's eyes were as big as olives, with a little frown between. Very slowly his face cleared, and he started to smile, then laugh, reaching out to me and dribbling. An armful of amphetamines couldn't have boosted me more than those few drachms of drool. The last thing I saw as his mother pushed him away was his delighted face craning past her legs. Audience satisfaction's a wonderful thing.

From Russia With Love led me, appropriately enough, into *Midnight in Moscow*. I was halfway through when a tall man with an enormous moustache erupted from a department store with his family in tow, pointed, and exclaimed 'I've got one of those!' It hardly seemed polite to blast him point-blank, so I stopped playing, and he bounced up to me like a Labrador puppy, overflowing with his story. The family watched wide-eyed. He'd always loved the trombone (a man of taste), he'd recently bought an instrument of his very own, now could I tell him how to play it? Six and a half minutes into the greatest adventure of my life, I found myself giving a trombone lesson in Canterbury Long Market. That's got to be some kind of record.

Things got better and better. If anyone wants an introduction to the noble art of people-watching, all I can say is, go busking. A massive American came up to me and asked, 'Is that an AH-64?' No, an AH-64 is an attack helicopter, this is a trombone. He forgave me the snotty answer and gave me a dollar, which will be a great boon to charity as soon as I find someone who'll change it commission-free. Two small children who'd somehow escaped the parental eye started to boogie in front of me, then ran right up to me and shyly dropped a lump of chewing-gum into my tin. Another, with parents in tow, ran towards me, ran back, hid behind his mother and finally allowed her to escort him forwards. Together they dropped a pound coin into the box. I bowed as low as I could without ramming the slide into the ground. He backed away wide-eyed, and fled to the shelter of his father's legs. The parents winked at me as they led him away. A young lady in sprayed-on black jeans and high heels hurried by, leading a colossal Rottweiler. The dog took one look at me and stopped dead, enchanted. Mistress hurried on two more steps and slammed to a halt with the kind of jolt you only normally see in Tom and Jerry cartoons. I fought down laughter as she hauled the beast away, leaning against the lead like a polar explorer dragging a sledge. I wished I'd set up a video.

The real problem was finding enough playing-time to finish a piece. Three separate women came to tell me that their husbands were trombonists. Shoppers of all kinds asked me where Santiago was, if I was starting or finishing (evidently 'Canterbury to Santiago' was too ambiguous), how long I'd been on the way, how I was going to get home afterwards. A passing tourist stopped to video me, then walked on without making a donation, which should be illegal; another, American, gave me a dollar, so I had enough to pay a commission. It was a start. Best of all, three Spanish exchange students who looked straight out of a fashion magazine came to wish me luck. 'We're from Santiago!' they said. 'We'll see you there!' One of them blew me a kiss as she walked away. I was looking forward to arriving already.

At last, after two hours, the quiver in my lip told me it was time to go. I finished off with a gentle rendition of *Danny Boy*, a tune I dedicated to Anna, and as the haunting echoes faded I ruined the effect completely by warming my lip back down with a series of the lowest and most flatulent notes I could excavate from the instrument. I felt quite light-headed as I packed away, and not just from oxygen starvation. The first busk of the entire trip had been a roaring success. People had stopped to listen. They'd smiled. They'd wished me luck. My collecting tins were half full of charity and chewing gum. I'd seen enough life to fill a book. If the rest of the walk was anything like that, I was in for the adventure of the millennium.

As I picked up my rucksack and headed for the Cathedral I was still whistling Dixie. Things don't get much more positive than that.

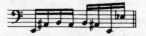

Every budding literary giant needs his dream, and mine is to be the next Chaucer. (A modest ambition.) Anyone who can get a dirty joke treated as literature for six hundred years has to be doing something right. It was nice to know that I was literally following in his footsteps as I lumbered up to the Cathedral gateway. The queue was only thirty feet long (it was early in the season), so I leant on my sticks behind a couple of art historians in fur-trimmed frock coats and sail-like flares, shut my eyes, and realized that I was shaking. I felt as if I'd just run a marathon. For a second Canterbury disappeared in a sparkling red mist. I shook my head and looked at the gateway: a medieval portal flanked by tourist boutiques, an orderly queue, green lawns, golden stone. It was as reassuring as the shipping forecast. Relax, I told myself. You did it.

The guard at the ticket-barrier beckoned me over.

'Are you a pilgrim?'

The question took me by surprise. I'd thought the Canterbury pilgrimage had died out at the time of the Reformation.

'Well, yes, but I'm only starting from here . . .'

'No problem, go right in, the pilgrim office is on your right.'

Pilgrim office? I was gobsmacked. He pushed me through the barrier with an encouraging smile, and before I knew it I was in the Cathedral grounds, standing like a muffin in front of a wooden chalet: the pilgrim office.

'You must be a pilgrim!' A photogenic young couple in airline-smart uniforms smiled at me. It was surreal. I hadn't expected a welcome like this before Santiago. They spotted my confusion.

'You are a pilgrim, aren't you?'

'Well, yes . . .' I shook my head to rally my wits, and started explaining. Canterbury to Santiago, in honour of Anna . . . Something must have shown in my face. The pilgrim team took one look at me and became all sympathetic attention. They gave me an official pilgrim's passport (they called it a 'credential'), wished me luck, asked me to send them a postcard when I arrived and offered to look after the rucksack while I went into the Cathedral. I wasn't seriously worried that some sneak thief would try to walk off with the thirty-kilo monster, but it was a nice thought. I left it leaning up against the counter, and fled.

Despite the crowds of tourists outside, the Cathedral was a haven of peace, and it was just as well. Memory had come back sharp and clear, driving away the present: the heat, the smell of the mangroves, the blue crabs clicking along the shore as my boss told me very gently that he'd just had a radio message . . . I could almost see Anna in front of me, strong and jaunty and grinning like a pirate. I would have given anything for just one minute with her; just the chance to say goodbye. I blundered down into the crypt, lit a candle for her, slumped in front of it. I was vaguely aware of visitors passing back and forth, but they weren't real to me. I was back in Belize, and seven months away.

I don't know how much later it was that I sat back, staring at nothing very much, getting my breath back. Slowly my mind reeled itself in from the far Caribbean and began to relocate itself in the present. A new thought drifted up through the haze: 'At least you're doing something for her now.' What else was I there for?

It was a comforting thought. I sat for a while longer thinking about her and letting the shaking subside. Slowly memories of the morning started to surface. I couldn't help smiling. It had been a good gig. As I stood up my knees cracked, one-two, like a double-barrelled shotgun. Without thinking I stepped back to stretch, and nearly kicked over a pew. Time to be going before I wrecked the place ... I touched the candle in farewell and went back out into the real world.

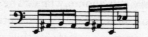

I'd expected the first step to be a big moment. I was wrong.

It was a beautiful Sunday morning, the first day of British Summer Time. The sun was just rising, barring the clouds with stained-glass scarlet, as I met my father at the Cathedral gates. He'd come down to see me off. Canterbury was silent and empty. The streets seemed twice as wide as the day before; the crowds forgotten, nothing moving but a burger carton scuttering about in the dawn wind. The Cathedral itself was closed, but it didn't matter. I wasn't there to see the sights. I went up to the wrought-iron gates and touched them briefly for the symbolism of the thing, but my heart wasn't in it. It all seemed so ordinary. I turned, walking-sticks clicking on the paving-stones, and there it was. I'd taken the first step. I'd been expecting elation. All I felt was 'One down, five million to go'.

We walked back through the pedestrian zone, down the ring-road underpass, past a glorious mural of scenes from the *Canterbury Tales* which didn't show any of the dirty bits at all, an impressive feat, and out into verdant suburbia. Fish and chip shops and semi-detached villas strangely failed to fill me with the wild joy of freedom. I might have been back in Birmingham. Where was the emotion of setting off?

It hit me when we said goodbye, just on the edge of town. I couldn't believe that I was going to walk for nine months. It was too far to imagine. What mattered was that I wasn't going to see Dad. We said a casual farewell on the pavement (we are

British, after all) and I walked on alone. I'd told myself I wouldn't look back, but I did. He was still watching me, lowering his camera. We both waved. I went on faster – I hate goodbyes. Then I rounded the corner and saw the road stretching away before me, and the elation struck. Books and plans and paperwork were all behind me. I was on the way.

It was a perfect day for walking. The sun was hot and the ground dry and firm, but the air was still cool enough to be comfortable; and it was spring. Half the population of Kent seemed to be out and about. A couple of joggers passed me with a cheery wave. Others followed, the enthusiasm of their greetings diminishing in direct proportion to the distance from Canterbury. I passed a few couples in long woollen socks and leather walking-boots out for a day's walk, and felt a sudden burst of nostalgia for my childhood days in Shropshire and Gwynedd. There's something deeply reassuring about the sight of Sunday ramblers. The twenty-first century might be howling outside the door, but there are still people within spitting distance of London who know that there's nothing to beat a really good stroll.

I'd never been in Kent before, but the phrase 'the rolling Downs' had been rattling round my consciousness ever since I learned to talk, and to my delight, they did. Long, wooded ridges curved down into shallow valleys, ancient churches peeped between stately trees. I could almost hear Elgar playing in the background as I walked past locals in Barbour jackets, gleaming Land Rovers, paddocks full of show-jumping barriers, converted barns with designer French windows – and, for some reason, pages torn out of a porn magazine. They lay scattered along the path for more than a mile, signalling every turn and junction with a profusion of images so adult you'd have to show your telegram from the Queen before you could buy one. It wasn't quite the waymarking I'd expected. Perhaps the National Trust was researching new ways of attracting walkers onto the footpaths. I tried to keep my eyes on the scenery, but it wasn't easy.

The day went by in a pleasant haze. It was so good to be moving at last that nothing bothered me much. Heat, thirst, weight, all bounced off the feeling of vague well-being suffusing my mind, without even causing a ripple. I ate lunch by the Canterbury-Dover railway, watching the world go by in green wellies and angora jumpers. I refilled my water-bottle at a stately home near the magnificent Piddle Wood, and was treated to a glass of punch. I got lost in the fields beyond – can't imagine why – and ended up happily sliding under barbed-wire barricades to regain the path. By the time I reached Dover it was sunset, and I hardly felt tired at all.

Dover was a pleasant surprise. Knowing nothing about the place, I'd been expecting a soulless industrial port, all concrete and container vessels, but the rather shabby town radiating out along the valleys was as warm and as personal as a well-worn shoe. No two houses looked exactly alike, the shops were scattered at odd intervals without much apparent logic, and even the waterfront had a character all its own. Admittedly it was the character of a waste of grey shingle, but character it was. It wasn't the sort of place to inspire anyone with poetic raptures – not unless you're the type to see bluebirds everywhere, anyway – but it definitely looked like the place where a complete stranger could go for a quiet pint and expect a friendly reception. I left my rucksack at the youth hostel and strolled around for a while, idly contemplating doing just that, but I wasn't in the mood for more alcohol. Instead, I climbed towards the castle.

The last tourists were leaving as I arrived, cooing and pointing at the golden horizon, and the guards on the gate had a no-nonsense look. I waited until they'd locked up, then went scrambling down into the grass-filled moat and contoured my way round to the cliff-edge. I sat with my back to an ancient wall, one leg swinging over the abyss, the other firmly braced against a solid outcrop (I'm not completely stupid) and looked dreamily southwards as the daylight died and the town lights started spreading. The stones at my back were still warm with collected sunshine. Below me, the cliff was green streaked with white. Seagulls swooped past, calling raucously. The sea was grey and laced with foam, and every now and then a ferry drew slowly out of the harbour and kicked up a rooster-tail of spray as it set its bow towards the Continent. Long after, the thunder of the engines reached me. I wondered idly about the passengers, where they were going, where they'd been. It's easy to slip into daydreams at the end of a long day's walk. Who else had sat here in years gone by, watching the ships? There's a Roman watchtower inside the castle, a Norman chapel, walls built under Henry VIII, a Second World War command bunker: half Britain's history summed up in a single monument. I sat watching the ferries draw away, and thought about Europe. It was a whole new land, as close to Britain and as far as a reflection. It was scary. It was exhilarating. Another ferry blasted off. Tomorrow, I'd be on that ship.

I could hardly wait.

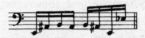

I knew when I'd reached the ferry terminal the next day. The first thing I saw was a man happily loading his Volvo to the axles with crates of beer. The second, on entering the building, was the bar, between the door and the check-in desk, presumably for those suffering souls who couldn't make it all the way across the foyer without a drink. It was eleven in the morning. Already the tables were laden with dreg-streaked glasses and dead cigarettes. It's a lie to say that the EU has done Britain nothing but harm. Alcoholics have never had it so good.

It was a cold grey morning, as bleak as a seagull's wing. Heavy clouds drifted across the sky, the same colour as the cliffs below, and the wind had teeth in it. Ice-grey spray showered over the breakwater. Just looking at it made me shiver. My nerves were fluttering again at the thought of waving goodbye to Britain. To calm them I took a stroll round the car-park, watching the Volvo merchant wedging the last beer crate in under the bulging roof. The water behind the terminal was a sickly green that looked like it glowed in the dark: there didn't seem a lot of point in the 'No Swimming' sign. I stood looking back at the land. A couple of kids were playing on the shore, that old childhood favourite of 'Let's throw stones at each other really hard'. Behind them the beachfront was almost deserted. Dover doesn't look half so snug in the daylight. I shivered, and went back into the warmth.

Someone was watching me. I could feel it the second I walked in. I looked around the bar. Half the tables were occupied, booze cruisers making the most of their limited time: at one table a man sat alone with his back to a pillar, watching the door. He was close to retirement age, a big, solidly-built man with a red-veined face, short-cropped grey hair and a bristling moustache. He was wearing a trench-coat belted tight against the cold, and there was a big empty tool-bag by his side. If the BBC ever need to cast a retired NCO for an Army drama, they could start with him.

He met my eye and jerked his head at me. Instant paranoia filled me. I went towards him, feeling my eyes and my wits grow sharp and suspicious as if I had antennae all round my head. He hoisted a half-empty pint in a meaty hand by way of greeting.

'That's a bloody big rucksack you've got.' His accent was pure South London. 'Where you off to?'

'Spain, I hope.'

His eyes widened. 'What, on foot?'

'That's the idea.'

'Well, fuck me!'

I decided I liked him.

'I'm doing a charity walk,' I told him, and pulled out a chair and sat down. Irrational fear faded as fast as it had come. He nodded approvingly and swung his legs round to make room.

'Who for?'

I started explaining, and he started interrupting, and the

more he interrupted the more I liked him. Raleigh and MS. Why Raleigh? Because I worked for them and they do a good job. What work? Diving instruction. Where? Belize. His eyes lit up. Where exactly? Nobody ever asks that about Belize. The normal question is, 'Where's that?'

'Do you know it?'

And the truth came out. He looked like a retired sergeant-major because he was a retired sergeant-major, an artillerist with thirty years' service behind him. He'd been to Belize three times in the days when the British Army was that little country's main defence against invasion from Guatemala. The conversation went into freefall. Halfway through we were interrupted by the boarding call, and he slugged his pint back and led me up the glass-roofed boarding ramp. It hardly seemed surreal at all to look back to the cold grey coastline while raving about Big Daddy's Belizean fried chicken. I never even noticed when we pulled away from the dock.

Rod led me into the upper saloon and calmly bagged a seat right at the back, halfway between the bar and the balcony door. 'Watch my bag,' he said, and disappeared barwards. As I stared out at the cliffs slipping quietly away beyond the window a trio came in and took their places beside me: a young, sandy-haired man in a bomber jacket carrying a *Daily Mail*, a slim girl with so much curly brown hair she looked like an advanced piece of topiary, and a giant of a man in a black leather jacket almost entirely hidden behind an immense black beard. They looked at me as if in surprise, nodded and settled down almost resentfully. Blackbeard immediately started jotting figures down on the back page of Sandy's paper, while Sandy and the girl conversed in murmurs. All three shot me suspicious looks. My scalp prickled with some thing more than reflex paranoia. Something was going on her, and I didn't know what. Then Rod came back, set a pint of lager in front of me and nodded at them, and the atmosphere cleared. Sandy and the girl leaned back and relaxed, and Blackbeard even

13

gave me a casual nod. I started to breathe again. I'd been accepted. I didn't know into what, but it was definitely acceptance.

'Cheers,' said Rod, hoisting his pint, and casually swallowing about half of it. Judging by the glasses he'd had stacked in front of him in the bar it was the fourth of the day already, but it didn't seem to effect him. He got through three more during the crossing, and they didn't effect him either. I never even saw him go to the toilet. They don't make men like that any more.

'Good seats these,' he added, looking around contentedly. They were leather-look easy chairs with tables carefully arranged at knee-capping height, the sort of thing that even the Inquisition would have banned as cruel and inhuman, but I didn't want to argue. 'I always come up here if I can.'

My ears pricked up. 'Come here often, do you?' I asked, which is about as unsubtle as nosiness gets, but he didn't seem to mind.

'Couple of times a week, normally. There's a friend of mine in London who needs stuff doing over here, and me being a gentleman of leisure . . .' He left the sentence hanging, and my eyes drifted down to the empty toolbag. It was the only luggage he had. Very slowly, a light began to flicker on in the back of my mind.

'You know Ostend pretty well, then?' I asked guilelessly. 'Where d'you stay normally?'

He didn't have to give me a straight answer, but Rod's an honest man. 'I get the last ferry back. The business doesn't take long. Don't even have to leave the terminal, really.' And he gave me such a carefully neutral look that it was like a jab in the ribs.

Realization dropped into my skull like a block of ice. I was sitting in the upper saloon of a cross-Channel ferry with the grey waves streaming away behind us and the gulls floating above our wake, having a quiet pint with a booze-smuggler. I was delighted. I'd wanted an adventure . . . I resisted the urge to lean forwards conspiratorially, and tried to keep my own voice neutral.

'Still, it's a bit of a fast turnaround, isn't it?' I'd checked the timetables in an idle moment, the ship wasn't in port for more than an hour.

He shrugged. 'I could do without it, but what can you do? Ever since they dumped the old Harwich service there hasn't been much of a choice. I hate the Dover run. The Customs are so bloody awkward . . .' And before I knew it I was listening to the tale of a smuggler's woes. The Dover Customs were a merciless set, utterly unsympathetic to the needs of the small businessman. Harwich seems an unlikely venue for Good Old Days nostalgia, but as I saw it through Rod's eyes it turned into a shining paradise of convenient ferry schedules, easy transportation and friendly Customs agents who knew better than to inconvenience the gentleman-contrabandists, and who spent their time watching out for the 'real bastards' who were turning smuggling into a criminal industry. He nodded at a group of black-jacketed men huddled on the after-deck smoking and talking on mobile phones.

'See them? They're the Mafia. Day after day on this bloody boat, they're taking the piss, they really are, and then who gets the blame? Guys like us.' He swigged his pint. He didn't seem unduly troubled by the thought, but it was hard to imagine anything disturbing him much. Whenever I looked at him the word 'solid' crept insidiously into my mind. You could anchor a medium-sized island with Rod.

Then the words caught up with me. Guys like *us*? I looked to my right. Our three neighbours had slowly drawn closer, drinking in Rod's words. Without my noticing it we'd become a single group, four rapt listeners around a chief, and the way the other three were nodding they'd already experienced what he was describing. I noticed for the first time that there was a little pile of empty bags leaning against Sandy's chair, and another penny dropped like the world's slowest jackpot. Rod was a smuggler. They were smugglers. The gentlemen outside were smugglers. I felt like I'd stumbled into a Victorian novel. Was I the only passenger on the boat who wasn't a merchant adventurer?

Rod saw me eyeing them, and broke off. 'Sorry, forgot the introductions,' he said calmly. 'Ben, this is John, this is Emma, that's Harry hiding behind the beard.' They nodded and muttered inaudibly, as Brits do. 'This is Ben, a friend of mine. He's walking to Spain for charity.'

Their ears pricked up.

'Nice one,' said Harry, the speech impediment clearing miraculously.

'Yeah, bloody good,' John added. Emma nodded, the hair bouncing around her brows like heather in a gale, and I felt myself grow warm. I'd never been welcomed into the underworld before.

The conversation became general. Never having smuggled more than an uneaten apple from my lunchbox (still a capital offence in the US), I was content to sit back and listen as a whole new world opened up before my eyes: buying strategies on the boat and ashore. (To prove one point, Harry scrawled on the back of his paper the kind of maths that would leave a computer stunned.) The evils of the Dover Revenuers. The delicate line between sidestepping the law and actually committing a crime. Every sentence was an education. I wished I could have recorded the conversation, but it didn't seem a likely way to prolong the friendship. If I ever really need a drink, I thought, I know where to come . . .

After a while the conversation petered out and the others returned to their amusements. Rod looked at me with a quizzical eye, took another swig of lager and asked out of the blue. 'How you going to cope when it gets hard?'

It was a fair question. I'd spent a lot of time worrying about that myself. I'm prone to spells of depression at the best of times (I keep telling people it comes of being a genius, but nobody believes me). What was I going to do when I was tired, wet, hungry, or in pain? Rod watched me as I mulled the question over, weighing me up. It felt like a job interview.

'Try to stop and rest before it gets too much.'

'And if you can't?' His face wasn't giving anything away.

I reached into my pocket and pulled out a piece of waterproof paper.

'Read that.'

He raised an eyebrow and took it. The other eyebrow raised as he started to read. It was my secret weapon, the spare backbone I'd prepared in Birmingham in case mine turned to jelly. This is what it said:

I'm walking for Anna.
Every step is another penny for charity.
I've survived worse than this before.
Tomorrow's another day.

And a list of names, more than a hundred of them: all the people who'd wished me luck and said they'd be thinking of me. If that didn't get me through, then I didn't know what would.

Rod nodded, folded the paper carefully and handed it back.

'You'll do it,' he said.

It sounded like a prophecy. My heart warmed further.

He looked out of the window. The horizon was growing nearer, a low, hazy line thickening and darkening above the waves: my first sight of the mainland.

'You'll do it,' he said again. 'I've been watching you since you came aboard, listening to you, working out the way you think. I've had a lot of men under my command under the years, and I can tell you this, Ben: if you were in my company you'd have two stripes on your shoulder already.'

Somehow I doubted that sobbing on his shoulder would go

down well; but I could have done. The praise of the praise-worthy is beyond all rewards, as Tolkien said. I bought him a pint instead, and we chatted, as outside the window the Belgian coast drew ever closer. I don't remember what we talked about: trivia, neither his business nor mine. It wasn't far to go, and we could feel the farewells looming. Harry folded up his paper. John returned from a tour of the fruit machines and nudged Emma awake. The endless wait of the last five minutes . . .

We docked, and the five of us watched as the inexperienced passengers bolted for the gangway. We waited in calm superior-ity, and when all was clear walked out like lords. At the foot of the escalator they turned to me.

'Good luck, mate,' said John, shaking my hand.

'All the best,' said Harry. Emma gave me a peck on the cheek.

'Cheers,' I answered. 'Safe journey back,' and they walked away.

Rod took my hand in a shattering grip. There didn't seem much to say.

'You'll do it.'

'Thanks, Rod. Don't get caught.'

'Have a good 'un.'

He followed them out of the terminal, upright and rock-solid in the belted trench-coat, still dead steady after seven pints of lager. A little pang struck my heart. He was a friend already. I doubt I'll ever see him again, but if he ever reads this – thanks, mate.

I collected my rucksack from the carousel, and stepped out of the terminal into Europe.

PART 2

Flanders

'In the midst of life we are in death . . .' (*Book Of Common Prayer*)

If you ever really want to wind up a Eurocrat (and let's face it, who doesn't?) tell him that you took the boat from Dover to Europe. The very least you'll get is a worried stare and the comment, 'But Dover is in Europe . . .', which just goes to show how vague a word can be. Ask many Brits where Europe begins and they'll tell you, 'Calais'. Every European I know (and how many people take that word to mean 'dweller on the Continental landmass'? – because I know I do) thinks of it as the geographical concept that reaches from Reykjavik to Istanbul and the North Cape to Gibraltar. Including, like it or not, the British Isles. Americans are famous for their inability to find the USA on a map of the world, but most Europeans can't work out where Europe is on a map of Europe.

This seems extreme until you look at Belgium. All I knew about that happy country when I started planning the walk was that it was famous for beer, bureaucrats and being the butt of half the jokes in France. By the time I left Canterbury I'd read so much that I was starting to doubt whether it actually existed. What is a country? If it's a tax-collecting and road-building organization, then Belgium's as real a nation as any other; but what does that make the EU? If a nation is the

19

expression of a feeling of unity, linked by common language, fashions, TV programmes, jokes, then you could be forgiven for wondering if the maps don't need re-drawing.

The history of Belgium is the history of western Europe writ small. At one time or another it's been ruled or militarily occupied by every major power on the continent: the Holy German, Spanish and Austrian Empires, the French Crown, the British Army, the French Republic, the Dutch House of Orange, and the Second and Third Reich. A short list of the battles fought on Belgian soil might include Ramillies, Waterloo, Ypres and the Bulge; a complete list would fill a volume. It's been a battleground every since Germanic tribes crossed the Rhine in the third century AD and did their level best to annihilate the Latin-speaking settlers they found there. According to some authorities, the war between French and Flemish speakers is still going on, each side trying to evict the other from their own 'historic' territory. Since the entire country has passed from hand to hand like a rugby ball over the years, anyone can lay an historic claim to anything, and the only reason Belgium hasn't degenerated into a second Palestine is that Belgians restrict their hostile takeovers to the board-room. Just like Palestine, Belgium was created by the Great Powers at the end of a major war to give them all a breathing space. It shows.

The country (if it is one) doesn't really have nationalism. It would be like getting worked up about Milton Keynes: it's theoretically possible, but nobody would do it for fear of being laughed at. What it does have is regionalism. A line runs through the country from east to west, just at the level of Brussels. Above it are the Flemish territories. They're like a hidden corner of Holland, complete with canals, polders, tall steep-gabled houses, interesting bread and a language which is almost, but not quite Dutch. They've also spawned a far-right Nationalist party, the Vlaams Blok or Flemish Bloc, whose graffiti are scrawled on every road- and canal-bridge in the north, calling for the expulsion of all immigrants: North Africans, Turks, Bosnians and Belgians. Logical stuff. South of the line is Wallonia, and if the nationalist voice is more muted there it's only because nobody wants to be called a Walloon on their passport. The southern territories are French-speaking, and the border between the two is as abrupt as the Iron Curtain. One side is wholly Flemish, the other a 100 per cent Walloon, baguettes and all. The divide governs everything from TV and radio to politics. Each side has its own regional parliament. The small German-speaking enclave in the east has its parliament. Even Brussels, a francophone city on Flemish soil, has a parliament. All of them deal with the national parliament (in Brussels), which then deals with the other governments of the EU (also in Brussels). Why are Belgians renowned as a race of civil servants? Because most of them are.

Then I reached Ostend, and even under the darkening clouds it looked as friendly as a smiling face. Despite being a popular seaside resort, it somehow managed to convey the impression that this was a place where real people lived, worked and took the piss out of the Powers that Be. The first thing I saw on leaving the ferry terminal was a splendid red-brick esplanade being dug up along its entire length, with cyclists and pedestrians blithely crossing the site in all directions. A couple of gentlemen in grey suits even broke off an animated discussion to admire a particularly fine shower of sparks from a screaming metal-saw, watching with interest as red-hot shrapnel peppered the tarmac around them. A workman shoving a barrow calmly backed up to let them pass, then stood watching as they leant their laptop cases on the far barrier and gave one another a leg up over it. How can you not like a town where that's allowed to happen? I walked along the waterfront and almost crashed into an elderly cyclist with the curliest moustache I've ever seen. He must have been eighty if he was a day, but he swerved round me and accelerated like Miguel Indurain, the wind whistling through his moustache.

'Great moustache!' I yelled after him. Some achievements demand recognition.

'I only take compliments from pretty girls!' The answer returned as he took the corner, one knee almost brushing the ground. Faceless bureaucrats? I walked on grinning as one preconception abruptly died.

The town improved on closer acquaintance. As dusk fell, the streets were still busy with an engaging mix of British holiday-makers and locals out for a stroll. Like Dover, Ostend has an agreeably lived-in feel to it: there were real shops on the waterfront between the multilingual bars (which included the 'Prince Charles'), late-night takeaways serving local customers, houses with peeling paint one street back from the esplanade, a traffic system rendered completely chaotic by the road-works. I had my first genuine Belgian meal in one of the takeaways, a carbohydrate-laden chip butty with mayonnaise further spiced by the Europop blaring out of the TV. My attempts to order the meal in French met with dismal failure . . . Once I'd eaten I strolled back out into the darkened streets. There wasn't much to see, but it was fun just to wander among the crowds. I ended up on the waterfront, looking down the breakwater steps, and on an impulse ran down them and dipped my toes in salt water for the last time. The gulls were crying above me. I didn't know it then, but the next time I was to hear that rusty call was on the ridge above Santiago.

Leaving Ostend was trickier than I expected. The long-range footpath on which I'd pinned such hopes led off in completely the wrong direction, north-eastwards along the coast. I wanted to head inland, south-east. According to my map, a canal led directly towards Bruges and distant Ghent, my first target. Unfortunately, the map in question was a 1: 100 000 without contour markings (a useless extravagance in Flanders) and using it was like trying to navigate across London with an Underground map. Within five minutes I was lost in a maze of mini-roundabouts, pedestrian bridges, abandoned factories and overgrown railway tracks. A few passers-by looked at me in bewilderment – how often do you see a fully-equipped mountaineer behind your local supermarket? – and hurried on, and I was left to the tried and tested method of picking a compass bearing and sticking to it, which isn't easy in suburbia. It took me an hour to find the canal, a stretch of mirror-clear water hemmed in between red-brick factories. Fighting down a sudden burst of nostalgia for Birmingham, I struck off south-eastwards in search of adventure.

It's unwise to go looking for adventure. You might find it.

I walked for four days in glorious sunshine, angling into the heart of Flanders. The canal was beautiful, bare poplars standing black and silver against an incredible blue sky with yellow blossoms flaming at their feet, an empty road beneath them – except during rush hour, when the towpath swarmed with rainbow-lycra'd cyclists. It led me to Bruges, where I spent a happy day busking and had my newborn opinion of Belgians as the friendliest people in Europe confirmed: in one day I received enough offers of hospitality to keep me sheltered for a fortnight. Beyond Bruges was the solid heart of the province, a long succession of villages stretched out along concrete-slab roads, a barking dog in every garden. They seemed heartless places, even under the brilliant sky: no town square, no church, just a ribbon of houses clustered by the road, but the heartlessness didn't stretch to the inhabitants. I got used to stopping at random houses to beg for water – always in English, the locals may have understood French but they weren't letting on – and coming away with enough food and drink for a platoon. I chatted with policemen, shopkeepers, a bank manager and a beggar. Everyone was friendly. Everyone knew about Santiago. It seemed that every other Belgian I met had made the pilgrimage on foot or mountain bike. Every hour hauled up a new facet of life before my eyes. I could have gone on drinking it in for ever.

My luck and the weather broke halfway between Bruges and Ghent. A wall of cloud rolled in from the north, and I followed the canal through a world of bleak grey clarity. Ripples dulled the water and the horizon seemed an arm's length away. Everything was drained of colour. Only the cyclists in their lycra fantasies brightened the monochrome monotony. Colour had frozen out of the world.

I loved it. I never get cold if I keep moving, and with the towpath devoid of life I wrapped myself in my jacket and let myself daydream. Following a dead-straight trail hardly requires great concentration, and since my mind's default-setting when I'm walking tends to be 'God this rucksack's heavy' and I haven't yet found the icon to change it, I have to keep myself occupied. That day I decided to watch films. I've never yet understood the way my memory works – I can still remember a lyric I wrote at the age of four, but not what I wrote this morning – but one of its great advantages is the ability to retain wholesale my favourite cinematic moments, sound-track and all. It seems a shame, sometimes, to turn my eyes away from the real world and switch on a re-run of *Indiana Jones* in the privacy of my own skull, but when it's a choice between that and aching shoulders, I know which way I'd go every time.

I was fifteen kilometres from Ghent and happily re-watching *The Princess Bride* when I saw something floating in the water.

The canal lay between high, steep banks topped with barbed wire fencing. A couple of hundred yards ahead of me a road-bridge arched over the water like a black metal sunrise. Short, stabbing wavelets gusted up the canal from behind me, and lapped against something deep red, knocking it against the crumbling bank. Deep red fabric, the only colour in the day. Cushion, I thought as I came nearer. It must be.

Something small and white protruded from it. The whiteness swayed in the ripples like weed. Weed on a cushion? I looked again.

The whiteness parted for a moment, and showed the scalp beneath. It was hair.

24

Shop dummy, I thought desperately. Has to be . . . I side-footed down the bank. The edging of concrete blocks was broken and half-submerged. I put one cautious foot on the edge, hooked the dummy with my walking-stick and pulled. As it rolled a blue-white hand in a sodden sleeve rose dripping from the water, as rigid as plastic. Mannequin, I thought, weak with relief. Then I saw the wedding ring.

Reality fled. I stepped back cautiously, retreated up the bank, dropped my rucksack and sat down on it hard. My brain was running on auto-pilot. It's a corpse, it's a corpse, it's a corpse . . . What do I do? Resuscitation? Not on someone that stiff. Phone for help? Don't know the number. God that wind's cold. Automatically I pulled my jacket on. What to do? Habit took over. There was no way I was going to reach my campsite. I grabbed my map and checked that there was another one nearer. There was. Food I had. Good. The tiny part of me still functioning nodded in satisfaction. Shelter and a meal were guaranteed. One less worry. I didn't even wonder about my own reaction until later.

I turned away to look for help.

I turned back.

The body had rolled back and was floating face-down, head-butting the stones.

I did hesitate, but only to work out if it was possible. Could I pull him out without going in myself? The edging had rocked when I put my foot on it . . . A little voice in my mind said to leave it for the police. I ignored it. I couldn't leave him in there. It would be inhuman.

So I walked back down the bank, hooked the body with my stick again, and pulled hard. There was a second's resistance, then his feet floated to the surface and the whole mass moved in side-on to the bank. He was wearing tights under his trousers, and no shoes.

I bent down, grabbed a handful of wool, and pulled. There was no give in the body, he was locked in position, arms out, legs half-bent, and the blue-white flesh was cold and flaccid. Any lingering ideas of resuscitation fled. As he came out of the water a yellow froth rose to his lips and bubbled over into his chin. His gold-rimmed glasses were fouled with mud. I tried to lie him down, but his limbs were as stiff as oak branches, so I sat him on the edge of the tow-path and started cleaning his face. I wanted to close his eyes, hug him, let him know he wasn't alone, but my body shrank from the contact. He was so cold . . . I put a hand on his shoulder.

'I'm going to call the police,' I told him. 'I'll be back.' The wind shook his hands as he sat there. He might almost have been resting.

I scrambled over the fence and onto the road. There was a little red-brick cluster of houses at either end of the bridge, impossibly suburban and normal. One looked like a café. I walked over, stepped into warmth and brightness. Half a dozen locals were sitting drinking and listening to pop radio. While a corpse shivered on the bank below . . . I went up to the barman.

'Do you speak English?'

'A little.' He was young and tall, with a red face and a black moustache. He was drying a beer-glass. 'What would you like?'

It took a second to find the words. Whatever part of my mind was still functioning, it wasn't the speech centre.

'I've just found a dead man in the canal. I need to call the police.'

His eyes widened. 'Oh! That is bad,' he said. How do you reply to that?

'Will you call the police?'

'Where is it? Show me.' He came out from behind the bar. Together we walked to the bridge and looked down. He was sitting just as I'd left him, staring into the water.

'Are you sure?' The barman looked at me doubtfully. He was still holding the glass.

'Yes! Will you phone the police?'

He hurried back to the bar. I scrambled over the fence and skidded down the embankment.

'I'm back,' I said, patting his shoulder again. It seemed important to tell him. I sat down next to him, wondering what to say. I was starting to shiver. It wasn't just the cold, the shock, the wet patches on my trousers where he'd splashed me. Memories of Belize were rushing back, and I could feel my control disintegrating.

Within four minutes the police were there. Blue lights flashed on the far bank. A patrol-car screamed into view, swerved onto the bridge, crashed to a halt on the road above me. Another followed it, then a fire engine and an ambulance. I stood up, touched 'his' shoulder as a couple of paramedics in navy jump-suits scrambled over the fence and hurried down the embankment. They threw one look at me, rushed to the corpse, prised an eye open, felt for a pulse. Oh God, I thought, should I have done that? . . . More heads appeared along the skyline, officials and locals. I stood back as policemen swarmed down. The cavalry had arrived. I felt as useful as a spare wheel on a fish.

The paramedics went into a huddle. A policeman was already shouting orders above us. Someone pointed at me. Cold, official stares raked me. Then one of the medics came towards me: young, tall, incredibly curly hair, bright eyes.

'You're English?'

I nodded, not trusting my vocal cords.

'You found her?'

Her? So it was a woman . . . I nodded again.

'Are you all right?'

I wasn't, but I knew I would be. Close enough.

'Could I have done anything?' I asked. I had to know.

'Nothing,' he said sympathetically. 'She's dead for a long time. She went missing since twenty-four hours. You saved us a search.' He gave me a long look, then went on carefully,

'The police needs a statementing from you. We know what happened, you're not suspishted, but . . .' He shrugged. I sniffed and nodded. I'd been expecting it. 'Why don't you go upstairs and wait?'

I swung my rucksack on, and there was a flurry of Flemish behind me. Two of them tried to help. I shrugged them off and scrambled up the embankment unaided. Machismo's a useful support sometimes. My paramedic accompanied me, helped me over the fence and shouted at the fire engine. A red face popped out, followed by a burly body in a red drysuit.

'This man is a *duiker* – diver, you know?' I knew. 'You did his yob for him, so he's going to take you for a drink until the police is ready.' Over his shoulder I could see a weeping middle-aged woman staring down at the scene: the dead woman's daughter. Her pain was like a stab in the gut. 'Are you all right?'

I nodded again.

'Let's go,' said the diver, and we made for the bar.

We sat by the window looking out at the road as the police set up tape barriers. The crowd grew. Where had they all come from at three o'clock on a Friday afternoon? The paramedics had covered the body, and were carrying it up the embankment on a stretcher; the daughter was huddled in a brown ambulance blanket, covering her face and crying.

'Did they tell you about her?' asked the diver. He'd unzipped his drysuit and pulled his head out of the latex seal, and was sitting there in a heavy thermal jump-suit. No wonder he was red in the face. 'She lived on the other side of the bridge in those houses there.' He pointed to the snug, smug brick build-ings. 'She has depression. Lots of people here do. She'd tried to kill herself many times. She went missing at 2 o'clock yester-day. Her daughter called the police at once.'

The paramedics lifted the stretcher over the fence. The daughter knelt down, lifted one corner of the shroud, turned away quickly. A policewoman moved to comfort her.

28

'You're a diver?' I asked hurriedly, looking away. 'I'm an instructor.'

His face lit up. 'Really? Where do you work?'

'Belize last year, the Red Sea before that.'

'Where in the Red Sea?'

'Sharm.'

'I was there last year!' He broke into a flood of reminiscences. He'd dived at the centre where I'd worked, he knew my boss, he knew the same sites I did. We talked blue water, sharks, wrecks and reefs while outside in the grey Flemish spring the corpse went into the ambulance. He asked me what I'd been doing in Belize, and I told him. I've loved working for Raleigh, and it showed. He sighed.

'It sounds great. I wish I could do that ... Why did you stop?'

Levelly, I told him. He looked at me, looked away, looked back.

'When did it happen?'

'Seven months ago.'

'*Gott verdumme*,' he muttered, the only Flemish curse I knew. 'And you had to find her today ... How long have you been walking?'

'Six days.'

He swore again.

'Good start!'

I was still groping for a reply when a policeman came in and beckoned.

'Can they interview you now?' asked the diver sympathetically. I nodded, and we went back into the cold.

The interviewer was waiting for me in a police Range Rover, talking into a mobile phone. He waved me to a seat, fired an order into the phone, and hung up.

'It's so much easier than radios,' he said. 'You're the man who found her, correct? I'm the officer in charge of the case. They tell me you're walking to Spain for charity. Well done.'

He stuck out a hand. I shook it automatically, wondering if anyone in the Flemish emergency services didn't speak fluent English.

He sat in the driver's seat, leg cocked uncomfortably over the hand-brake. 'Firstly, I've been asked by the Commissioner to thank you for helping us,' he said. 'I'll have to take a statement from you, but I hope you understand that you're not under any suspicion.'

'Thank you,' I said, and meant it. I couldn't have faced a hostile interview at that moment. 'What do you need to know?'

He led me through the story: who I was, where I was going, what I'd seen, how I'd reacted. Then I wrote it all down in my best English and my best handwriting, and signed it. He read it through, nodding to himself.

'Thank you,' he said at the end.

'Will you need me again?' I asked nervously. The last thing I needed was a court appearance.

'In your case, it might be difficult,' he replied drily. 'I'll take your phone number, but I doubt we'll use it.'

I gave him the number, shook his hand and climbed out of the car. Ambulance and police-cars were gone and the onlookers were drifting away. The tape barriers flapped mournfully in the wind. The fire engine's motor was already running as my diver looked out. As I walked over to him the Range Rover pulled away; the driver gave me the thumbs-up as they passed.

'I've got to go,' the diver said. 'I told the others what you're doing. They made a collection.' He poured a double handful of notes and coins into my hands. Someone shouted from the cab. He patted my shoulder, swung back on board, called 'Bon voyage!' and was gone. I was alone again, clutching a pile of cash on a cold grey canal-bank in Flanders six days' walk from the nearest friend. Bad Sack Day.

It pissed it down that night. When I reached my back-up campsite it was closed: I climbed the gate and pitched my tent miserably in the pseudo-shelter of a pine tree. I would have given anything for a smile and a hug, but I was in a dripping tent under a dripping tree a very long way from home. Everything hit me at once, homesickness, shock, grief, fatigue. I huddled in my sleeping-bag and howled.

When that was done, I phoned home. Four answer-machines in quick succession nearly set me off again (what do you say, 'Hi, I've found a corpse, give me a ring'?), but Emma was in, God bless her. I don't even remember what we said: I wasn't at my most lucid, and nor was she, which is fair enough under the circumstances. It's not quite your everyday call. She promised to let the family know – they all rang during the evening – and made the sort of soothing noises that are worth more than their weight in pharmaceuticals. Gradually I felt my sanity return. There wasn't a lot we could say after that. We promised to stay in touch, and I rang off, feeling much better.

There's a lot to be said for necessity. If anyone had been around that evening I would have let myself go completely and curled up like a hedgehog in the headlights, with about the same effect. As it was, I was alone, and a voice somewhere in my stomach pointed out that if I didn't get on with the cooking it was going to be a long, hungry night. I got my stove going and brewed up a huge pot of macaroni cheese, then lay in my sleeping-bag and ate to the music of the lashing rain. The only thought I had left was, 'At least it wasn't a friend of mine this time.' Is that callous? I don't know. I'd seen the daughter's grief, but she and her mother were strangers to me. With a hot meal inside me, I stuck the washing-up out into the rain to soak, and quickly fell asleep.

The bad weather continued for three days, and carried my mood with it. Flanders isn't at its most scenic when the clouds bounce along the treetops, and what with the weight of memories and the weight of the Pack From Hell, it was hard to keep my spirits up. Long-distance walking isn't a thrills'n'spills activity. I'd shift my rucksack, walk, look at the scenery, walk, check my map, walk, and try and stop my 1990s-trained mind running so far ahead of me that I lost it. Modern man isn't designed for pedestrianism. So much of life is instant, from e-mail to mashed potato, that braking down to the pilgrim's ten-miles-a-day mindset is all but impossible. Even language struggles to express it. 'That day I walked to Ghent.' One curt sentence to describe ten hours' effort? It should go like this.

I left the campsite. Plod, plod. I turned onto the towpath. Plod, plod. I crossed the bridge. Plod, plod. I listened to the radio news. Plod. For an hour. Plod, plod. When I turned round I could still see the bridge. Plod, plod. It was two hours to lunch . . . And so on. Gripping reading, you'll agree, but that's what it's like. I used to dream of writing a book that would let the reader share the walk. It's possible, but nobody would read it.

Nevertheless, I walked. Eastwards along the Bruges-Ghent canal, jumping every time I saw something in the water, then across the narrow strip of farmland between Brussels and Antwerp, and south towards Leuven. A week's walking. Seven nights of campsites (open and closed), houses, a barn, a hotel. Breakfasts sitting on my rucksack overlooking the Meuse with the sun rising to warm my bones. Cheese sandwiches, chocolate sandwiches, ham sandwiches, sausage sandwiches, basking in the sunshine, sheltering from the rain. Cars hooting and flashing as they went by, the drivers sticking up their thumbs in a complete reversal of the natural order. Blisters developing overnight, half-crippling me as I lost the trail and hammered along iron-hard roads north of Brussels. They didn't last. Nothing did. I was just passing through.

I was standing on the battlements of Ghent castle. It was Easter Monday, one of those luminous silver-grey days when the air is like a focused lens: the tight cluster of the city's spires seemed

close enough to touch, the streets shone, and away in the west
a bar of silver light was spreading on a cold breeze. The canal
glittered in the distance. Ostend was already out of sight, and
I wished Ghent was too.

I'd gone busking on Easter Sunday in the perfect location:
a little square lined with tall thin town houses and restaurants,
just opposite the castle. A steady stream of tourists flowed by.
Locals came and went, hurrying into the restaurants, staggering
reluctantly out. They didn't even acknowledge my existence,
which is pretty impressive when it's a trombone that's going
off at point-blank range. The only human contact I had all
morning was with a beggar, come to see if he could share my
pitch. I laughed bitterly.

'You're welcome to, but do you want to be the Invisible
Man?' He didn't get it.

I played for two hours and made twenty-five pence and
not a single smile. I'm not sure which hurt more.

I didn't have the heart to play on the Monday. My morale
still hadn't recovered from finding the corpse, and I couldn't
face more indifference. It's not nice to put your heart and soul
into music and be treated like an unpleasant smell. All I wanted
was to leave Ghent as fast as possible. I was on my way out
when the castle caught my eye. Why not? I thought I'd come
all this way to see the sights of Flanders, after all. It would be
a shame to miss them entirely.

So I paid the entrance fee, left the rucksack with a pop-eyed
guard, and walked into the beautiful skeleton of a building.
Ghent was a mighty city when England and France were bleed-
ing one another to death, but when those nations settled their
differences and started making trouble for the rest of Europe
its days of greatness passed. The birthright of the glorious
dukes of Burgundy passed into Habsburg hands, thence to
their ever-less-efficient representatives, was ravaged by French,
Spanish and Dutch armies and at last fell into disrepair. The
broken shell of a once-proud fortress was bought for a song

in the nineteenth century, and converted into a textile mill. Stone and mortar have been lovingly restored in the last twenty years, but the treasures that embellished it have been scattered beyond recall. Halls and chambers stand empty and echoing. I walked through in gloomy silence, too wrapped up in my own resentment to feel more than a vague desire to climb on the walls.

The visitors' route took me out onto the roof. I stood sulking for a while, then decided that I might as well start walking. Ghent was enemy territory, and the sooner I got out of there, the better. I was at the head of the spiral staircase leading towards freedom when I heard music drifting upwards: a medieval song, played on a solo harp. Ten seconds later, resentment and resolve both forgotten, red-faced, bright-eyed and with my ears spread like radar dishes, I lurched through the archway into the castle chapel.

The player looked up, startled, as well he might. The chapel was a long, high-ceilinged room lined with pillars, the walls cold, grey and bare. He was sitting in one corner behind a full-sized orchestral harp, staring dreamily into emptiness as he pulled magic from the strings, and the eruption of a travel-stained backpacker into his private communion must have been a severe shock. His finger kept going automatically as his eyes swept me from head to muddy boots. I leant against a pillar, shut my eyes and let it wash over me. I've always been a sucker for harp music, and this was as subtle and as magical as raindrops falling. I could almost feel him shrug as the music lifted and intensified. 'Listen if you want,' it seemed to say. 'I'm going to play anyway.'

All of a sudden I couldn't have cared less for the failures of the day before and the trauma of the week. I was standing in a medieval chapel listening to a medieval song. How could anything possibly worry me? He played on. My hand started to beat time and my feet to dance, or as much of a dance as you can manage in size eleven boots. The music grew stronger, more complex. He was improvising to my dance steps, as I was improvising to his music. Briefly my eyes flicked open. He was watching me. We smiled. Then he played on, and I danced.

We stayed like that for half an hour. Once a trio of tourists came clattering in and stopped to stare; one brought his VCR up by reflex. When they were gone, he stopped to stretch. I sat on a stone window-seat and waited. Neither of us was in a hurry. I had music, he had an audience. We were happy. It was a long time before I even thought of moving. When I did at last, I went towards him. There was a low table at his side, covered in tapes and CDs with his picture on the cover: a stout middle-aged man with a neat grey beard and bright eyes. He looked at me quizzically, and brought the piece to an end.

'Do you speak English?' I asked.

A head-shake. 'Français.' He was the first French-speaking Fleming I'd met.

'*Impeccable!*' I love speaking French, it makes me feel supple and sexy, which is a nice change. 'Listen. I can't take anything, but can I leave a donation anyway?'

He looked surprised. He didn't know the kind of Sunday I'd had.

'I know how it feels to play to a dead audience.'

Light dawned. 'Was that you playing the trombone yesterday?'

'You heard it?'

'It's a trombone.' He grinned impishly. Point taken.

His name was Marc. He'd been a harpist for thirty years. I leant against the pillar facing him, watching him as we chatted. All the while we spoke he played very gently, an odd note here, a rippling chord there, punctuating the mutter of our voices with sudden stabs of colour. No musician's career is easy, and harpists have it harder than most. He'd played at one time or another for most of the orchestras in Belgium. In between times he'd kept himself alive by playing on most of the country's streets. Twice when he was in his thirties work had dried up completely: he'd let his house and taken off on a motorbike with a small harp strapped to the pillion. God knows how he kept it in tune, but he'd carried it to the Syrian border and back seeking his fortune. Voice and eyes were meditative as he described his life on the road, the accidents and near-misses, mechanical breakdowns and physical illnesses, friends he'd made and gigs he'd played from Biarritz to Istanbul.

'How do you cope when it goes wrong?' I asked. He gave me a long look.

'I stop. Why?'

My bitterness boiled over, and the story came flooding out. He listened, not speaking, fingers running idly over the strings. I told him why I was walking, I told him about the corpse, I told him about everything that had been bothering me that morning, and the sense of relief was like lancing a blister. It's good to talk.

'What do you think of when you start playing?' he asked when my rant ran down.

I thought about it.

'Raising money,' I answered.

He nodded. 'Forget about it. Music doesn't work that way.' He hesitated, groping for words; his fingers struck a blues chord, stilled it. 'Look at it this way: in every town, 1 per cent of the people will be interested in what you're doing. If you're lucky, they'll be on the street when you're playing. If they aren't there, it doesn't matter how well you play. You'll never get a good reaction.'

It wasn't very encouraging.

'Do you ever enjoy what you play?'

'God yes!'

He smiled. 'Then try this. Don't play when you're tired and unhappy. You won't play well. Do it when you're in the mood, play the pieces you want, and enjoy yourself. Forget the money! If you meet the 1 per cent, you'll do well anyway, and if you don't – at least you'll have a good time.'

His fingers started picking out the first movement of Rodrigo's *Concierto de Aranjuez*, fast and light-hearted, and I felt my mood swing up to meet it. I'd been concentrating so hard on the serious things that I'd forgotten to have fun. I almost joined in, but harps and trombones don't mix that well.

'Listen,' he said suddenly, stilling the strings with his palms. He took a cassette off the table. 'I'd like to give you this. It's got my address on it. Will you sent me a postcard on the way?'

'I promise,' I said, touched. 'Thank you.'

'It's nothing,' he replied, and stood for the first time. We looked at each other, and quite unexpectedly hugged. I felt better than I had done in days.

'*Au revoir.*'

'*Bon voyage.*'

As I walked away he struck up again, a ringing dance. I wanted to stay and listen, but suddenly I was buzzing again. The enthusiasm for adventure was back. I whistled my way out of the castle, and went looking for roads to the east.

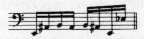

Three days later I crossed the Antwerp-Brussels motorway in pouring rain. A blister was growing under my heel, but I was whistling. Marc's magic was still with me.

A BMW roared past me in a wall of spray. It slammed to a halt, crashed into reverse, hurtled towards me. The window opened and a man looked out.

'Want a lift?'

'Thanks, but I promised to walk.'

'Oh.' Short silence: man contemplating maniac. 'Good luck!'

Gears crunched and he shot away, screamed to a halt, roared backwards past me, read my rucksack, and kangarooed forwards as I stared. The window jerked back down.

'Walking for charity?'

'Yes . . .'

'Well done. Here!' A meaty hand thrust something at me. The window juddered upwards and he took off as if catapult-launched, showering me again. I looked down at the five hundred franc note in my hand and started to laugh.

One by one the villages went by like a Spike Milligan poem: Boom, Reet, Duffel, Donk, Binkom, Wommersom. I began to feel at home in the Flanders scenery: long, narrow roads between heavy fields, chapels and calvaries at every corner, naked beech-trees rising out of a mist of crocuses. Daily the spring weather grew kinder. Daily I became more confident. I became adept at finding camping-space in woods and the corners of fields. I learned to vary my pasta meals with different flavours of soup and cheese, so that they became almost original. I learned that chocolate and oranges make the perfect dessert even when you've had them every day for a week. I learned to cope with blisters, cramp, fatigue, Bad Sack Days. I learned a few halting words in Flemish and a whole vocabulary of smiles. Everywhere I went, I was made welcome. It made the miles fly by.

After two weeks on the go, I passed through Leuven and set my head towards Wallonia. In fact I pissed through Leuven, or at least got pissed there. It's the home of Stella Artois, and the locals are proud of it. One of them intercepted me when I was busking and bought me a pint. Several hours later we were still drinking. It was a great day, but I don't remember much of it. The next day I got up late. Six pints had had an oddly soporific effect. It wasn't until the morning's third coffee that I felt human enough to walk: better living through chemicals.

It was a hot day. At least, my overloaded metabolism was having difficulties coping with the pale sunshine, which comes to the same thing. Every step was an effort. For all that, my heart lightened. South of Leuven the landscape changes, starts rolling with the merest hint of slopes and dips. It brought tears to my eyes. Hills at last! I'm the son of a Scotsman, and Edinburgh is my dream city: I don't feel at home on less than a forty-five degree slope. Every now and again a lark took off from the furrows, rising higher and higher on a pillar of song. Buzzards circled against skim-milk clouds, alone, in pairs, once five in a loose-stacked spiral far to the south. I'd never seen so many before. I leant on my poles and watched entranced. One shifted a lazy wing and drifted in my direction, so close that every feather stood outlined against the shining sky. You can't buy moments like that. I was glad to be on the way.

An hour south of Leuven I found my first waymark: a red-and-white flash painted on a tree. France and Belgium are covered with long-range footpaths, *sentiers de grande randonnée* or GRs, and with true Gallic thoroughness they're all marked and numbered: the GR1 *tour de Paris* (for lovers of the savage wilderness), the GR5 from Ostend to Nice which inspired my route, the GR10 Pyrenean traverse which was later to haunt me, the GR20 Corsican crossing, and a hundred others. Literally. They're all marked with the same red-white blazons on trees, walls, gates, even wheelie-bins when all else fails, and they intersect in a muddy web all across the western half of the continent. Follow the waymarks faithfully, and you could end up anywhere from Gibraltar to Schleswig-Holstein. Meeting my very first one, I was intoxicated. (Again.) Suddenly the whole vast continent seemed to open up before me. What was to stop me walking clear across to the Bering Straits? Well, time, energy and a little practicality, but in the first flush of enthusiasm those factors seemed terrifyingly weak. If I hadn't been hung over, who knows where I might have ended up?

Hung over I was, and by 5 o'clock I was definitely flagging. It takes a better man than I am to sink Belgian beer with impunity. The countryside grew more welcoming at every step, but the steps themselves were increasingly reluctant. I followed a stony lane over the fields, longing for a break and a drink.

My bottle was empty and the nearest campsite was two hours away. Then, ahead of me, I saw a little cluster of houses: old, solid, red-brick farm buildings that might have come straight from Shropshire. Beyond them was another long, slow climb. Right, I thought. Water and a sit-down, and then I'll go on.

The first two houses were empty. Loud music was playing in the third and I felt too shy to interrupt, so that left the last: smaller and newer than the rest, tucked back from the track behind a low privet hedge, the back garden full of saplings. The front garden was a clayey excavation surrounded by piles of marl, a shovel leaning crazily out of the debris. As I gathered my nerve to call, a man came out of the house, saw me, and stopped dead.

'Er . . . *parlez-vous français*?' I asked with my usual fluency. He smiled. He was past forty, with a high, balding brow, bright eyes and the sort of lean physique that screams 'marathon runner'. His hands were covered in gardening gloves, his feet in mud.

'I speak English too,' he said with the barest hint of an accent. 'Where are you going with that lot?'

'Spain, I hope.'

For the first time, it failed to shock.

'How long will that take?'

'Nine months.'

He nodded thoughtfully, then looked up at the sky.

'It's still early. It's a shame you're going on, I'd like to invite you in.'

I made the fastest decision of my life.

'I'm not in a hurry.'

His face lit up. 'Would you like a cup of tea?'

'I'd love one!'

We kicked off our boots, I dumped my rucksack and he led me into the house. Of all the rooms I've ever seen, I think that one appeals to me the most. Half the walls seemed to be window, looking out at the hills beyond and the woods behind the house. The floor was tiled and scattered with rugs and books. More books were crammed on an enormous shelf between a stereo system and rack upon rack of CDs. In one corner a wood-burning stove glowed and pinged merrily to itself. In another was a compact kitchen, complete with massive wooden table. And more books. What little wall-space remained was covered in framed photos of mountains, rivers and trees. Beneath them a hand-painted mural showed Calvin and Hobbes resting on a boulder under the world's finest motto: 'The world isn't so bad if you can just get out in it.' If I ever decide to grow up and get a house of my own, that's how I want it to be.

'Where were you planning to sleep?' asked Bart, as he plugged the kettle in. It was the first kettle I'd seen since crossing the Channel. Was there anything this paradise lacked?

'I was going to camp somewhere,' I told him, still admiring the room.

'Would you like to camp here? There's room in the garden.'

I turned to him. He seemed to mean it. I was delighted. Anyone with a house like that has to be worth knowing.

'Brilliant!'

'Well, go and pitch your tent, and I'll make the tea. What would you like?'

There was a *choice*?

He opened a kitchen cabinet, and my joy was complete: Lapsang Souchong, Earl Grey and Chinese Fruits. The collection took up half a shelf. I was still chuckling in amazement as I made camp behind the garden shed.

I'd arrived there just after five. At seven o'clock we were still talking, our stomachs seething pits of tannin, and nothing short of ruptured bladders could have shifted us. I'd thought Marc the harpist was a good story-teller, but he paled beside Bart. Bart was born in Zaire when it was still the Belgian Congo, the eldest of ten siblings. The first time he saw Europe was at the age of ten, when he was sent to boarding-school. After a ten years' battle with the education system he decided modern life was too stressful, left university and promptly got a job as a mechanic at a Volkswagen factory. It financed an incredible series of foreign trips. He'd been trekking in Indonesia twice, teaching himself the language on the way. He'd walked and climbed in every European mountain range except the Caucasus. In between times he'd bought a derelict farm outhouse and converted it into the home I admired so much, complete with solar power, rainwater storage and garden cuttings harvested from all over the continent. He spoke English, French and Indonesian fluently and was teaching himself Spanish. He wrote poetry in all his languages, and loved French music, Spanish wine and Belgian beer. Two hours weren't enough to hear half the things he'd done.

We were poring over maps of the Ardennes when his wife came in, and suddenly I felt a strong desire to be elsewhere. She didn't sound angry, and she didn't look angry, but I knew in the pit of my stomach that I wasn't welcome any more. To be fair to her – and she deserves fairness – there are very few women on this planet more generous and affectionate than Tine. It's just that there are even fewer who'd be happy to see a complete stranger on the doorstep when they're nine and a bit months pregnant. Besides, she had visitors already: Bart's younger brother Karel and his wife Anna. I think she was worried that another little guest might be planning an appearance.

Bart made the introductions, looking rather embarrassed. To judge by Tine's expression he'd be hearing more about it later. I tried to make myself as unobtrusive as possible, but Karel wasn't having any of it. He wanted to hear all about my adventures, where I'd been, where I was going – and why. There was a sudden silence when I told them. Bart and I hadn't got that far yet. How would you react if the aforementioned undesired stranger turned out to be walking across the continent in memory of a murdered friend?

42

For God's sake don't react as Tine did. Come to that, please don't tell me that my words did it. Her eyes shot very wide, her hand went to her stomach and she leant over to Bart and whispered urgently. He went white. His jaw dropped. He looked from me to Karel and back to Tine as if not quite sure who we were. Then a connection clicked, and he shot up from the table like a Harrier jet.

'Erm . . . erm . . .' His eyes were white round the edges. 'Can you look after the house? We've got to go to hospital . . .' And he was thundering up the stairs as Tine sat back, breathing hard. Anna (a nurse) was by her side in an instant, gripping her hand and muttering Flemish wisdom; Karel and I sat and gibbered. Within three minutes Bart and Tine were gone, blasting off down the rutted track at a speed that can't have helped at all. The three of us were left gaping. What do you do at a time like that? Eventually Anna went looking for a hoover, and Karel and I cleaned the table and washed the dishes. Simple, unchallenging work, and it was just as well.

Then we locked up and drove back to their place. If anything, Karel's house was even more welcoming than Bart's, a poem in pale wood that he'd planned and constructed himself. They poured me into a shower, kidnapped my clothes for the unsuspecting washing-machine, made me a colossal plate of bacon and eggs and generally made me feel like an honoured guest. As Karel's English warmed up he turned out to be a one-man entertainments programme. Work in the Belgian fire brigade, accidents, call-outs, the evils of management; politics and regionalism ('of course the Walloons are unfriendly. They live next door to Vlaams Blok'); Belgian society as it seemed to him when he, in his turn, was shipped home ('I could never work out why people always lock their doors here'); above all, travel. He'd continued the family tradition of trekking all over Europe from the Canaries to the Carpathians, he knew the Ardennes as a walker and mountain-biker, and he was one of a very select few who'd seen the Pyrenees from all angles as a walker, caver and paraskier. He had a joke for every occasion. He called himself 'the fool' and 'the joker', and any king would have been proud to employ him; but it wouldn't have worked. Half his stories were Homeric accounts of his battles with management, bureaucracy and convention. Life with him would never be peaceful. I wondered how Anna coped. 'You know what?' he said as I sat there in a borrowed dressing-gown devouring pig. 'You must have been sent to be the godfather. Can you do Marlon Brando?'

I laughed. Acting's not one of my talents.

It was close to midnight when we drove back to Bart's, and we were still talking like madmen. I'd been on the go for two weeks and I was already feeling lonely: company like his was heaven-sent. In fact Karel was so busy talking he almost missed the turn into Bart's drive, swerved into it at the last moment and came within an ace of crushing his elder sister Els, who'd come round to see if there was any news. Neither seemed surprised. Karel introduced me ('This is Ben, he's walking to Spain with a trombone and some memories'), and Els, a beautiful forty-something-year-old gave me a warm hug. I was definitely starting to like this family ... We chatted for a few minutes, but it was too late and too cold to linger. Brother and sister drove off in convoy, and I staggered into my tent and crashed.

Bart came back at 2 a.m. By a miracle I was awake and heard him. I bounced out of my tent, doss-bag and all, and hurried over to hear the news. He gave me the palest smile I have ever seen.

'No news yet, but I'm not worried.' His hands were, they were shaking.

'I'll put the kettle on,' I said. Two in the morning is one of the few times at which my brain really functions (it's the jazz bandit in me) and I couldn't leave him there to suffer alone. He sat on the floor, wrapped in his sleeping-bag. I took the armchair, wrapped in mine. The stove rustled and creaked.

44

The cold wind flapped my tent outside. With mugs of tea steaming before us, we talked the sun up into the sky.

We'd known each other for less than twelve hours, but somehow, that wasn't the point. He was waiting for the birth of his first child. I was walking in Anna's memory. Neither of us was in the mood for strict social convention. We talked about the things that really mattered: birth and love and friendship, loss and grief and joy. He told me of his favourite spot on Earth, a farm in the Ardennes run by long-dead friends. He was going to name the child after them. I told him I didn't have a favourite spot yet, I just wanted to see everywhere, and he understood. We talked of Tine, of Anna, of other meetings and friendships, of fatalism, of belief. We could have talked about anything that night . . . I said what Karel had said about godfathers. He said it was a good idea. I said I'd be honoured, and meant it. We never forgot what was going on in Leuven; but the conversation travelled far away.

It was after five when we crashed out, and neither of us slept for long. We met in the kitchen at seven, bleary-eyed and tense. His nerves were infectious. I made the tea while he mixed the muesli, and we sat and munched in silence. His thoughts were with Tine. Mine were running through check-lists: route, food, packing. The second Bart finished he was on his feet. We shook hands, I wished him luck, and he was gone in a shower of mud, leaving me alone in the house. I did what I could do wash and tidy up, left my phone number on the table, locked up, and legged it. Hanging around to greet the new mother and child didn't seem like the world's most tactful plan.

I crossed the linguistic divide early that afternoon, and it was like changing countries. The last Flemish town I saw was Goetsenhaven, full of the now-familiar signs: *Bakkerij* on the baker's, *Het Volk* newspaper, *Het Laatste Nieuws*. Two miles later I walked into Hélécine: *boulangerie*, *La Dépeche*, *Café du Domaine*. The first passers-by greeted me with '*Bonjour*' and my heart jumped with delight. At last, a local language I understood! I hurried into the café with a ringing '*Bonjour*' of my own, so they probably thought I was nuts, and who am I to argue? My very first French conversation ran roughly thus:

'Hi! Can I get some water here?'

'Of course. With or without soap?'

'Without. My stomach's clean.'

'Where are you going?'

'Spain.'

'What, today?'

'I walk fast.'

'Did you walk across the Channel?'

'Just call me J. C. Can I visit the castle here?'

'Yes, it's free. The water's a hundred francs.'

'Really?'

'Swiss.'

'I'll drink slowly.'

'Bon voyage!'

There was a spring in my step as I left. Walloons were hospitable too! One less thing to worry about.

And that evening, as I slept on a Sunday-school table in the village of Orp-le-Grand, the phone went.

'Allo?' I mumbled. When in Wallonia . . .

'Hey Ben, it's Bart!'

I jolted awake.

'What news?'

'My daughter! She's born, she's beautiful, you can be the godfather!'

Whatever the conversation that followed, it wasn't coherent. I was as overcome as he was, but we didn't gibber for long. He had too many calls to make.

'Where will you be in September?' he asked.

'The Pyrenees.'

'Great! We'll come to see you!' He rang off, leaving me gaping. It was a long time before I dropped off again, laughing with delight. I was looking forward to autumn.

PART 3

The Ardennes

'And crossing the Channel, one cannot say much
For the French and the Belgians, the Danish and Dutch . . .'
Michael Flanders, *The English are Best*

They call Namur the gateway to the Ardennes. It's not much of a distinction. They say the same about Liege and Aachen. It's a cut-throat world out there. But Namur can at least enjoy the modest distinction of being the Ardennes' wettest gateway. It lies at the confluence of the Meuse and Sambre rivers, a steep-sided little town looking down to the water and up to a magnificent fortress, designed – like most of the other fortresses in Europe – by Vauban, military architect to Louis XIV. Swans cruise along the rivers as cyclists whiz by above, apparently oblivious to the first real slopes I'd seen in Belgium. Stately willows line the banks, and above them on the heights the beech trees sing to the wind. It's all terribly civilized, and I liked it the first time I saw it.

It also taught me a lesson.

I came to Namur for one reason: its museum. Forget the Louvre, the V&A, the Guggenheim. The finest museum in Europe is the *Musée des Trésors d'Oignies*, a humble collection of sheer medieval genius clustered in a small back room in the convent of Notre-Dame. It celebrates the lives of two thirteenth-century personalities: Bishop Jacques de Vitry, and Brother Hugo, a monk at the monastery of Oignies west of Namur, and one of the finest goldsmiths who ever lived. Jacques was a patron of the arts, collecting and commissioning things of beauty from all over the known world, and especially from Hugo. He bequeathed his entire collection to the monastery of Oignies. Eight hundred years later, despite invasion, rebellion, Reformation, fire-bombing, and thirty years bricked up in a wall to escape Napoleon's armies, the legacy remains safe and sound in Namur, the responsibility of a single nun who loves it like a child – and admits to trying on the bishop's rings when no-one's looking. A room the size of a squash court holds a tenth-century Byzantine cross, eleventh-century Arab glasses, a gold-embroidered twelfth-century mitre showing the martyrdom of Thomas à Becket, and half a dozen pieces by Hugo which are so delicate they take the breath away: a two-foot-tall filigree cross, a crescent reliquary holding a fragment of St Peter's rib, a beaten gold chalice that I still think of as the Holy Grail, a gigantic Bible written, illustrated and covered by Hugo's hand. I went because I'm a medievalist. I stayed to admire the beauty.

In more than one sense.

The museum had another visitor that morning: a classic backpacker, in a fleece jacket and bush trousers, her rucksack leaning against the umbrella-stand. She was a slim, athletic, twenty-something, and blonde. She greeted me in fluent Australian and smiled bright-eyed, and my heart took off and started dancing. 'Pleased to meet you,' I said, while my eyes implored, 'Be my friend!' Whenever I looked at her I could hear bluebirds tweeting, which seldom happens in Namur when the spring sleet is falling. I say this as a compliment to Hugo: his craft is so beautiful that it even distracted me from her. Occasionally.

When the hour-long visit was over she smiled again and said, 'Fancy a waffle?' – a question very few beautiful women have ever asked me. It wasn't much of a decision. I would've joined her for a glass of engine oil. We collected our rucksacks and struck off in search of culinary gold.

Belgium really only has two culinary specialities. One is *moules-frites*, mussels and chips, the only foodstuff known to unite Flemings and Walloons in patriotic fervour. No other nation's fries quite attain that combination of golden shell and sensuous interior, they claim, and wince when I extol the merits of chips soaked in gravy. The other is the waffle, and oddly enough, pretty much the same adjectives apply, which leads to a few questions about Belgians' relationship with the deep-fat fryer. Namur is full of waffle boutiques, and soon Kathy and I were ensconced behind platefuls of concentrated carbohydrate laden with sugar, cream and a wood's-worth of fruit, chatting as backpackers do. I don't remember half of what she said, being far too busy staring deeply into her eyes. Her face had a curious luminosity that flashed into life when she smiled, and I would have been happy to sit and watch her all day. Romantic towers raced skywards in my head. Why not join forces for a few days? I was in no hurry, and she was on holiday. And beautiful. We could visit Namur together, look at the fortress, maybe even share a part of the walk! My pulse accelerated at the mere thought of a couple of days in her company. My mind had built up a beautiful friendship before we'd even finished the whipped cream.

'Fancy strolling around for a bit?' I asked her hopefully at the end of the meal. She gave me a dazzling smile.

'I'd love to, but I'm meeting my husband in Ghent this afternoon.'

I visited the citadel alone. It was closed for repairs. Bad Sack Day.

I left Namur in a thoughtful mood. I've always been a fan of feminine beauty and a hopeless romantic, a combination which kept Interflora in business while I was at college, but even I normally tend to wait more than half an hour before swearing undying devotion. I'd even learnt a measure of self-control in the last couple of years, a necessary defence mechanism in an industry where everyone wears tight rubber suits practically all the time (it's a tough life): what had made me so susceptible to a beautiful smile? I'd been walking for two and a half weeks, but I hadn't been that isolated, had I? My memory was studded with the faces and stories of the people I'd met. Isolation? Surely not! And yet . . . I thought about it. Few of the meetings had lasted more than an hour. They all followed a pattern: say hi, chat, say 'bye, and leave. I was crossing one of the most densely-populated countries in the world, but for all the long-term human contact I'd had I might as well have been in Alaska. It was a bizarre thought, and a disturbing one. I would have been happy to jettison my entire timetable in order to spend time with Kathy. The loneliness was already that intense. What would I be like in six months' time? It didn't bear thinking about. Wilderness isolation – in Belgium. It's not a common complaint.

I was still pondering the meaning of loneliness as I got my stove going that evening. I was sitting on a harrow in the yard of a palatial farm (complete with crenelated watch-towers). My kit lay spread out neatly on a pile of hay-bales in the barn behind me, watched by a herd of drooling cows. The farmer had been very hospitable. 'Sure, you can stay the night! Just don't set fire to my barn.' Sound advice. I made sure I was well outside and downwind of anything flammable before I stuck a match to the petrol. It exploded with the normal satisfying woof and took most of the hairs off the back of my hand. Business as usual, I thought, as the scent of *chef flambé* filled the air. I reached for my pasta.

Then I saw the eyes. Five pairs of them, level with my own, peering warily over a low wall; five short-cropped blond heads above. They stared at me unblinkingly. I nodded and turned to my stove, which was spitting incandescent white flames. Feet scraped on the concrete as I opened the feed-valve. Slowly the flame dwindled and tightened to a roaring blue inferno.

Small, muddy boots crept into my peripheral vision. I started whistling through my teeth, dropped my pot onto the flame and clipped the fire-shield in place around it. Only then did I look up.

Five boys were watching me, enthralled. The eldest must have been eleven or twelve, a tubular young man with white-blond hair and heavy glasses, the youngest five or six. They started like wild animals as I met their eyes, but they didn't bolt.

'What are you doing?' asked one: not the eldest, but something in his stance proclaimed that he was their chief. He was small and upright, and as vigorous as Napoleon. He spoke so fast that I barely followed the words.

'Cooking supper,' I answered slowly, hoping he'd take the hint. 'Macaroni cheese.' Nothing if not inventive.

They inched closer as the pot started to steam. 'Why?'

'I'm hungry.'

'Why don't you eat at home?'

'Because home's in Britain.'

They stared. 'What are you doing here?' asked the eldest, as Napoleon groped for words.

'Walking to Spain.'

'Why?'

It was an awkward moment. How to explain my mission to a group of prepubescent farmers? The same way as to anyone else of course.

'In memory of a friend.'

'What happened to him?'

'She was murdered.'

Long silence.

'What if someone kills you?' asked Napoleon brightly.

'I'll be dead.' I bent to the pot again as a rogue penne made a spirited bid for freedom.

'What's your name?' asked Napoleon. Their eyes were following my spoon around the pot as if hypnotized.

51

'Benoit.' Which is approximately true, since my Dad's been calling me that ever since I can remember. The Youngest Son jumped.

'Mine too!'

I grinned at him. Napoleon gave him a black look.

'I'm Frédéric,' he said sternly, recalling the ranks to order.

'I'm Adrien,' added the eldest. The others – Nicholas and Ludovic – chimed in and they fell over each other to explain. Adrien and Nicolas were brothers who lived in Brussels 'a long way away', and who came here with their parents for the holidays. The other three lived here. They were astonished when I said I'd walked from Ostend.

'But that's even further than Brussels!'

I showed them my boots. The soles were already wearing smooth. Five simultaneous indrawn breaths nearly hoovered the mud off.

'And you're walking to Spain?' Adrien asked. It was slowly sinking in.

'Did you walk across the Channel?' added Nicolas. It kept them laughing for five minutes.

They lost interest in me as I started eating, which was a relief. Heavy-duty pasta consumption is not a spectator sport. One by one they drifted into the barn and started scrambling around on the stacked bales. I ate quickly, not wanting to miss the show. Sure enough, within minutes the hay was flying. A five-cornered guerrilla war broke out, something between King of the Castle and tag-team wrestling with handfuls of prickly stems thrown in. Treble cries of '*au secours*!' and '*vengeance!*' filled the air and the bales rocked and crumbled. Hastily I moved my sleeping-bag out of the danger area. I was stuffing it back into my rucksack when a flying clump hit me on the back of the head.

'Hey!' I yelled.

There was a sudden silence. Five bright pairs of eyes regarded me narrowly. I could see the cogs whirling. I backed away, hands raised, starting to laugh. The five looked at one another.

Would anyone dare? Would they? Then Nicolas smiled ador-ingly and hurled a fistful of straw at me. I hadn't even begun to duck when the ramparts erupted. Small hands hit me all at once, grappled my knees, shoved me sideways. The bale I was standing on teetered. With a despairing yell I toppled to my doom. Two young thugs tickled me as a small hand rammed yet more straw down the back of my neck. Next second they were fleeing, breathless with laughter, and I charged up the bales after them howling for blood.

We were still playing tig round the rafters when the farmer came in to investigate the disturbance.

Five juvenile warriors and an infantile pilgrim stared aghast as cold eyes raked us. A fine rain of straw settled slowly around us. I risked a quick look sideways. Three bales were disintegrat-ing and the whole stack looked as if an earthquake had hit. A frown crossed mine host's brow: Zeus reaching for his thunder-bolts. They led me astray, your honour! Benoit giggled ner-vously. Nicolas slipped an anxious hand into mine. The silence lengthened.

Then the farmer burst into the deepest belly-laugh I've ever heard.

'Bedtime!' he said firmly. 'It's almost 9.30.'

Already? We were appalled.

'Sleep well,' he added to me as he shepherded his charges towards the house. 'It looks like you've earned it.'

My playmates were nearly at the house when Nicolas slipped away from Adrien and ran back.

'Bed,' I said. Hypocrite!

'When are you going tomorrow?' he asked anxiously.

'7.30.'

His face fell. 'Oh. We get up at ten.' He gave me a quick, hard hug. 'Bonne nuit, Benoit.'

'Bonne nuit, mon ami.'

It wasn't. Unseen hands had doctored my sleeping-bag. I was still picking straw from it a week later.

I awoke to the sound of whispers. The night was as black as pitch, the dawn the merest hint of grey on the horizon. What . . . ? I rolled over blearily and looked at my watch – 6 o'clock?

'He's awake!' A hiss from the bales.

'Ssh!'

I groped for my glasses, looked up, saw five blond heads duck out of sight, 6 o'clock? I had to be dreaming. Excited giggles cut through the barricades around me.

'*Bonjour, les gars,*' I croaked. '*Bien dormi?*'

They popped up out of hiding like a Punch and Judy show. '*Oh oui, merci, monsieur!*'

'We wanted to say goodbye,' added Nicolas proudly. 'We got up specially.'

Greater love hath no man than this, that he shall get up hideously early to see a friend off. I put on the closest I could to a happy morning face and clambered to my feet. They emerged from cover, wreathed in grins. All five were carrying plastic bags full of food. A gift? No, their breakfasts. We sat and ate side by side on the bales, swinging our legs and watching the sun come up. Everyone wanted to help me pack. Everyone wanted to carry something. It took a long time to get everything sorted. When I heaved my rucksack on at last, they lined up like troops on review.

'My God, what a load!' muttered Adrien.

'Shit,' said Benoit proudly.

I shrugged. 'It's my house.'

'You're a snail!' Nicolas laughed, then looked worried that he'd offended me. I grinned.

'That's right! The Pilgrim Snail.' We stood smiling at one another. Then someone called from the house, and we jumped.

'*Au revoir, mes amis.*'

'*Au revoir*, Snail,' they chorused. The parental voice was raised again. The three locals fled. Nicolas and Adrien lingered a moment longer.

'We talked about you and your friend Anna last night,' Adrien and Nicolas nodded eagerly. 'We wanted to give you this.' He reached out a small hand and dropped a few coins into mine. Nicolas did the same, and touched my hand affectionately.

'It's the last of our pocket-money.'

Then the voice called again, and they bolted.

That night, huddled over a torch in my tent, I translated my rucksack cover into French: 'Canterbury to Santiago for charity, in memory of Anna,' I signed it, 'The Pilgrim Snail.'

Thus the legend was born.

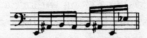

I marched into the Ardennes. And up, over, down and through them. I've never been quite sure what an Ardenne is, but the hills that cover Wallonia and Luxembourg are full of them, and they're worth seeing. The entire land is hacked and ploughed by deep river valleys running between colossal cliffs, covered in rich forests and carpeted with flowers. It looks like a film-maker's version of Transylvania. Boar still roam the forests as they did a millennium ago, i.e. running like buggery from hunters, and the skies are full of birds: herons, buzzards, falcons, woodpeckers, pheasants, and owls. Spring burst upon me as I followed the GR5 east, and I walked beneath canopies of blossom. Often the joy of travelling overcame me and I found myself whistling: *Consider yourself at home*, *Waltzing Matilda*, *Tipperary*. Heaven knows what the birds thought of it, but nothing swooped from the trees in desperate attack, so it can't have sounded that bad.

Three days after leaving Namur I discovered that not all Belgian kids are friendly. I passed through the town of Hotton at dawn, crossing the Meuse yet again and stopping to gaze in awe at water like liquid light. I was sweating my way up the far side when I saw a small boy playing with a large dog, a picture of youthful innocence. My heart warmed nostalgically, and I waved. He waved back happily as I went by, flinging back a halo of golden curls, then bent to whisper conspiratorially to the companion of his childhood. Ah, youth and its carefree joys!

Two seconds later pain erupted in my right ankle as the son of a bitch took a chunk out of my Achilles.

Somewhere in Hotton, cowering behind a wall as I write this, is a golden retriever that's never going to bite anyone again. Especially not large backpackers with – this is the important bit – two walking poles. I'm still not sure what happened. One second I was walking along without a care in the world. The next I was charging back down the road with both sticks raised, foaming at the mouth and screaming obscenities while dog and owner took off for the horizon like scared chickens. I've never gone berserk before. You think I'm exaggerating? I know I was foaming. I found the spittle on my shirt afterwards, and as for seeing red, the blood rushed into my head so fast it's a wonder my scalp didn't detonate. But they breed brave kids in Belgium. When I stopped cold and turned to march away, suddenly aware that committing homicide in the public highway wouldn't be tactful, a whistle and the scatter of claws on tarmac brought me up short. I turned just in time to score the hit of my life on the hell-hound's flank. He catapulted backwards, picked himself up and shook his innards out barking. '*Viens*!' I bellowed, sticks raised. 'Come on!' The kid was watching from a safe distance. If he'd been in range I might have reconsidered my leniency. The dog came one step nearer. I jumped towards him and he bolted, tail between his legs. '*Viens*!' I yelled again, but nothing stirred. The field was mine. I marched proudly round the corner, checked that they were out of sight, and sank down swerving onto the verge. The wound wasn't as bad as it might have been, two bloody furrows where his teeth had nicked me. They soon disappeared under assorted plasters and a pint or so of iodine. When the throbbing subsided I went on, swearing to myself. I didn't meet another soul all day. It's probably just as well.

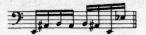

Pines rustled in the breeze above the valley of the Meuse, and the track was a scented carpet winding between their trunks. Far below, the river lay blue beneath the sky, flecked with yellow canoes drifting on the current. White moths like flying blossoms streamed up the river. I sat on the plinth of a desecrated cross, the Christ above me broken and covered in graffiti, pondering the Belgian countryside. Every other crossroads sported a shrine, a cross or a statue of the Virgin. In between them lay war memorials: the Ardennes were the scene of some of the most savage fighting in the Second World War during the winter of 1944–45, and the countryside remembers. Here and there concrete bunkers dot the woods, and the street names evoke past heroes: rue Patton, Place Eisenhower, Carrefour du 1,718 Airborne ... Everywhere there are Dutch tourists. The Ardennes are the heart of French-speaking Wallonia, but you wouldn't always know it. Every campsite I found in the area was Dutch-owned and Dutch-speaking. The few locals I met warned me: 'Watch out! The Dutch are everywhere!' as if the Plague had broken loose again. When I did meet them on the tracks, they seemed human enough. Perhaps I was missing something.

The image I'd once had of the Belgians as a race of bureaucrats had crumbled too. What few lingering doubts I entertained vanished on my last night in the country. I'd gone busking in the town of Houffalize, not far from the Luxembourg border. It's a pretty town in spring, full of life and colour, though since the whole place was bombed flat during the Battle of the Bulge it doesn't have a lot to boast in the way of architecture. I was playing in the gleaming-new town square when a middle-aged man jumped out of a middle-aged Renault and ran towards me.

'Can I help you?' I was having a polite day.

He stood there looking embarrassed, a dishevelled figure in a worn brown shirt and dirty trousers. I waited, leaning on the trombone.

'Do you play jazz?'

I just had been, but he seemed too nervous for irony.

'Yes.'

'Wonderful! Will you play in my pub this evening?'

A month ago, I wouldn't have accepted the invitation at gun-point, but the trip was mellowing me. 'With pleasure,' I said.

'Excellent! I'll collect you in an hour!' And he turned and ran for his car.

Two hours later I was in his pub, somewhere at the end of an incredible tangle of country lanes, and I could see why he was so nervous. The hamlet around us had a population of three, and two of them were teetotal, but somehow two separate optimists had seen fit to open bars there. Joseph, my host, had the distracted look of one who hears the wolf at the door. To block it out, he talked. Non-stop. This was going to be the most English pub in Wallonia. (He had horse-brasses on the wall to prove it). It was going to make his fortune. The band this evening would set the countryside alight.

'Band?'

'I've asked a friend to come and play the piano.' He didn't meet my eyes. 'I thought you could play together. You know, folk songs, a bit of atmosphere...' He trailed off, looking despondent. 'That's okay, isn't it?'

'Yes,' I reassured him, and hoped like hell that the pianist knew the same pieces I did.

He did.

One and a half of them.

All of *Yellow Submarine*, and half of *Strangers in the Night*.

Not a logical half. He kept on jumping bars in the middle without warning, as if he'd learned it off a skipping CD.

Oddly enough, the audience seemed to like it. Richard the pianist kept them happy with a string of Jacques Brel classics, prefacing each by turning to me and saying, 'But you *must* know this one . . .' Whenever he got tired or thirsty, I took over with what I thought was an international repertoire. How can anyone not know *Tipperary*?, I thought; but it hasn't reached Wallonia. In despair I reverted to school song-books. I wouldn't have believed it possible to improvise a swinging blues to the tune of *Frere Jacques*, but that night I managed it. It went down a storm.

Richard got nervous when he heard the applause. He hurried back to the keyboard and started in on some lugubrious folk tune, and I took advantage of the pause to prop up the bar. Joseph, anxious to convince me that it was a fine gig poured out a generous dollop of wine, and threw an anxious glance at my neighbour. I looked, and shuddered. He was about my age, a tall, spindly, pale-faced lad, and his eyes were so deep in alcoholic oblivion that I would have needed radio to reach him. One hand was clutching a bottle of Johnnie Walker, the other clenching and unclenching on the bar.

'Wha' you thi' o' reeshun?' he slurred, gaze oscillating around my face.

'Pardon?'

'Wha' you thi' o' reeshun?' Irritation snapped in his voice. I didn't like it.

'There's a one-eyed yellow idol to the north of Kathmandu,' I began amicably, in English: not one of my smarter moves. 'There's a little marble cross below the town . . .'

His eyes zeroed in on my face, and there was a red light in them. 'Wha'?' The hand was definitely a fist now. Eight months' vengeful aggression ignited inside me. *Just start*, I though. *Just start*!

Joseph saw us in the nick of time. 'Come on, Steve,' he said. Not Stéphane, Steve. 'Leave him be.'

Steve swung round and threw a punch. By sheer accident, it

glanced off Joseph's shoulder. Mine host went red and tried to hit back. Steve grappled him and they crashed against a pillar.

I ducked as a flailing arm whistled past my nose, glimpsed a blur of movement on my right, and jumped behind the bar as Steve's brothers arrived in midair and pinned him.

'Out!' yelled Joseph. 'I'll call the cops!'

'Call them! Call them!' It took two men to hold Steve back.

'Out!'

The rest of the audience watched with clinical detachment as the skirmish moved towards the door. Joseph was shouting threats, keeping well out of range. Steve was just shouting. As his brothers forced him out of the door Joseph rushed up and kicked him in the backside. Steve's obscenity shook the windows, but the door was shut before he could get inside. The frame shivered. Joseph laughed.

'It's toughened!' He shouted. 'Fuck off!' There was a scattering of ironic applause from the onlookers. Something told me they'd seen this before.

'Did he pay his tab?' asked Joseph anxiously. Someone nodded.

'Same time tomorrow, then.' He sounded almost resigned. 'Come on, Richard. Play something.'

And the show went on.

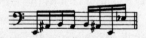

Ten days after crossing into Luxembourg, I was still there.

This is unusual.

I'd decided it was the most fascinating country in Europe.

This is unheard-of.

Everyone knows about Luxembourg. It's a city full of bankers. No, it's a country full of Eurocrats. No, it's the EU headquarters. Isn't it?

No, it's cool.

It takes an hour to drive across the country. At rush-hour. Even on foot you can do it in a week. Luxembourg is so small it barely shows up on a map of Europe. There are only two 1:50 000 maps in the country: North and South, and they mainly show Belgium and France. For anyone who hasn't got it yet, Luxembourg is a *very small country*.

In three days in this pocket-sized state, I slept in a French-speaking monastery, a Portuguese restaurant and a German-speaking farmer's barn. I talked jazz trombones with a Danish theologian and listened to a monk blaming all society's ills on cable TV. I visited the twentieth century's finest photographic exhibition (*The Family of Man*) in one twelfth-century castle, and was invited to lunch by a TV crew in another. They were filming *Pinocchio II*. I walked past a farmer hand-sowing his crops behind one of Europe's biggest electronics factories. I saw a town so full of Portuguese immigrants that the May Day parade followed the Portuguese flag. (The town's ever-so-Iberian name? Echternach.) I was even sworn at by a local motorist for the first time on the walk – in Italian. Anyone still care to tell me that Luxembourg's boring?

Good.

After a week of kaleidoscopic cultural experience, I walked up the hill into Luxembourg city. This is harder than it sounds. The city's built on the cliffs overlooking the Alzette gorge, and I mean *cliffs*. If the public transport system didn't include a handy lift from Upper town to Lower, commerce would grind to a halt. I knew about the lift, but I walked anyway. Stubbornness is an amazing thing, and besides, I knew I could do it.

I wasn't the same Ben who'd set off from Canterbury such a short-long time before. For six weeks I'd been on a learning curve so steep you couldn't ski down it, and the effects were starting to show. When I set off I'd been nervous about every-thing: fitness, camping skills, languages, people. All those worries had died in the blossomed hills. It seemed natural to walk up to a complete stranger and ask for whatever help I needed. It seemed natural that they would comply. In six weeks I'd been refused one request. Who says we live in a selfish society? I'd grown so used to planning my days that it had become routine: food-shop, water-stop, route, rests. I'd stopped bothering to plan campsites at all. I'd never had a problem finding somewhere to sleep, and I was starting to believe that I never would. Not even language scared me any more. I'd spoken English once since Namur. The rest was a glorious mixture of French, German, fractured Spanish and Dutch, mixed in with plenty of hand-waving. My confidence grew at every step. I knew I'd make it to Santiago.

I'd been planning to spend a day in the city. I ended up spending four. It's a combination of Vauban fortress, sophisticated capital and park, and it would have been a crime to hurry through. Much of the Alzette gorge is too steep to build on. The locals gave up trying centuries ago, and have converted the entire stretch of precipice into a series of terraced gardens. Behind them is the old town, a maze of courts and streets as steep as stairs, and behind them is one of the most exclusive shopping areas in Europe: heaven for happy buskers. I was still adapting to Marc's philosophy, fighting against a natural desire to make buckets of cash at every stop, and it wasn't easy; but the shoppers of Luxembourg are generosity incarnate, so I had the double delight of playing well and raking it in. For all that, I didn't do much playing. I was tired, physically and mentally. It was a pleasure just to do nothing.

I did it at the youth hostel, a barracks-like building caught between a verdant garden and a motorway bridge in the low town. It was half-full of backpackers speaking the strange jargon of their sub-culture: words culled from a dozen languages, acronyms based on half the world's transport networks, knowing references to this hostel and that. For me it was the first chance I'd had in six weeks to feel completely normal. Nobody batted an eyelid when I staggered in under my load. Nobody remarked on my bizarre Anglo-Franco-Flemish accent. I felt at home, with those who had no home. It was one more measure of what I was becoming.

Of all the family of backpackers, I spent most time with Chris. Bizarrely – given my experience in Namur and the number of attractive single women in the hostel – this Chris was a Christopher, a nineteen-year-old actor and lobster-fisherman from Nova Scotia, treating himself to a grand tour of Europe before getting on with some serious thespianism. Not that he treated it seriously. He never treats anything seriously, and he's probably the funniest human being I've ever met. Rowan Atkinson is famous for getting a laugh from reading school registers, but Chris could make a tax bill sound entertaining. It's impossible to reproduce his humour on the page, and I'm not going to try. Suffice to say that if my eyebrows were half as eloquent as his, I'd be a sex symbol by now.

We spent two days wandering around the city, sitting in the parks and laughing. I hadn't realized until then how much I'd missed English. I love speaking other languages, but they're not my own. We visited the cathedral and admired the appallingly over-decorated tomb of John the Blind, the King of Bohemia who died at Crécy, and the imposingly minimalist tomb of the late Grand Duchess Charlotte. We stood gazing up at the gilded statue of the Liberation, a Greek goddess holding a laurel wreath who looked as though she was about to make a swan-dive into the Alzette, and tried to count the tourists giving themselves cricks in the neck filming her from all angles. We took my boots in to be resoled, a sorely-needed operation. (I then spent a happy day strolling the richest streets in Europe in my slippers, and collected more funny looks than I've ever received in my life.) We stripped and reorganized my rucksack and posted five kilos of kit home. We indulged in huge lunches of bread and brie and local wine, starting on the stroke of noon and ending, immobile, some time after three. We spent two hours in the municipal museum looking at illuminated medieval manuscripts, then retired to an Irish pub near the hostel. It was a different world. Concrete underfoot, street-lights overhead, running water, all the company my heart could desire: it was the perfect holiday.

Four days in Luxembourg. They might easily have become more, but as my mental energy returned I felt the itch to con-tinue. It was still an unimaginably long way to Santiago, and summer was drawing near. On the fourth night Chris and I went for a traditional Luxembourgeois pint (Guinness at the Irish pub), and I said, 'I'm moving tomorrow.'

An eyebrow quirked. 'You're moving *now*.'

I tried to give him a stern look. The other eyebrow wiggled, and I cracked.

'Where to?' he asked, as if he couldn't understand what all the fuss was about.

'South. Over the French border.'

I expected another smart-arse answer, but he only said, 'Want a bit of company?'

I stared. 'Are you sure?'

'Sure I'm sure. I'll walk a ways with you, then get a bus back. No sweat.' In addition to being funny, he was cooler than a polar bear in shades.

'Fancy carrying my rucksack for me?'

'I wouldn't want to deprive you.'

'Too kind.'

But he carried lunch for us both, when we left in the morning. As he said, 'It's the least I can do.'

We followed the Alzette southwards, upstream, past man-sions and old mine-workings, factories, wrecks and ruins. The shadows were pleasantly cool after the hot spring sunshine, and the river made liquid music on our right. We chatted as we walked, about politics and politicians, Kosovo and the fall of the European Commission, and then the interesting stuff:

women, gigs and travel. It was the first time I'd walked with anyone, and it was a pleasure. I felt a pang when we reached the road early in the afternoon. There was just time for a final lunch before the bus drew up. Chris climbed aboard, waved, and was gone, leaving me strangely desolate. But the sun was shining, the birds were singing, the flowers were bright. After five minutes' moping I struck out southwards.

Two hours later I was in France.

PART 4

Lorraine and Alsace

'The natives were friendly, so we stayed the night' (trad. British)

I'd wondered what reception I'd get in rural France.

It wasn't what I expected.

I crossed the border some time in the early afternoon. It was hard to say exactly where. The trail I'd been following vanished under the earthen ramparts of a new motorway. Beyond it lay mile upon mile of fields: thick green pastures, golden oil-seed rape, stands of oak trees heavy with their full foliage. The sky was blue, studded with blinding white clouds, as warm as an English August. I slogged on due southwards, ducking and climbing fences and gates, and at last came out into a muddy country lane. It had to be France. There was writing all over the tarmac:

Brazil 0 – France 3

They wouldn't forget that in a hurry.

Half an hour later I crossed my first French village: a cluster of farms at one end, a long strip of ruined outhouses, then an incongruous patch of modern cottages, their pale bricks and rigid lines absurdly out of place. As I walked past a red Peugeot blasted by me and swerved into a gravel drive.

All four doors crashed open at once like a Thirties' gangster film, and four incandescent locals sprang out: two young men in dark suits and open collars, and two young women in cocktail dresses that might just have been decent on someone four sizes smaller. All four were swigging champagne from the bottle. Two plunged into each others' arms without even seeing me, and stood there kissing furiously. The others staggered towards me, waving their booty.

Mademoiselle bumped into me, bounced off and put a hand on my arm to steady herself. She leant forward and stared deeply into my eyes. Her young man was busy with his bottle.

'Are you Philippe?'

'No,' I said, as my senses reeled from a blast of Chanel and champagne. She pouted.

'Oh.' Then she brightened. 'Well, have some champagne, anyway!'

She thrust the heavy bottle into my hand, and giggled.

'*Santé!*'

'*Salut!*' I answered, and sipped cautiously. Not cautiously enough. I'm not used to drinking champagne from the bottle, and the bubbles overflowed, up my nose and down my windpipe. As I spluttered she snatched the bottle back protectively, took a practised draught and smiled beatifically.

'Congratulate me! I've just been confirmed!'

'Congratulations!' I said heartily, and wished I were French. They did it in style.

'Are you going somewhere?' asked Monsieur, eyeing me narrowly as he wavered on his feet.

'Spain.'

He didn't even blink. 'And where are you walking to now?'

I checked the map.

'Antilly.'

His mouth opened so wide I thought he'd dislocate something.

'But that's *miles*!' He was still gaping when his demoiselle decided to take advantage of the open mouth and threw herself enthusiastically into his arms. I waited for a second longer to see if they'd come up for air and continue the conversation, but I reckon her ladyship had gills. When I looked back from the road five minutes later, they were still entwined. I walked on ruefully, wishing I were French.

If anyone had asked me what I knew about popular French culture before I started walking. I would have said 'food and wine'. I'd been hoping to encounter something of each on the way. After all, I was planning to cross Alsace, the Cotes du Rhone and Languedoc. I was looking forward to a little constructive sampling.

After a few days in Lorraine my liver was praying for sobriety. French hospitality is in a league of its own.

Most of Lorraine is farmland. After the savage ridges of the Ardennes it was wonderfully gentle walking, an endless succession of easy hills and rolling vales, all decked out in green and gold. East of the Thionville-Metz conurbation and north of Nancy, the fields stretch unchecked clear into the Vosges. For a long-range walker, this has the following important implications:

1. no campsites
2. few tourists
3. bored locals
4. home cooking

It was perfect. Since there were no campsites, I had to ask the farmers' permission to pitch in their fields. Since there were no tourists, I was a novelty. Since they were bored, they usually invited me in to eat with the family. And, since they combined traditional home cooking with traditional home produce, I ate like a king. Every night. Only one farmer in the whole province refused to let me camp on his land. He'd just sprayed the lot with pesticide. If anyone ever tells me that French farmers are a xenophobic bunch, I'll hit them.

The problem is that the farmers of Lorraine are renowned throughout the Hexagon (as the French call continental France) for one thing: home-distilling. It's their proud boast that they can make white alcohol out of *anything*. And they do. One diary entry sums up the story of my first two weeks in France as no amount of polished prose ever could. It's written in red biro on a sheet of airmail paper in a hand that utterly fails to follow the lines on the page. The reason should be apparent:

Friday 14 May:
PISSED! After an evening's homebrewed hospitality chez Patrick, Christiane, Willy and Maxime (aged 5) – pastis, wine, and le cru (schnapps to you). Peach, apple, orange, normal pear, Williams pear, quince, myrtille (bilberry?). And the rest! Bottles lined up on the table like a monument to the brain-cells I've just killed. God help my head tomorrow . . . Followed the Roman <squiggle> this a.m., turned into classic over-bush-over-<squiggle>. Falling over streams, into nettles, soaking feet, scratched legs . . . Give up. Rejoin road. Bloody tarmac! L-driver slows as he goes by to read my rucksack. Slow reader. Traffic jam forms. Angry hoots. Gives two fingers to them, thumbs-up to me. Style.

Reached <name illegible> 3 p.m., shopped, invited in for a café by Olivier the shop assistant. Europe: he thinks Brits still have island mentality, not part of Europe. 'Les anglais sont spécials'. I keep hearing that. Buy toothpaste at chemist's, given a free bar of soap. Hint? Five <squiggle> later chatting with 5-yr-old girl by roadside. 'Where do you live?' 'In my tent.' 'Can't you even wash then?' HINT??? Paranoia . . . Tired, stop at this farmhouse, invited in – marvellous! Shower, tent in orchard, play Gameboy with Maxime. Annihilated (I am). Shame!

Shame! Rebuild reputation with trombone lesson. He's delighted. Parents less so. Eat with family, discuss weather (tres anglais!), Europe, neo-Nazi problem in E. Germany. Dutch buying up villages in the Cévennes, Patrick's trips to Argentina, Mexico, Chile, Uruguay (steel industry), charity work in S. Africa. Sit and drink. And drink. 'Dumbo' on TV (dubbed). Dastardly and Muttley. Maxime enthralled. Rest of us trolleyed. Vive la France!
   Wonder if this'll be legible demain?

It was, but only just.

I spent a lot of time talking about Europe. The Continent had me hooked. I'd been there for less than two months, and already I'd crossed five different language zones (six if you count the Echternach Portuguese) and three major frontiers, meeting monks and jazz musicians, farmers, foresters and factory workers, tourists from Holland and Germany, immigrants from all around the Mediterranean. I looked back on the last twenty-seven years and realized that I'd been blind. How else could I have missed the cultural kaleidoscope just across the Channel? When I left school the concept of the year out was just gathering momentum. I spent mine in New Zealand. So did ten out of the thirteen of my fellow students. By the time we graduated there seemed to be few students who hadn't spent a year in Australia or Nepal. Four years later, the young volunteers on Raleigh already viewed South-East Asia as passé. South America was the place to be. 'Europe? Who wants to go to Europe?' Okay, Prague was cool, but what lay beyond? Grey post-Communist depression. And as for the West, what was the point? It was all the same anyway, from Biscay to Berlin.

By the time I reached Lorraine, that prejudice was as dead as the soles of my boots. Continental Europe wasn't just as rich and as varied as Britain, it was more so, because there was more of it to be varied *in*. France alone may not look much bigger than England north to south, but it's got double the surface area, and there are no seas to stop people crossing the borders. The borders aren't even fixed. Alsace and Lorraine were German until the fifteenth century, briefly became Burgundian, reverted to German rule, were conquered by France under Louis XIV, and remained French until the Franco-Prussian War of 1870–71. Then Germany took them, and 'Alsace-Lorraine' became the war-cry of French nationalism. France took them back after the First World War: 'Elsass-Lothringen' promptly became a German nationalist slogan. Both Hitler and de Gaulle viewed the disputed territories as theirs by historical precedent. Even now there's doubt. I've lost count of the number of Lorrainers who told me, 'We're proud to be French, but everyone else calls us half-German.' One twenty-year-old graduate from Metz even spoke of a school exchange to Paris where she was asked, 'Metz? That's in Germany, isn't it?' It's even worse in Alsace. The local dialect there is Germanic, and it's not dead yet.

I'd read about French regionalism before I left. It was all about Paris against the provinces, especially the separatist ones: Corsica, Catalonia (there's a Catalan province in France too), the Basque country, Brittany. I'd never heard of the regional rivalries. Alsatians are the butt of half the jokes in Lorraine, and vice versa. Toulousains curse Parisians as 'northern invaders'. Pyreneans call the Toulousains the same. Auvergnats are legendary as country bumpkins. Normans are indecisive. Provence wine-merchants can't even say 'vin'. (They pronounce it 'ving'.) The town of Bourges in central France claims to have the purest accent in the country. You can't be a southerner unless you drink *pastis*, or a Breton if you don't drink cider. The further I tramped through provincial France, the richer the differences grew. All the same? Britain was homogeneous by comparison. France was messy. It was human. I was hooked.

Europe was the same, but bigger. I'd always seen it from a British perspective: the Franco-German monolith whose sole purpose in life seemed to be banning our beef and measuring our bananas. 'Europe' was an *entity*. It never occurred to me that people who lived in geographical Europe might not like political Europe either. I had a lot to learn . . . Half the farmers in Lorraine have gone bust. Who's to blame? The EU. They claim their taxes are the highest in Europe. Why? The EU. I asked a German what she thought: same problem, same culprit. The EU to them was a Hispano-Italian rip-off, with Britain on the sidelines helping itself to whatever it could get. Nobody believed I was British: 'But you speak French!' The automatic assumption was that I was German. As for loving Europe, that earned me astonished stares. Walking with a trombone seemed normal in comparison.

I fell in love with the tiny differences. It was so close, yet so far from home. Only one family between Ostend and Metz possessed a kettle. The rest brewed water on the stove. ('How can you not have a kettle?' I thought. 'Even *students* have kettles!') Everyone ate breakfast directly off the tablecloth – but the 'cloth' was plastic. One wipe with a damp sponge and that was the housework done for the morning. They break-fasted on baguettes, jam and hot chocolate, the classic 'conti-nental' that you could get in any hotel in Britain, but the quantities were *huge*. They drank wine every evening, even the ten-year-olds. The kids stayed up until midnight and nobody batted an eyelid. They got dressed up in their best clothes to go to Mass on Sunday. They knew and loved the song *My Way*, but with French words, 'Comme d'habitude'. They knew a million songs that I'd never heard of, by writers I didn't even know existed. They divided the country into *départements*, they numbered them alphabetically, and the numbers took over everything from car licence plates to phone numbers. It wasn't unusual to hear conversations along these lines:

'Where's he from?'

Glance at address. '68.'

'Oh, down there!'

Post offices were all equipped with free minitel stations, the

French equivalent of the Internet. Post boxes and vans were yellow, phone boxes silvered metal with double doors, motorway signs green. Everywhere I looked there were differences. The fact that France is so similar to home only made them stand out the more. It was baffling, alien, and yet so close that I felt I might come to understand it one day. That's a feeling I doubt I'd get in Thailand.

As I followed the GR5 eastwards towards the loom of the Vosges, I was already dreaming of exploring the rest of the continent. Europe had me seduced.

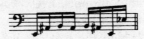

Europe's a kaleidoscope. It holds dark as well as light. I discovered that on my last night in Lorraine, in a little village huddled beneath the first ridge of the Vosges. It was a small, steep-sided place, the houses stretched along the road with their backs dug into the cliff-face, and the slopes above were dark with pines. It was the need of the day, and I was looking for a campsite.

A woman stood by the roadside, taking the air: tall, thin and blonde, perhaps in her late thirties. She looked at me curiously as I approached, without shyness or suspicion, so as I came closer I called out:

'*Bonsoir*! Is there a campsite near here?'

The inevitable conversation followed: where are you going, how long will it take, how will you get home, did you walk across the Channel?, hohoho. She was aggressive, quick, sharp as a needle, but she seemed friendly.

'Would you like to sleep at my house?' she asked. 'It's not very luxurious, but we can give you a meal and a hot shower.' It had happened to me so often that I wasn't even surprised.

'If it's not imposing, I'd be glad to,' I said. She laughed and led me towards the house.

It was a small place, with whitewashed walls. The garden

73

was at one side, a tiny terraced affair thick with weeds, over-grown bushes, and animals. Three dogs pressed themselves up against a chicken-wire enclosure. A couple of cats looked through us from the wall. A vortex of young ferrets clung to the wire facing of their cage. Mrs Needle threw a few soothing words to the menagerie and led me into the ground-floor store-room, dark and grimy under dusty beams. We dropped my rucksack between piles of split logs, and I followed her upstairs.

I've never seen a house so full of herbs. The rafters were hung with onions and strings of garlic, the kitchen work-surfaces littered with plant-pots. Every kind of herb I'd ever smelt was there, with a rich overlay of cat. Kitten heads kept popping up from behind the sofa. As we came in a puppy scrambled out of a basket and skidded towards us. My hostess crashed to her knees and gathered it in, crooning. I waited for her to notice me again. It took some time.

She was a fine hostess, when she remembered to be. She showed me the bathroom, gave me a clean towel, offered to do my washing, asked what I wanted to eat, and as I answered turned away to talk delighted baby-talk with one of the cats. I didn't mind. She'd said the magic words 'hot water'. No mere fixation with animals was likely to bother me. She crooned. I washed. It wasn't until we sat down to a huge meal of horse stew and potatoes that we really started talking.

Mrs Needle is a German. She'd married a French forester and come to live in Lorraine, and I don't think I've ever met anyone so full of hatred. Listening to her was like reading a National Front manifesto. Her fellow-villagers: 'They're all evil, they don't like me because I'm German, they try and poison my dogs.' When I asked where all the dogs came from, she said, 'I rescue strays.' We talked about Egypt: 'I think it's disgusting the way Western women go over there wearing nothing but bikinis, trying to seduce the innocent Arabs.' Later, we talked about Paris: 'It's disgusting, it's full of Arabs and they're all sex maniacs. They should send them home.'

I used to work in Egypt. 'Don't you like Arabs?' I asked barbedly, and received a wide-eyed stare.

'They're all right where they are, they just shouldn't be allowed in France.' And while I pondered she added, 'I'm not racist. I like belly-dancing.'

I bit my lip a lot that night. I didn't want to argue with my hostess, but she hit nerve after nerve. East Germany: 'they're skinheads and racists, we should put the wall back up.' Lorraine: 'they're nothing but egoists, they hate foreigners.' Alsace: 'they should all learn German.' France: 'the French are too arrogant, they should be made to learn English.' She also spoke Russian, and thought that everyone east of Berlin should be made to learn that. I couldn't help thinking that if that was the way she normally talked, it was no wonder she'd had problems with the locals.

It was a relief when the talk turned to travel. She was full of questions about my trip, and it gave me the chance to fight for my friends: the kind families I'd met everywhere I'd been. She listened neutrally, as unwilling to argue as I was, but just as unconvinced. Eventually the dread question came: why was I doing it? I didn't want to say. It could only lead to trouble, but silence would have been as bad. I told her as bluntly as I could, and my tone said that comments weren't an option. She pursed her lips.

'Where did it happen?'

'Central America.'

She shrugged. 'Oh, that explains it. They're all blacks.'

I lost the plot at that point. I was on my feet and protesting before I even knew it. She stared at me in hostile amazement. If she'd said one word more I would have been out of there, rucksack and all, no matter how late it was. But after a second she nodded stiffly, and said, 'Perhaps you're right.' She didn't believe a word of it, but you should never argue with a guest . . . We steered clear of the subject for the rest of the evening. I was glad to go to bed.

She'd forgiven me by breakfast. She met me with a smile. We sat in the early sunshine sipping herb tea and eating muesli, talking about her animals. Even that led to an impassioned attack on the villagers of Lorraine, those heartless animal-abusers. There must be two Lorraines in France, I thought; this was the first I'd heard of it. As we washed the dishes she came out with another gem: 'I could never kill for a human, but I could for an animal.' I left soon after that. She kissed me goodbye and wished me luck, then stood waving from the doorstep. She'd been kind to me. She loved her animals. It was just everyone else she hated. Meeting her was like taking a step sixty years back in time, to the heyday of Hitler's Germany. I'd never met anyone like that before. I was still thinking about her as I followed the footpath up into Alsace.

I reached a milestone that day: the Donon, highest summit in the northern Vosges, a sandstone cone jutting out of the great darkness of the pines. A forestry trail led towards it, thick with the strange mud that comes of mingled earth and pine-needles. It was sheer pleasure to have soft earth underfoot again, after so long breaking my ankles on the roads. If I'd had the breath I would have broken into song, but despite all the exercise, I wasn't Julie Andrews yet. I concentrated on walking and navigating, never an easy task on forestry tracks, and tried to ignore the summer flies.

I was eating lunch on a rocky ridge with a strong wind surfing through the treetops when I heard a sound like a rusting bicycle squeaking below me. I put down my sandwich (quark and chutney, a present from Frau Needle) and looked downhill. A cyclist here? It seemed unlikely . . . The sound drew nearer, more insistent. I could see the vehicle in my mind's eye already: a heavy, rusty butchers's bike, ridden by a Frenchman in a Breton beret with a string of onions round his neck. Something small and brown teased my vision between the pines. Then it trotted into sight: a fawn, standing knock-kneed and uncertain on the trail, calling plaintively. I could have tossed a twig to it without effort. I sat there, not daring to breathe, as it tottered a few more steps and stopped to call again. Its fur was a rusty brown, dappled with lighter spots across the rump, its eyes vast and liquid. The ears swivelled like radar antennae. I didn't move. It must have felt my eyes on it. Suddenly it looked round, saw me and rocketed away into the woods. It was a long time before I carried on eating. I'd never been that close to a wild creature above the water before. The memory stayed with me all day.

I reached the summit just before four-thirty, ten minutes ahead of schedule, and sank down on a sandstone block to get my breath back: the last two hundred metres are volcano-steep, and like a twit I'd gone directly for the top. The view was breathtaking anyway. No other peak in the area comes within a hundred metres of the Donon. On a good day, you can see the whole of eastern France from the summit. It's a strange hodge-podge of a mountaintop. One end rises to a pinnacle of sandstone slabs, crowned with a Gallo-Roman temple built in the late nineteenth century when the Vosges were a part of Germany, and undermined with fox-holes dug in 1914–18 when the French tried to take them back. Below that crest is a broad col rising to a secondary summit, thick with Celtic ruins, plus a TV and weather-station, half-screened by the trees. The whole mountain-top is criss-crossed with tourist trails, each with its own waymarks and information boards. There's a car-park behind the TV station. Litter sparkles between clumps of heather. It's as tame as Hyde Park. It was hard to believe that wild deer still lived just below the summit.

I sat there, looking back eastwards. The plain of Lorraine stretched out like a map before me, dim and grey, the magical green-gold wealth of the fields a memory in my mind's eye. Cloud-shadows drifted by. Water gleamed fitfully. Roads drew ruler-straight lines across the fields and forests. I traced them back and back, picturing the way in a million disjointed images of places and people. When vision failed and floundered into the anonymous blue distance, imagination took over, following my trail past Metz, past Antilly, across the border into Luxembourg and beyond. For the first time, I realized time was passing. Life had become a scatter of images as brilliant as stained-glass shards. I'd lost track of the days, the weeks, everything but the *now*, bright and compelling. I hadn't admitted that the world was moving on; but it was. Suddenly I was sitting on the Donon, with the eastwards trek behind me and the southwards road ahead, and the spring was almost gone.

The breeze curled around me, carrying the song of the trees. The sun came and went across the warm stones. I sat, staring westwards, letting two months' passion fall into order in my mind, and found myself talking to Anna. We'd so often shared quiet moments in Belize, canoeing up the river behind Field Base, sitting on a log in the jungle, jolting down the Southern Highway on the way to our project sites: it seemed natural to share that time with her as well. I could feel her sitting next to me, grinning. It seemed natural to talk. I told her how I was feeling, a little dazed, a little confused. I told her about some of the people I'd met on the way. Just thinking of them made me smile. I asked her how she was getting on, wondered what her family were up to, asked if she remembered the last bus ride we'd taken together. She'd been so full of enthusiasm for what she was doing and planning that it was infectious. It filled me with undirected fire. She always had that effect on people: her legacy was a boundless energy looking for a purpose. I told her that, too, asked if she was proud of it. I don't remember half of what I said. The words mattered less than the fact that we were sharing them. She was with me on the hilltop, as if she'd never left.

It was hard to leave the Donon. I wanted to stay up there overnight with her, but the clouds were blowing up from the west and the wind was strengthening. By the time I left the first drops of rain were already falling. For a while I could feel her with me as I hurried down through the twilight. Then, quietly, I knew she was gone.

So I entered the Vosges, the mountainous rampart standing between the bulk of France and the flood-plain of the Rhine. Romance and Germanic tribes have been meeting here to bargain and battle for two thousand years, and the mountains' history lies only a scratch below the surface. The ridges of the Vosges where the GR5 runs are lined with medieval castles, nineteenth-century border-markers and First World War trenches, all showing in their own way the shifting patterns of power along the hills. The local identity is strong here. Time and again I heard the words I'd heard in Lorraine, 'We're French, but they don't believe it in Paris'. Alsatians put Alsace first. The ones I met didn't seem to think they had much choice.

It's beautiful walking territory. Steep-sided hills sweep up to broad rolling crests, some wooded with pine and beech, others bare grass and flowers rippling in the wind, and over and round and through them wind a hundred long-range paths. The GR signs are only the start of the waymarking here: every trail has its own symbol, yellow circle, blue triangle, yellow-and-red flash, black cross. The 'club Vosgien' which maintains the trails claims to have laid its network a decade before the rest of France caught on to the idea: this is the only part of France in which the GR sign is a single red bar. No true Vosgien would countenance a change. What, lose their regional pride? Fans of an integrated and centralized Europe, take note . . . The trails are certainly used. Even in May, the most popular summits are black with walkers. And yet it's the history which dominates, lingers, captivates. I remember the Pyrenees for the mountains. The Vosges I remember for the monuments.

The first after the Donon, and by far the most evocative, is Struthof. It's not a word to be used lightly. Drop it into the conversation anywhere in France and it's like throwing a pebble into a pool: an instant's shock, a lasting unease. Shout 'Auschwitz!' at a party in England, and you'll see the same. Struthof is the only Nazi concentration camp built on French soil. When France surrendered to Hitler in 1940 it was divided into two political entities, the Occupied Territories under direct German control and Vichy France under Pétain. Alsace was quietly written out of the treaty. From Hitler's point of view it was part of Greater Germany, with all the rights thereto: conscription, rationing and racial cleansing. Pétain submitted. Whatever his motives – and he's still the most ambiguous character in French history – he gave the invaders a free hand in the Vosges. Few locals of that era that I talked to have forgiven him.

Struthof camp stands at the head of a wide green meadow on a sweep of hillside above the town of Schirmeck. The monument behind it is visible far across the mountains: a brilliant white finger shining against the pines. I'd been walking towards it for a day and a half. A broad road leads up to the camp, and there's a car park below it big enough for fifty coaches. It might be a film set: double fences, machine-gun posts, wooden huts in terraced rows, all looking as bad as new, but above them stands the memorial, and at its feet are the graves. Surprisingly many graves. Struthof was never an extermination camp like Auschwitz. Many of the inmates were political prisoners, *résistants* and hostages, whose internment was designed to break the spirit of Alsace. Their deaths were as it were incidental to the camp's proper function, rather than its aim, so the disposal of the remains was haphazard. Many were burned, and their ashes scattered over the vegetable garden; but others were buried in graves that the immates themselves had to dig. Looking down from the road above it, Struthof is framed by rank upon rank of crosses. Somehow, it's appropriate.

I was lucky to visit it when I did. That afternoon the camp had other visitors: a group of school-kids from Bonn. They'd been in the Vosges for a week, combining short rambles with visits to monuments and vineyards, and this was the last day of their trip. The first sight of them as they piled off their bus appalled me. Young, rowdy, dressed in tattered jeans, many of them with close-cropped hair and army boots: what were they doing here? I let them go ahead, following when I judged the coast was clear. As they piled in under the gateway laughing and jumping on one another's shoulders, I felt a little sick.

I found the first stragglers behind the garrison kitchen. Two couples were standing wrapped around one another as though vacuum-sealed, and the sight blew a fuse in my oh-so-tolerant mind. Snogging in a memorial ground! Every traditionalist nerve was burning for retribution, when I saw that they were crying. As the berserk fury stopped roaring in my ears I heard their sobs. Seconds later another young lady staggered out of the kitchen white-faced, looked around desperately and threw up all over the gravel. A skin-head followed her, knelt down and took her head in his hands, talking quietly. She looked up, and I've never seen a face in such misery.

There was a water-heater in the kitchen. The firebox below it was over six feet long, and human-shaped. Firewood had been critically short in the last year of the war, and the guards had turned to the most abundant alternative: prisoners. Once you've seen that, you've seen all you need to know about Struthof.

I hardly bothered with the rest of the displays. I was too busy talking with the visitors. How must it feel to be a German going round a Nazi concentration camp? I asked them. They were appalled. They called it madness, sick, perverted, impossible. One lad with a face like a declaration of street warfare turned away from a picture of Belsen and said to me simply, 'Never again.' His girl-friend added, 'It makes me feel guilty.' And their teacher chipped in, 'My father was a policeman during the war. He never joined the Nazi party, he always said he never knew what was going on here. How can they not have known?' She swept an arm round the room-full of pictures: Belsen, Dora, Dachau, Treblinka and the rest. 'The whole German race was guilty of not looking. We've inherited their shame.'

I found myself arguing, trying to talk them out of the over-whelming guilt. They were saying that the entire Holocaust was the fault of their ancestors, and I'd read enough to know how untrue that was. Every country in Europe had its share of Nazi collaborators, just as every country had its Resistance, and they weren't just people scared of violent death: France raised an entire SS division, the 'Charlemagne', which fought for Hitler right until the fall of Berlin. Even Britain had its traitors. The Nazi terror couldn't have taken hold as it did if it hadn't found willing support wherever it went, from small-time thugs to Pope Pius XII. Germany can claim much of the guilt, but it can't shoulder it all.

Not so, argued my teenagers, and it didn't seem incongruous at all to be standing in a concentration camp listening to the garrison's compatriots defending their guilt. Even if nobody was innocent, the Germans were *worse*. They organized the death-camp system. They created the conditions which allowed evil to flourish, and then turned a blind eye to it. Yes, I countered, but so did everyone else. The German people didn't design the death camps, Hitler's circle did. Ah, replied the teacher, but who gave Hitler power? The Germans. Yes, I answered, but who created the resentment that he embodied? The First World War Allies. We were going in circles. We had to agree to differ. In the end a young man with a crew-cut, combat boots and a face that I never want to see in a dark alley summed it up for all of us:

'Let's just make sure it never happens again.'

There were a lot of Germans in the Vosges that May. I met another group only days later, but in far happier surroundings: the castle of St Ulrich (another fine French name) overlooking the town of Ribeauvillé. I've called the Vosges the rampart of France, and I'm not kidding. The last ridge of the mountains towers over the Rhine flood plain, and every hilltop has its castles. Plural. On the ridge between Andlau and Ribeauvillé, a day and a half's walk, there are seven: Bernstein, l'Ortenbourg, Ramstein, Haut-Koenigsbourg, Haut-Ribeauvillé, Gierstein and St Ulrich. Ramstein is a complete ruin, its crumbling walls choked and throttled by brambles. Haut-Koenigsbourg is a masterpiece of restoration, completely rebuilt in the 1890s in honour of Kaiser Wilhelm, and the biggest tourist attraction in the Vosges. The others are a fantastic playground for children of any age. Overgrown courts, crumbling chambers, soaring towers, each one dominating a town on the plain ... I dropped into the towns a couple of times to go busking, but it never really came alive. The locals didn't seem interested. I left them to their urban amusements, and climbed back up to play.

St Ulrich stands on a rocky spine above the red-and-green roofs of Ribeauvillé. Beech-woods cluster thickly about its base and sweep in a sea of green to the watchtower of Gierstein, half a mile to the east. Beyond Gierstein the plain is a chess-board of light soil and dark vines like some giant and complex cross-stitch, and far away across the Rhine rise the blue-hazed hills of the Black Forest. Most of St Ulrich is intact. The roofs are gone, the elaborate stones of door and archway long since plundered for houses in the town, but the original walls and chambers still stand open to the sky, carpeted with grass. The keep has been reinforced in recent years. A wooden stair leads up inside the hollow tower, and the roof is a concrete slab. As soon as I saw it I decided to camp there.

I also decided to strip. It had been a hot day, and my clothes were soaked in sweat. One thorough check all around to make sure I wasn't going to embarrass anyone, and my kit was off. Stark naked, I draped it over the warm parapet to dry, then sat down on my camping-mat and got my stove going. Soon the merry scents of petrol, scorched chef and packet soup were mingling in the warm air. I sat back and started writing a letter, keeping about half an eye on the proceedings. The pot bubbled, the cooker roared, the birds sang, and I completely failed to hear the footsteps on the stair.

'Bwooah!' A head popped up through the floor and recoiled. Most people climb that tower for the view, but I don't think he'd been expecting the eyeful he got.

'Bollocks!' I exclaimed in shock, starting and nearly knocking my tea flying. Seldom can I have sworn so appropriately. The head vanished abruptly and I heard voices ringing out in consternation from the tower as I fled for the safety of my shorts. I've never dressed so fast in my life.

'Okay, come up!' I called in English as I struggled into my inside-out T-shirt. 'I'm decent.'

After a long second thick with whispers, a woman of my age peered cautiously over the edge. Her face cracked into a grin like a tectonic fault as her eyes travelled across the rooftop: boiling pot, scattered papers, drying underwear, flushed me. Then she leaned back down and called 'Kommt mal!'

Half a dozen teenagers in jeans and walking-boots climbed up warily and stood clustered around the stair-head, uncertain what to say. I wasn't at my most eloquent either, and no wonder.

The pot saved us, as Vietnam veterans would say. Just as the embarrassed silence was becoming unbearable (and the woman's grin threatened to meet behind her head) it boiled over with a huge hiss and a cloud of stream. Three of us jumped to save the meal and my papers, and in the ensuring chaos all awkwardness was forgotten. In no time at all we were sitting on the parapet, passing around bars of chocolate as I waited for the pasta to cool. Slowly the full moon rose from behind the Gierstein tower. The horizon was golden behind us. Quietly we introduced ourselves: shouting in that deep-blue twilight would have been a crime. They were a group of scouts from near Heidelberg, out for a week's walking. Who was I?

'I'm Ben.'

One of them grinned at me slyly. 'Would that be as in Big Ben?' He'd been the first to climb the stairs.

Modesty forbids.

History came alive with a vengeance a few days after St Ulrich. The whole southern half of the Vosges is a memorial to the First World War. The trenches were blasted out of the solid rock and shored up with rubble and concrete, and they've barely changed in eighty years. When historians say the Front here was set in stone, they're not exaggerating.

I climbed the Tête des Faux on a blisteringly hot morning at the very end of May. The sun blazed down on the pine-woods, filling the air with resinous scents, and the heather-choked hillsides shimmered in the heat. The summit was a broad sweep of moorland bare to the sky. The bushes were thick with half-concealed shapes: bunkers and dug-outs hacked out of the bedrock. I dropped my pack in the shade of a half-grown fir and went exploring, crawling down overgrown trenches and into iron-roofed tunnels. It's another paradise for boys, and I made the most of it. My memories of that morning are of sounds: broken stone clinking underfoot, moisture dripping in the cool darkness of the dugouts, the scratch and scrape of overhanging branches on the trench walls as I forced my way by, the crunch of a rusty tin collapsing underfoot. A Heinz baked bean tin with a scrap of label still intact. Not all the artefacts there are vintage.

It must have been a couple of hours before I returned to my rucksack in No-Man's-Land. The opposing strong points were literally a stone's throw apart. I stood on top of the German bunker and lobbed a piece of concrete onto the French one to prove it. It was hard to imagine what that war must have been like. When I came back I saw an old man sitting in the shade by my rucksack. He was staring at the French command bunker just behind us, a smooth concrete roof reinforced with a star-burst of steel beams. He didn't look up as I threshed through the heather.

'See that?' he said, nodding. 'That's where my father was captured by the Germans in 1915.'

I sat down on my sack and offered him a drink. He swigged absently, eyes far away. I waited for more comments, but none were forthcoming. I'm not sure he even realized I was there. After a while he stood up and walked back down the French lines. I watched him go, awed. I was trying to imagine how it would feel to look around an historic site and think, 'My Dad was here.' I couldn't do it. History's about books, papers, modern actors in modern cinemas. It's stories, not people. At least it was until then.

I left the hilltop in a thoughtful mood. The path was a stony rut zigzagging towards the forest. I couldn't be bothered to zigzag, so I took to the heather, thrashing my way through the tussocks in a cloud of perfume and butterflies. I've done more intelligent things in my time. Think 'First World War'. Think 'battlefield'. Think 'trench warfare.'

Think 'barbed wire.'

I was plunging down through the heather when my left foot caught in something unyielding and pain stabbed into my shin.

My right foot jolted forwards to catch me, twisted on a bunch of heather, and slammed down at an awkward angle, propelled by twelve stone of idiot and almost five stone of luggage, and the crunch as my hip slammed up into my pelvis was probably audible in Poland.

It still wasn't as loud as my curse.

'*Merde*!' I commented. I was lying on my side in the heather, the branches sticking into my face. '*Merde alors d'un bordel de connerie de putain de merde*!' The total-immersion technique was doing wonders for my French.

I managed to wriggle out of my backpack and get my right leg free. The hip hurt like blue buggery every time I moved, but at least it was still functioning. I tugged at my left leg. The heather heaved and parted, and my foot came into view wrapped in a fetching anklet of rusty barbed wire, 1915 vintage. There was a large tear in my trousers and a small gash in my shin, which I drenched with iodine and TCP, but that was all. After a few minutes' ginger stretching my hip hardly hurt at all. Cautiously I shrugged on my rucksack. Bearable. Leaning as much weight as I could on my sticks, I ploughed my way back to the path and kept on going.

Having made one stupid mistake already that day, I went for the record. Walking with a heavy sack when you've just wrenched your hip is *not* something I'd recommend to anyone with an instinct for survival, but it pales beside the idiocy of sleeping under the stars on an exposed mountain ridge just because the forecast has said the weather will be good. The evening found me on a long escarpment high above the world, with a rustling forest at my back and another golden moonrise ahead. There aren't many truly isolated spots in the Vosges any more, and I was determined to make the most of this one. It had been hot all week, and the forecast promised another clear night. I didn't bother to pitch the tent, I just wrapped myself in it and fell asleep in the heather.

The wind woke me at 2 a.m. All around me the heather was tossing like waves in a gale, and no wonder. The forest was roaring, the jagged pines back-lit by lightning. As I shot out of my sleeping-bag a flurry of sleet hissed across the leather. In three seconds I was drenched. This wasn't a storm, it was a bombardment! I jumped to my feet. Instant agony seared into my hip and I fell heavily. Half-kneeling, twisted with my back to the blizzard, I battled the flapping tent into something like its proper shape and rammed the tent-pegs home. The flap gaped like a hungry mouth. I bolted in, dragging my sleeping-bag with me, thanking God that I'd had the sense to pack everything else in my rucksack. Hail rattled across the canvas. Inner and outer tents billowed and stuck together, letting a slow trickle of water through. As I lay down an unseen rock jabbed into my hip. The joint was locked solid, it flared with pain every time I moved. What had I got myself into? I lay there staring into the dark, and tried to fight down the panic. Thunder whip-cracked overhead. Lightning flared. The confidence born of two months' walking melted. Sometimes the divide between adventure and disaster parts like a wet tissue and you see through to the other side. I didn't sleep much that night.

At dawn, I looked out onto blindness. Clouds whipped by on either side as grey as ghosts. The woods were dark and threatening. My tent shivered at every gust. I tried to stand up cautiously, and my leg buckled. Not a good start. Looks like I'm staying, then, I thought. Better get warmed up. My shirt was soaked through and the wind had teeth in it: I'd been shivering for hours. Stove and food were in the rucksack. Where was my water-bottle? I couldn't see it. Flinching from the cold, I crawled outside. There it was, lying against a stone. The stopper had come out. I had half a cup of water left.

I grabbed it and scrambled for the tent. Warmth, quick! I fumbled with my rucksack, excavating my thermals from the very bottom of the pile, and trying hard not to panic. I was soaked. So was my bedding. I was frozen. I had enough water for maybe three mouthfuls of soup, I had a leg that didn't work. I was a day's walk from anywhere. Suddenly the Vosges didn't seem tame any more. If I screwed up here, I was in trouble.

Calmly. I forced myself to go slow. I'd taught enough diver-rescue courses to know that panic was a quick way to disaster. *Am I going to die right now? No.*

Then take your time.

Warmth was the priority. I peeled off my wet shirt, rubbed myself as dry as I could, and pulled on every stitch of clothing I had left. The pain screamed as I moved, then eased just a fraction. Maybe there was hope yet. I had one bar of chocolate left. I wolfed it down, trying to ignore the dryness of my mouth. The wind hammered on the canvas. For a second I considered lighting up my stove then and there, but not even I'm that stupid. High-pressure petrol in a one-man tent? I think not . . .

Eventually I pulled on my waterproof jacket over my woolly hat and poked my head and hands out of the tent to work. Getting the stove to light in that wind was no fun, but I managed it. As soon as the water was on I ducked back inside.

The leg was the problem. If I could just get up and moving, I'd be fine. Walking in sleet and gales isn't exactly pleasant, but lying shivering in a sodden sleeping-bag with no water and a knackered hip is a really good way of winding up in hospital. As the pot began to steam I lay on my back and waved my bad leg in the air, groaning at every movement. My tent's far too small for proper physio: it must have looked very strange from outside, a moving bulge running around the canvas. For five minutes my world was a pinpoint of concentrated agony. Then, very gradually, movement became easier. The conflagration in my hip dropped from white heat to red, and back down to jumping embers. I tried standing up, *very* cautiously, which is no easy task in a one-man tent. It hurt, but I stayed upright. The howling wind blew streamers of steam in under the tent-flap: nature's way of telling you soup's up. As I sat and slurped, warmth returned. The dread slowly receded. It was as close as I'd ever come to a real mountain accident.

When I hobbled onwards half an hour later, I was almost cheerful. It wasn't so much that I'd survived a potential disaster. The hills were covered in clouds, rain gusted sideways and the temperature had dropped ten degrees. Proper mountain weather at last! I felt at home for the first time since Canterbury. My Scots blood's got a lot to answer for.

It's a week's walk from the Tête des Faux to Belfort, the southern terminus of the Vosges, and in between there's not much but mountain. The high pastures where the GR5 runs are dotted with scattered farms, and a main road runs across the hill-crests, but the only population centres are down in the valleys. It was decision time: was I going to risk another week on the heights with a dodgy leg, or should I head for a village and rest? And, even more crucially, what was I going to do when I reached Belfort? I'd been planning to cross the Belfort Gap and head straight up into the Jura and the Alps, but the thought of doing that with my hip in its current state brought me out in a cold sweat. It would have been sensible to stop for a week, but I thought: if it's really bad I'll rest in Belfort. I was so close to the end of the Vosges I couldn't bear the thought of stopping.

So I plugged on. Sometimes my hip hardly hurt at all. Sometimes, on long steep climbs, it was so painful I had to stop. Mostly it just ached, a low-level discomfort shot through with odd sparks of sharper pain. Climbing hurt far more than walking on the level, so I kept to the ridges as much as I could. Even though that meant carrying four days' food at a time, since there ain't no shops on the tops, it was a pleasure. The Vosges are ideal for high-level walking. Their broad open backs offer wide paths and even wider views, and I got used to seeing clear across the eastern plains to the glimmer of the Austrian Alps. The weather cleared within a day, and I went on with the sun and the wind through meadows thick with flowers. If I hadn't been worrying about the Alps it would have been a perfect week. Even as it was, I loved it.

There was only one incident worthy of note that week. One night I camped in a field just below the summit of the Grand Ballon, second summit of the Vosges. The farmer, a cheery soul, invited me in to share a bottle of wine from his brother's vineyard, a sweet, almost syrupy white which we found extremely drinkable. We drank. A bottle later I staggered back uphill to my camp below a flowering blackthorn, stumbled into my tent, and crashed.

I awoke to the sound of heavy breathing, which is never a good start if you've gone to bed pissed. Didn't I go to bed alone? . . . I rolled over blearily, pushed the tent-flap back and came eyeball to eyeball with the biggest bull I've ever seen.

'MMOOAAH!'

'AAGH!'

Our cries came simultaneously. I recoiled into my tent. He lumbered backwards and galloped ponderously away. Until *The Guinness Book of Records* proves otherwise, I claim the world record for striking and packing a tent. I was out and the thing was down in seconds. The field was alive with cattle. The farmer watched from the foot of the hill. Even from there I could see him grinning. I was just considering reprisals when I heard the bull bellow. He was looming amidst his harem, shaking his head. The gate was directly behind him. I looked up, across the slope. The fence was thirty metres away. Two bovine idiots were grazing between me and it. All right. I swung on my rucksack. Hooves thudded behind me. Three heifers cantered fecklessly away. I picked up my sticks. The bull bellowed again. The hairs prickled along the back of my neck. I started walking. Slowly. False pride's going to get me killed one day, but there was no way I was going to run with a French farmer watching. Thundering hooves failed to shake the earth behind me, though my heart was going so fast I probably wouldn't have noticed if they had. It seemed a very long walk to the fence. I climbed over as elegantly as I could, which wasn't very, and walked down to meet my audience with homicide in my heart.

He grinned at me and spat carefully over the fence.

'Fancy some breakfast?' I looked at him stonily. His grin broadened, and he led me to the kitchen. The table was laden with steaming plates: home-cured bacon, free range eggs and his wife's special sausages. I'd forgiven him by the end of the first plateful. We had a second anyway.

He was the last Alsatian I met. Four days later I was in Belfort.

PART 5

Burgundy

'I will lift up mine eyes unto the hills . . .' (Psalm 121)

I spent a week there. It wasn't easy. There's not much in Belfort except yet another Vauban fortress, but I badly needed a break. My leg ached severely, and everything else was starting to grumble. After three days' soul-searching, I decided that the Alps were out. I simply wasn't in a fit state to face them. Instead I'd follow the River Doubs westwards into Burgundy, rich with medieval monuments and fine wine. There are worse silver linings . . . The decision made, I spent a lot of time sitting in local cafés rebuilding my energy reserves with enormous plate-fuls of steak and chips, and sprawling on my bed in a cheap hotel, writing letters and reading. I must have showered three times a day. Hot water and clean towels! It was a paradise on earth.

When the hedonism got too much, I went busking. It was an effort. Marc had warned me that only 1 per cent of the population would ever be interested in my music, and he was right. I'd played diligently all the way through Luxembourg and down the Vosges, but it had never quite taken off, and I missed the excitement. I was used to the buzz of big band stage shows. Somehow my trombone solos didn't have the same impact. I was doing my best to raise a response from mid-week shoppers in an anonymous pedestrian precinct when a six foot four Ghanaian walked up to me and asked if I'd be around for long.

'I'm leaving tomorrow.'

His face fell. 'That's a shame.'

'Why? It was the first human contact I'd had all day.

'I run a jazz trio. We're playing on Friday night. I was wondering if you'd like to join us for a jam.'

By the time he left, he was running a quartet.

It took a bit of planning. After a week of inactivity and carbohydrate stacking. I was itching to be gone. Could I bear to sit around for another two days? I checked my maps and sighed with relief: I didn't have to. My new route ran parallel to the local railway line. I wasn't quite sure if it was in the spirit of the pilgrimage to hop on a train at a wayside station and pop back for a gig, but it was certainly in the spirit of the trombonist. Once I'd found an appropriate train the only challenge was making sure I caught it. A chatty nonagenarian on the footpath almost sabotaged the whole operation, but I managed to escape and hurtled onto the platform, sweating and gasping, with two minutes to spare. Having walked for two days to get there, it took an hour to get back. Welcome to 1999.

We met in a smoky L-shaped bar a few blocks from the station. It might have been anywhere in Europe: beer-stained floorboards, half-panelled walls hung with fading posters, Bottles of All Nations gleaming behind the bar, low round tables scarred with cigarette burns. We set up at the toe of the L, wedged between mike stands and speakers. I've never yet played in a pub that was big enough to hold the band it hired: this one was unusually spacious, we had room to sit down. The rest of the L was jammed with drinkers waiting for the show. A few were seated, privileged witnesses to an endless sea of buttocks; the vast majority stood around them like a besieging army. There seemed to be an inordinate number of pretty girls there, or perhaps my wilderness-heightened senses were refusing to take interest in anyone else. The air was thick with smoke and noise.

Alphonse the Ghanaian made the introductions over the noise of clinking glasses and clanking metal-work as he put the PA system together. He was the band's founder, a bass guitarist specializing in African soul. Seated behind him in the corner was Luc, a professional big band drummer in a beret with an unsmoked roll-up hanging from his lip. As I slid onto my stool in front of him he looked up and grinned. 'Don't fart,' he said. Kneeling at the front taping wires to the floor was a young guitarist in a Metallica T-shirt and a baseball cap. Alphonse introduced him as Jan, from Prague. A Ghanaian, a Frenchman, a Czech and me. African soul, big band jazz, heavy metal and street improvisation. 'Eclectic' doesn't even begin to describe it.

'Electric' does.

We played free jazz that night. There wasn't much choice, anything else would have required rehearsal. Alphonse kicked off with a bass riff in 10/8, one he'd made up while the rest of us were setting up the mikes. Luc joined in after four bars with a heart-racing scatter on the tom-toms. I could see Jan's left hand tapping the frets, driving the rhythm into his brain. My fingers drummed on the slide. He launched after sixteen bars, hammering the up-beats with snarling chords. I followed in four bars later, bouncing off his treble stabs with shock-notes of my own. It was barely music. It was raw rhythm, alive, caught up in our heart-beats, pulsing in our brains. As Alphonse dropped the initial riff I picked it up, low down in my register, trying to match him sound for sound. His teeth flashed. Then Jan took off on a flying flurry of scales, and fireworks detonated in my mind.

I used to be a classical musician until I discovered jazz. It didn't matter what we played, whether it was Telemann quartets or big romantic symphonies, I loved it. Sometimes it was the pride of playing with absolute precision, in perfect harmony with the musicians around me. Sometimes it was the heathen delight of playing unbelievably loud. Always it was the joy of being part of something bigger than I was, drawing beautiful pictures with the sounds. Classical music, I thought, was it.

Then I joined a jazz band, and it was like moving from black and white to technicolour. It's the difference between Oslo and Rio, Jane Austen and Irvine Walsh, Latin and Spanish, a Viennese waltz and *West Side Story*. It's the difference between being at someone else's wedding and being at your own. Classical and jazz are different languages. There's beauty in both – but only one is *mine*.

It starts with a rhythm and a chord sequence, the simpler the better. The less you start with the more you can add. Your ears pick it up. Your hands work out how to play it. You wait and you listen harder, until every cell of your body is filled with it and your heart shudders to the beat. Someone else starts playing and your being splits in two, the mind holding that first rhythm and the ears following the rest. What's he doing, where's he going, how do I fit in with that? The third player joins in. Three skeins wind round one another, and there's no time to think any more. Stop to wonder what note you're on, and you'll lose it. You play as if you're singing, and hope that the note you hear in your head is the one that's about to come out of the instrument. They say great jazz is better than sex. That may be an exaggeration, but it's impossible to get more passionate with all your clothes still on.

We'd barely exchanged three words before starting, but we made up for it in the set. Whoever had the lead played head down, blind and inspired, and the others stood back and talked with their eyes. I matched Alphonse's bass riff note for note. A glance and a grin, and he left it and started improvising as if the guitar were a third tom-tom, eyes locked with Luc's. After a minute Jan came back down to earth. Alphonse picked up the bass line, Jan looked up, both nodded to me and I swept up into a blaring solo. It was the first time in months that I'd had a backing band, and I was alight. As I came back down I saw Jan lay his guitar aside and pick up a trumpet. He started mimicking my cadenzas, a bar behind. Our eyes met and we carried on the game, climbing back up, leap-frogging each other a semitone higher with every phrase. Anything you can play, I can play higher . . . Alphonse and Luc were playing as if they were psychic, driving us onwards. We'd almost forgotten the audience. In the end my lip cracked. Trombones just don't go that high. I went for a stratospheric ending, missed it, shivered back down through the harmonics, heard Jan follow me with a sound like a horse neighing, heard the crowd cheering, plunged all the way back into the bass register, and caught Alphonse's eye again as I took the bass-line and let him break free. Luc threw me a wink and nudged my glass nearer with his foot, and I ducked down to gulp a little more liquid inspiration.

We played for hours. The first fast number lasted twenty minutes, and we followed it with a slow blues based on an African folk song. Halfway through Alphonse set the bass aside and started singing in an astonishingly high voice, and Jan and I swung our bells close together and blended quiet chords underneath him as Luc stirred the skins with brushes. After that it was fast again, a piece that started out as a riff and somehow went through *In the Mood*, *It Ain't Necessarily So* and the *Marseillaise* before swirling back down to the original theme. Jan picked up his guitar again, working himself into a frenzy as the scales screamed higher and higher. I've never seen anyone play as he did that night. Halfway through the number his cap fell off and a great curtain of blonde hair dropped down over his face. His frantic nodding made it jerk like a puppet, but his playing never even flickered.

The first set lasted an hour and a half, then there was half an hour's drinking time before we got back down to work. I alternated orange juice and scotch, both purely medicinal (there's nothing like whisky as rocket fuel for jazz), and tried to chat with the others, but the landlord had turned the stereo so far up that we couldn't hear ourselves shout. The second set, when it came, was mellow, but we wound up with a salsa that would have powered the national grid for a week. Halfway through, Luc launched into a frenzied assault on the drums. In the grandest traditions of jazz, we left him to get on with it and nipped to the bar for a final round. He didn't care. I'm not sure he even noticed.

Midnight was long gone by the time we finished. The last reluctant punter staggered home, and we set to stripping the kit away and loading it into Luc's van. Clearing away after a gig is a melancholy task, but it provides a useful buffer between exaltation and normal life. The clocks were striking one as we strolled back to Alphonse's place just off the charmingly-named *rue des bons enfants* for a final whisky and a cigar. There, in the dim light of scattered candles, with the soft notes of Chet Baker drifting from the stereo, I received the highest honour of my playing career so far, to be declared the fourth member of the Alphonse Trio in perpetuity, the vote carried unanimously. I was still grinning and hugging my trombone case as I boarded the last train, back to my tent and my mission.

For three weeks I walked westwards with the river my constant companion. I sat beside it through the long hot afternoons, cooling my feet in the shallows and watching life go by, kayakers and river-boaters, cyclists and joggers, herons grey against the green banks, dragon-flies clashing round the reeds. I camped beside the river in the deep blue dusk as bats flitted overhead. One by one I passed its cities: Montbéliard, smelling of tyre factories and burnt rubber, its castle like an imitation Edinburgh; Besançon, Vauban's masterpiece, looming sheer over the green meanders; Dole, pinned to the fields by its white cathedral. Then came the plain, a dazzling tableau of golden corn and blazing poppies rippling in the sun, the colours blindingly intense. The heat was brutal. Even bare-chested, I was overwhelmed. Soon I took to walking at night. I was constantly aware of my hip, never quite hurting but never quite comfortable, a feeling that was to last another seven months. My rucksack straps were starting to wear out, slipping and straining my shoulders, and my resoled boots were once again worn smooth. All the same, I was happy. Every night I slept like a rock, and by morning the aches were gone.

The idyll carried me all the way to Dijon. Just after Longest Day I stopped at a little farm not far from the city and asked permission to camp. As always, I was welcomed. As always, the farmer's four children came to watch, shy at first and then increasingly demanding. What's this? What's that? Why do you walk with sticks, are you blind? Ooh, a trombone! Go on, let me have a go . . . Once the tent was up we sat in a row on a hay-bale and took it in turns to shatter the silence. Echoes rang around the horizon.

'What about the neighbours?' I asked nervously after one particularly vigorous fanfare that scared the birds out of the trees.

'Three kilometres away,' answered the eldest, fifteen-year-old Damien, and kept on blasting.

They invited me in for supper. As a special treat the kids were allowed to stay up late, and bombard me with questions about my travels. Where was I going, why had I come that way, how would I get home, did I walk across the Channel? Ten-year-old David couldn't pronounce my name. The first time he tried it came out as 'Bean'. His siblings dissolved in laughter. The parents, Georges and Irene, tried to calm them, but it was too late. 'Meester Bean, Meester Bean!' I was labelled for life.

The kids retired at midnight. So did I. Red wine after a full day's walking is more effective than any sleeping-pill I've ever known. As I stumbled towards my tent David caught my hand.

'Monsieur . . .'

'Bean,' corrected nine-year-old Charlotte, and collapsed in fits of giggles. David ignored her loftily.

'Monsieur, we're going fishing tomorrow. Do you want to come?' He smiled at me appealingly. I couldn't refuse.

'With pleasure!'

He beamed. 'Great! We'll fetch you at six o'clock!'

He ran off up the stairs before I could protest.

I dreamt of Anna that night. We were kayaking up the Belize River past the mangrove swamps, talking utter rubbish as you only can when you trust one another completely. It was like a surprise visit from a long-missed friend. I woke up feeling as warm and happy as if I'd been hugged. I wanted to go back to sleep and see her again. The sun was low and red, shining through the wall of my tent. A long shadow grew up from the ground: a head, shoulders, a fishing-rod.

'Monsieur?'

'Mister Bean?'

Giggle giggle.

'Bonjour, mes amis,' I called out wearily. It was quarter past six. They'd let me lie in.

They led me down the white dusty lane to a bridge. The river ran below, bright and clear. We could see the dark fish flicking in the current beneath us. Damien baited my hook as David told me how to do it. The dawn breeze rippled the water and brought the scent of rotting weeds and mud. It was Belize again. I was still half-dreaming. I felt that if I turned round I'd see her sitting beside me, grinning. All I had to do was reach out and touch her hand. David noticed my abstraction and broke off his chatter.

'Are you all right?'

I stared into the water and told them my story. At the end there was a long silence. Then, shyly, David took my hand.

'Were you in love with her?'

'A little.'

'Was she in love with you?'

'No.'

He put his arm around me. 'You're my friend. I love you.'

Slowly the sun came up. Ripples danced and dazzled beneath us as we tried and failed to outwit the cunning fish. By ten o'clock we'd caught two branches, a patch of weed, and sunburn. My plan had been to leave before lunch, but my heart wasn't in it. I was too comfortable. What was the point in hurrying? When Irene came out with a huge jug of home-made lemonade and asked me to stay for lunch, I took no persuading at all. After lunch the boys took me on a tour of the farm, the milking-shed, the combine harvester ('I know how to drive it!' declared Damien proudly, elbowing David out of the driver's seat), the soya silos ('Do you have soya in England?'). We were kicking a football around the yard when Georges drove by in the tractor. The boys whooped and ran after him. He stopped, and we swung aboard, jolting our way to the riverside hay-field. For half an hour the boys and I paddled through the shallows looking for fish while Georges chugged up and down the field turning the new-mown hay. Then the boys ran off to watch the river-boats pass. I was dozing off under a tree when Georges came over and asked me if I'd like to drive. The rest of afternoon was a whirl of roaring engines, flying dust, and delight. I'd never driven a tractor before. The sun shone. Swallows swooped on disturbed flies. A sparrow-hawk swooped on the swallows. The boys came running back and cheered me every time I passed. By the time the field was done my ears were numb, my throat dry, my skin gritty and my eyes shining. Driving a tractor! A childhood dream come true.

David drove us back under Georges' laughing supervision, and we careered into the yard and came within an ace of crashing into the combine. We laughed and jumped down from the cab. The football lay in the gutter. Georges raced for it with Damien on his heels. A game of grown-ups versus kids erupted and shouted its way into the near pasture, narrowly missing my tent. Charlotte and her five-year-old sister Emilie came out to see what all the fuss was about, saw me and promptly dragged me off to give them another trombone lesson. Irene came out with the half-time lemonade and stopped to applaud her daughters' musical talents and her menfolk's footballing skills. We were still at it when the red sun sank behind the distant escarpment of the Côte d'Or.

Anna was still with me when I went back to the tent that night. It had been a magical day, and I was glad she'd shared it. It was only when I came to write my diary that I realized it was the twenty-fourth of June. It was a year to the day since I'd met her.

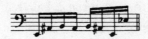

It was hard to return to my solitary path, and the fact that I'd said goodbye so often only made it harder. But after a day the old habits reasserted themselves. Self-sufficiency is a skill, and I'd had a lot of practice. I kept my mind busy with daydreams and marching-songs and made for the Côte d'Or.

Flanders had been grey as steel, Lorraine oil-seed gold, the Doubs valley a gentle green. The road along the Côte d'Or was white and glaring, so fierce that all colour died. White dust powdered my path, stones and soil were bleached by the sun, even the sky seemed blind. Only I was red, sun-burnt and prickly despite all my precautions. I was walking in the razor-thin shade of a high wall just north of Gevrey-Chambertin when a gleaming black Mercedes purred to a stop beside me. Tinted windows hissed down and a huge man in a black suit and shades stared out at me. God, I thought, it's the Mafia . . .

Expressionless, he read my rucksack.

'Pilgrim.'

'Yes, Godfather,' I quavered. He didn't get it.

'It's a long way.'

'Yes, Godfather.'

'You must have sinned a lot.'

No comment, Godfather . . .

Cold shades raked me from head to heel. 'You'll need courage.' One big hand reached for a thigh pocket. 'Go and buy yourself some wine.'

He handed me a hundred-franc note (about £8) and drove off before I could answer.

I walked into the village: stone houses clustering around the castle, unchanged in three hundred years. Every building sprouted adverts for quality wine. I wondered if my hundred francs would be enough. I was standing by the village well wondering where to start when a battered Renault drove by and stopped abruptly.

'Are you lost?'

'I was looking for a wine-tasting.'

The driver laughed. He wasn't much older than me. 'That's my vineyard there. Come on in and I'll open a bottle!' It was nine o'clock.

Three hours later we were still there. François was a keen mountaineer, and when he heard where I'd been and where I was going there was no stopping him. He led me into his office, tastefully furnished with a computer, a fax and a wine-rack, and pulled a mountain of maps off a shelf. Sweeping a pile of invoices merrily onto the floor to make room, he poured out two glasses of priceless vintage and proceeded to reminisce about every GR in France. Halfway through a description of the Vosges he stopped short, grabbed a marbled sketch-book off the shelf and slid it towards me. Reverently I opened the crackling yellow pages. It was a diary, in beautiful handwriting. The first date was 1 September, 1914.

'My grandfather's war diary. He was a stretcher-bearer.' François touched the page affectionately. 'He was on the Tête des Faux, Verdun, the Somme, he survived them all. I remember him talking about it sometimes. He said he lived because he refused to give up. I've always treasured those words.' He gave me a meaningful look. 'Think about them when the going is hard.'

I was still groping for an answer when the phone went. An angry voice barked down the line. François paled.

'Okay! I'm on my way!' He slammed the phone down. '*Merde*! I was supposed to be in a meeting at twelve!' He looked around desperately, grabbed the papers from the floor. 'Sorry, I've got to go . . .' He sprinted to the car, gunned the engine, jumped out again, ran past me into the office, grabbed the bottle we'd been tasting, ran to his car *again*, pulled out a plastic Vittel water-bottle, tipped its contents onto the drive, emptied the wine into it, screwed it up tight, ran back to me and shoved it into my hands.

'Have it for lunch! Just don't shake it up too much!' And he bolted for the car and took off in a cloud of dust.

I ate in the shade of a row of vines, sipping warm ten-year-old Gevrey-Chambertin *grand cru* from a plastic bottle and munching baguette and brie. It's a hard life being a pilgrim, I thought as I finished the bottle and lay back against my rucksack. When I shut my eyes the world spun around me. Never mind, navigation's not that difficult . . .

I got very lost that afternoon.

For two days I walked southwards with the limestone bluffs on my right and endless perspectives of vines spilling onto the plain to my left. Villages and chateaux passed like a wine-taster's dream: Pommard, Volnay, Clos de Vougeot, Beaune. Every *vigneron* in Burgundy was out pruning his vines, and the air was sharp with the scent of cut leaves. Far away to the south-east Mont Blanc gleamed like a tooth; out on the plain shone the diamond-patterned roofs of Beaune. Somewhere south of Beaune I turned west and climbed the back of the Côte d'Or. The change was astonishing. Below were the vineyards, orderly and tame. Above them was a limestone wilderness of rubble and thorns. Heat rose from the stones like a kick in the face. There were paths on the ground, but the map didn't recognize them: I got used to losing my way and forcing my way through grappling thickets. It took two days to cross the heights, and by the end my clothes and my temper were ragged. But beyond lay paradise. I'd reached the southern edge of the Morvan, a wet, wild land of tangled forests and lush pastures. Land and people were much poorer than their eastern neighbours, the roads rutted, the paths barely maintained, but after the furnace of the vineyards it was like coming home. Again, my diary tells the story:

3 July:
  over fields in blistering heat. No paths. Barbed wire everywhere and I'm too stubborn to go back – end up crashing through bush for half an hour, oh for my machete! Then emerge twenty metres from path. Just mildly annoying. Stamp on to monastery of Val St Benoit, arrive at sunset. Medieval buildings nestled in a wooded valley. Cool shade. Everything green. Idyllic. Greeted by prioress. Prioress? Nunnery not monastery – oops. Can't let me in, doesn't want to turn me away: puts me in a caravan behind the priory. Peeling paint, sagging ceiling, surrounded by nettles, but sisters bring me a huge bowl of HOT water – bless! Invited to matins tomorrow. Tempting but it's at 6:15, groan groan ... Brew up on my doorstep then sit and write letters by candle-light, watching spiders play on the ceiling. Share bed with a grasshopper. St Francis would be proud.
  4 July: up at 6, stumble over to the chapel. Glorious. Ancient stone refurbished with beautiful simplicity: white wooden stalls, altar of white stone, sisters all in white robes, dawn light coming through lacy Gothic windows.

*Worth waking for. Nobody comes out to see me off –
leave letter of thanks. Set off up into woods. Map wrong
again – there's a track going in exactly the right direction!
How handy. Sit and eat on ridge in sunshine, enjoying
scents of pine, taste of tomatoes. Lovely view of Autun
and its cathedral through the trees. Reach town
early p.m., large late lunch and mending (boot heels,
trousers) then visit the cathedral. SUPERB! The best I've
seen yet. A symphony in stone: high Gothic vaulting,
sculpted arches, bare walls, an elegant forest of winter
trees. Well worth all the trekking to see it. Amble outside,
walk straight into the finals of the European Champion-
ship of Boules with Square Balls. How bizarre?! Building
blocks thrown with skill ... Final pits junior against
senior champions. Juniors aged about 11, capture all
hearts. Younger has arm in plaster. Superb players! Ten-
sion mounts with every boule (Bloque?) Cries of 'Let the
little ones win!' But they lose on the last throw. Enormous
applause, prizes all round. Walk home grinning. Glad I
came this way.*

After Autun, I went mad. There's no other explanation. I'd
been walking through farmland and across country lanes for
a month in the summer heat. Quite suddenly, I'd had enough.
So, with the kind of logic that puts people into padded cells,
I checked my map, decided that the Auvergne volcanoes were
the nearest available mountains, guesstimated that they were
two hundred and fifty kilometres away as the pilgrim walks,
and decided that since there didn't seem to be much of interest
on the way I might as well aim for speed.

I walked. How I walked! The trick of doing something insane
is to approach it systematically. I left my campsite at eight each
morning and walked until nine-thirty. On the stroke of the

half-hour I dropped my sack, pulled off my boots and socks to let them dry and ate a few handfuls of dried fruit and chocolate. It didn't matter if I was on a thundering roadside, I stopped, much to the amusement of passing truckers with loud horns. At ten precisely I'd be off again, shoving with my poles for maximum speed. Every hour and a half I'd stop for another half hour, and I kept up the rhythm until sunset. I would never have contemplated it in the mountains, where the important thing is to go slowly but steadily, but down on the plains it was the only way. After an hour my feet ached from hammering the tarmac. More than an hour and a half would have been unbearable. As it was, the last leg of the day was always a killer; but the distances flew by. My record for a single day was thirty-five kilometres, and I never did under thirty. I was amazed. Looking back on it, I'm appalled. How my hip and shoulders survived I'll never know.

There were no campsites. It's too flat for walkers and too rural for anyone else, so I had to improvise accommodation, but it's amazing what you can find if you just have the nerve to ask, and after three months of pilgrimage my initial embarrassment was long gone. In swift succession I camped in the grounds of a parish church, a Buddhist temple, and a retired engineer's back garden. The hospitality was as warm as ever. The engineer gave me beer and a hot shower, a priest gave me beer and bacon, two ladies outside the church brought me beer and a bowl of soup, the Buddhist monks offered me beer and whisky. Evidently Burgundy's fame wasn't limited to wine. Would Britain be this welcoming? I wondered. It was an unanswerable question. One day, I vowed, I'll go and find out.

After a week I could see the mountains on the horizon, a blue wave shimmering above the corn-fields. My heart lifted. I was longing for a rest. Walking had stopped being fun the moment I began to hurry, and it had become a mind-game. Could I overcome the pain? For the first time in months I found myself thinking of the morale-boosting list I'd once shown

Rod, the smuggler. It was still in my breast pocket, as it had been for a thousand miles. To my amazement, I didn't bother to read it. Every day I ached more. Every day my body longed to stop, but my brain was simply too stubborn. I'd promised myself I'd rest when I reached the mountains, and by God I was going to reach them ... I'd never thought of myself as macho, but the mere thought of admitting defeat had me spitting fire and brimstone. Give up? It was inconceivable.

On 13 July I reached Chatel-Guyon, northern gateway to the Auvergne hills, and sank into the campsite with a groan they could have heard in Autun. I'd covered two hundred and fifty kilometres in a week and a half. The roads were behind me. From there I could follow mountain paths all the way into Spain. It was a triumphant moment. I'd taken on the plains, and I'd won. How to celebrate? I asked myself. Dancing, alcohol, food?' I rejected the lot and plunged my feet into the finest footbath of my life. I won't say it was better than sex, but not even jazz could have beaten it.

PART 6

The Auvergne

'Never look at the brass. It only encourages them.'
(Sir John Barbirolli)

The Auvergne is a land of volcanoes. More than two hundred ancient cones jut out of the wild wet forests like upturned cups, from barely-visible hillocks to the mile-high horseshoe of the Puy du Sancy, and between them sulphurous springs gush from the rocks. Chatel lies at the very edge of the range, a little spa town flowing down the sides of one such cone. On the very pinnacle is the war memorial. Below it is the church. Below that, in a tangled web of narrow streets, is the old town. At the foot of the hill is the fashionable new quarter, built and sustained by money from the spa complex. Half of France still comes here to take the curative waters, and the main parade is lined with jewellers and fashion boutiques. Every afternoon fine ladies in evening dress and pearls take their constitutional walks under the stately plane-trees. Every one carries a little gourd of *l'eau de Chatel* in a wicker basket. Walking there was like stepping back into another age.

I spent two days in the local campsite, recovering from my exertions. Then I went busking in the old town market. It wasn't a spectacular success, but the sun was shining and I was playing well, so I didn't really mind. After half an hour a traveller stopped to watch: dreadlocks, scarred and stubbly face, camouflaged jacket, army boots, dog. He waited politely until I'd finished a piece.

'How's it going?' he asked.

I shrugged. 'Not bad. The people are okay here. How about you?' I'd seen him begging that morning, and given him what change I had. Nothing increases generosity like a dose of fellow-feeling.

He shrugged. 'Not bad. Good luck, *mec.*'

He wandered off. The dog gave me an inquisitive sniff, then followed.

I bumped into him on the main parade two hours later, and he invited me for a drink. Evidently the begging had gone well. We sat in wicker chairs on the pavement, watching the curists pass and chatting about life on the road. He'd taken to travelling when he was eighteen, eleven years before. He'd crossed France on foot and by thumb a dozen times, going wherever fancy and casual work took him. He was a fund of stories.

'What are you doing here?' I asked. His accent was a ferocious mixture of northern speed and southern twang, mangled by missing teeth: he'd been in a few fights in his time. It was hard to follow him.

'Looking after a friend who squats here. He broke his leg a week ago, he can't move.' He gave me a sidelong look. 'If you're around for a few days, why not come and stay?'

I hesitated. I'd learnt a lot of faith in human nature in the last few months, but not that much. Share a squat with a traveller? My bourgeois soul blanched. Then I laughed. I had more in common with him than anyone else I had met on the walk.

That evening I moved into the squat: a half-ruinous house behind the church, just below the war memorial. Jimmy welcomed me with a gap-toothed grin and introduced me to Didier, a deep-chested Belgian with one leg swathed in plaster up to the hip. He was happily installed in front of the TV with a case of beer, and there he remained while we cooked sausages and eggs, providing a running commentary on such French classics as *Buffy Contre les Vampires, Le Texas Ranger Walker*, and *Friends*. So much for cultural purity. The next day Jimmy and I tidied the flat from top to bottom. It needed it. The paint on the walls was cracked and streaked with dust, the bare floor-boards rolling in mouse-droppings, the antique electric stove caked in grease and culinary archaeology. By the time we'd got things shipshape it was evening. We sat up until the small hours, swigging beer, eating pizza and throwing the crusts at the screen. I hadn't had such fun since I was a student. I was sorry when the time came to leave.

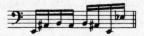

I left Chatel on 18 July, refreshed and raring to go after so much healthy living. Forget energy bars and a balanced diet: if you ever need to pack in the calories, nothing beats beer and pizza. I dropped down the hill from Didier's squat, crossed the main parade just after 8 o'clock, and set my head towards the wooded hills, the very picture of a man on a mission.

I made it as far as the outskirts.

The road dipped down to a slender bridge, climbed steeply between balconied houses glowering at the plain, and turned into a forestry track. As I passed the last house a middle-aged man emerged from his garage, stared at me and said, 'You've got to be a pilgrim.'

I stared back. He tapped himself proudly on the chest: a stout, powerfully-built man with a silver beard and a balding dome.

'I'm a pilgrim too. I walked to Santiago last year. Do you fancy a drink?'

I'd come seven hundred metres. It was time for a break.

He led me into the house. It was a delightful place, alive with his wife's pot plants and illuminated by his photos. As I straightened up from pulling off my boots I found myself face to face with the one picture that every Santiago pilgrim comes to recognize: the statue of the saint above the Portal of Glory, a bearded, smiling pilgrim carrying a staff and a gourd, with a cockle-shell on his hat. Leaning against the wall beneath it was a carved staff as tall as I was. Guy picked it up, beaming with pleasure.

'I carved it myself.' He held it out, nearly cracking me on the forehead. 'Look.' One horny finger traced the designs: a key, a cockle-shell, a palm leaf, the traditional symbols of Rome, Santiago and Jerusalem. Above them was the word '¡Ultreia!', and below 'Calla y anda'.

'Ultreia.' He gave me a sharp look. 'You know the word? It was the pilgrims' motto. Ultreia y suseia, onwards and upwards. They say it all the time in Spain.' He grinned. 'The other one is a phrase I learned from a doctor from Menorca. It's Spanish. It means, "shut up and walk".'

He put the staff back in the corner, then turned suddenly. His eyes twinkled.

'I've got a question for you. You'll laugh.' I waited. I hate it when people say things like that. 'How are you getting home afterwards?'

I burst out laughing. How many times had people asked me that along the way? Guy slapped me on the shoulder, laughing with me.

'Ah, I knew you were a pilgrim! Come on, let's have some wine.'

It was almost 9 a.m. Morning drinking was becoming a habit.

I was still there at one, groaning as my stomach stretched. His wife Marie had taken one look at me and decided I needed feeding up. A light lunch followed: salad, macaroni cheese, and *then* the main course: steak and potatoes. It was delicious, but not half so good as his company. He'd already made pilgrimages to Rome, Santiago and Lourdes. Jerusalem was next, if he could find a partner. (Marie winced when he said it, but remained silent.) He'd been a successful businessman once. Then he'd grown tired of the materialistic life and gone looking for something different.

'And I found it.'

'What did you find?'

'You decide.'

The stories came flooding out.

'I was caught in a snow-storm in the Aubrac, south-west of Le Puy-en-Velay where the pilgrimage starts. I was walking by the road, and I thought: God, I wish I could hitch a lift. But that would be cheating. I heard an engine. I didn't put my thumb out, but the car stopped anyway and carried me to safety . . .

'On the fourteenth day I got lost. My sack was too heavy, my legs hurt, I couldn't go on. I prayed to my dead brother Gabriel: send me some help! Then a pilgrim came down the path towards me. He had a map and a compass. He helped me to the nearest hostel. His name was Gabriel.

'There was a seventy-seven-year-old Swiss millionaire. He'd got tired of working and sold his bank, and he was cycling to Santiago. He was very slow. Everyone knew about him. In all the pilgrim hostels people left messages for him, encouraging him. All the *hospitaleros*, the hostel-keepers asked about him. One night he slept in a hotel. We'd been expecting him in the hostel, so we were worried. Three of us went back to find him the next day. He was laughing. When he walked into the hotel with his bike the receptionist looked at him and said, "You'll find somewhere cheaper opposite." He said, "I want to see the manager." "Why?" says the receptionist. "To buy the hotel and fire you," he says, and puts his platinum credit card on the desk. He laughed about it all week.

'I was in Spain. It was winter. One boot had split and my toes were frozen. All I wanted was a hot bath and a bus home. I got down on my knees and prayed for a hotel. Then I saw a hair-grip lying in the mud. It wasn't even dirty, someone must have just dropped it, but there was nobody in sight. I mended my boot with it. That was all I needed to carry on. That's when I decided there must be a God. Fate doesn't have much humour.'

Those were just some of the stories. He showed me his photos in two immense albums. He showed me his guide-book, battered and stained, and the worn-out boots. The hair-clip was still there, rusted half through. He warned me of the perils along the way: loneliness, fatigue, dogs. 'The Galician dogs are really dangerous. Are your sticks heavy enough to stop one?'

'Yes.'

He looked surprised. 'Are you sure?'

'Pretty sure.'

I'd come a long way since Hotton.

I left at three, groaning and bloated. Guy accompanied me as far as the woods, scrambling straight up the slope like a ten-year-old. I lumbered after him with my normal grace. As we said goodbye he looked up at the sky. Black clouds were boiling in from the west. 'Look out on the hills,' he said. 'This is the lightning season.'

Marvellous.

Two hours later the clouds burst. I was well into the hills by then, winding my way between great strands of mossy oaks and ferns. Heavy golden light came and went between the trunks, breaking into glorious fans that blinked and vanished. Slowly it faded to a sickly grey. The first fat drops began to fall. I stopped, unshipped my pack, stripped down to my shorts. There was nowhere to hide, and no point in getting my clothes soaked. I was just packing away when my phone went off. I'd arranged two daily one-hour slots when it would be switched on. Guy's hospitality had driven the thought of switching it off again clear out of my head.

'Shit!' Thunder was grumbling over the hills. 'Allo?'

'Ben!' Dad, cheerful as ever. 'Is this a good moment?'

Lightning blazed overhead. 'NO!' I shouted over the crackle of thunder.

'What? Speak up! I'm getting interference!'

'I bet!' I was breathing hard. 'I'll call you back!'

'Is everything all right?'

It won't be if you don't bloody ring off! I thought. 'Yes! Later!' As I killed the handset lightning flared directly overhead. The flash and the bang came at the same moment. It sounded like the world ending. My heart almost stopped. Somewhere ahead of me came a scream of tortured wood, snapping and crackling, the appalling reek of burning. Then the trees flung up their branches, and the gale hit. Behind it came the rain, solid as bullets. Flying twigs pelted me. The horizon disappeared. As I ducked behind my rucksack a three-inch branch crashed down where I'd been standing.

I picked up my pack and ran, poles held protectively over my head. Standing still in that bombardment would have taken more courage than I've ever had. The slope clawed at my legs. Soon I was walking, gasping, flinching every time the thunder ripped the sky. A bloody haze pounded before my eyes. My legs and torso were bruised and scratched by hurtling debris. The rain was a wall. I was slogging up the middle of a river. Is this *eau contraire*? I thought hysterically. The storm seemed to last for ever. Terror does strange things to the mind. It can't have been more than half an hour before the sky began to clear. I picked my way upwards between fallen branches and drowned birds, shaking. The sunlight began its slow dance between the trees. The branches were dripping diamonds. It was beautiful. I stood leaning on my poles, staring around. I wasn't dead after all. Blood and rain mingled on my chest, a strange light-rimmed redness. Suddenly I felt very glad to be alive.

I camped that night on a lightning-proof col between two

volcanic craters, high above the world. The woods steamed and dripped mournfully through trailing veils of moss. Far below me the lights of Chatel were twinkling, but the great sweep of the west was dark, lit only by the stars. I sat staring at them for a long time. I'd forgotten how beautiful they were. It was late when I got round to calling home.

'Was everything all right?' asked Dad. 'You sounded a bit stressed.'

There wasn't much I could say.

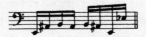

It took three weeks to cross the mountain ranges, and it was the happiest time I'd had in months. The Auvergne is France's equivalent of Wales. It's been a bastion of oppressed tribes since Celtic times, and, as in all Celtic homelands, the weather was bloody awful. I had one sunny day just after my thunderstorm, and two more the weekend I stayed in le Mont-Dore, but for the rest it was just like home. The clouds whipped along the ridges and curled down into the valleys. Rain came in diagonally, horizontally, even straight up on the more exposed crossings. Night-time temperatures dipped so low that I had to zip up my sleeping-bag for the first time since my scare in the Vosges. My northern-bred physiology responded with delight. Gone were the sullenness and fatigue of the plains. Gone were gritty eyes and prickly scalp. Even the residual ache in my hip, not now severe but never quite forgotten, diminished. I slogged my way up slick, muddy slopes and along cloud-blind ridges, and loved every moment of it.

July was almost gone, and the holiday flood was at its height. Every major peak in the great chain of volcanoes was crowded with tourists: the Puy de Dome overlooking Clermont, the Puy du Sancy horseshoe like a second Snowdon, the Puy Mary at the southern end of the chain, with its neighbours Peyre-Arse, Roland's Crack and Venus' Nipple. A major road runs by the

Puy Mary and up the Puy de Dome, whilst a cable-car leads to the Puy du Sancy's summit, so the numbers were no surprise; but even the grass-filled crater of the Puy de Come, miles from the nearest road, was flooded with screaming school-kids. The tracks between the peaks were so full that traffic-jams formed on the narrower sections. A couple of times I caused the jams, as bewildered ramblers looked at the Pack From Hell, and asked why I was carrying a parachute. The numbers were overwhelming. I found myself longing for solitude, or at least a single friendly walker going my way. No such luck. I'm sure I wasn't the only walker going from north to south that summer, but it certainly felt that way.

After a week I reached le Mont-Dore, and my mood rocketed. It's another spa town nestling at the foot of the Sancy horseshoe, as full of genteel wealth as Chatel, but local enterprise here has branched out into outdoor pursuits. Each morning a flood of elderly curists in cardigans and pearls strolls down the hill to the thermal baths, and meets a flood of booted hikers heading for the heights. The juxtaposition delighted me. I took one look at the place and decided to stay and busk.

I went to the town hall to ask permission. It started well.

'Excuse me, I'm a trombonist.'

'You *are*? *Formidable!*'

The moustached functionary spread his arms to embrace me. This very seldom happens.

'Do you want to stay for a few days?' Eager sincerity rang in his voice.

'Err . . .' Fluent to the last. As I stood there yammering, he explained. The town was celebrating the fiftieth anniversary of the Auvergne-Belgian Friendship League that weekend with a parade and a giant party. Half the municipal band was on holiday. They desperately needed players. Could I, would I help?

I was cautious. 'Will I have to march and play at the same time?'

'Of course not!' he lied heartily.

'Excellent! When do I start?'

'This evening at seven, in the rehearsal room.' He showed me a map, shook my hand repeatedly, bowed me out of the room like a high-class butler. I was buzzing with anticipation. A gig! I could hardly wait.

I passed the time happily busking in the main square – actually more of an oblong, as the town's built along the foot of the valley and is seldom more than two streets wide. The mere thought of playing with a band lit me up like a bottle of whisky, and my improvisation reached new heights. I'd never thought it was possible to slip straight from the *Frere Jacques* to *The Great Gate of Kiev* and thence to *Waltzing Matilda*, but I managed it that day. The locals seemed to like it. Two small girls petitioned me to be allowed to play, an elderly woman who had always wanted to walk to Santiago gave me a blessing, and a menacing-looking gendarme told me politely that there was a vacant busker's spot just round the corner where I could guarantee a good reception later in the day – true community policing. I decided I liked le Mont-Dore.

The municipal band room was at the head of a dingy staircase just opposite the public toilets in one of the town's less salubrious squares. I arrived ten minutes early, and stood gazing nostalgically at scattered music stands, battered instruments and tattered scores sliding off ramshackle shelves: the universal face of municipal music. Gradually the band drifted in and started warming up: three teenage girls with clarinets and sulky expressions, a young and enthusiastic couple of saxophonists firing Dave Brubeck quotes at each other, a tall, thin tuba player who looked far too frail to carry his instrument, a balding percussionist with lopsided specs. There didn't seem to be any trombonists yet. I was just starting to worry about that when the tuba player came up to me.

'You must be the trombonist! I'm Alain.' He gave me a beaming grin and shook my hand.

'Er . . . Where's the rest of the section?' I asked.

'You *are* the section.'

Right . . .

Jean-Yves, my contact from the town hall, arrived just before seven. He hurried over to me with a huge smile, crushed my knuckles with an eager hand-shake, and dragged me to the teetering stack of music. The first piece he dragged from the pile was a medley of folk tunes in a wind band arrangement that I'd first played when I was fourteen. My heart jumped with delight. I might be all alone, but at least I knew the repertoire! He dropped it into my arms, and followed it with a shower of yellowing parts. *Hello Dolly*, good, I knew that one . . . *The Liberty Bell*, less good, I'd only played it once and that was on the sousaphone . . . *La Marseillaise*, well, at least I knew the tune . . . *Aces High*, *Pasa Doble*, *Chanson d'Ete*, very bad, I'd never played them in my life . . . Piece after unfamiliar piece followed. I hadn't sight-read music since leaving College. My nerves started fluttering like a bat in a blizzard. Thank God we weren't planning to march as well!

'You'll need a lyre.' Jean-Yves hadn't noticed my abstraction. 'Have you got one?'

A lyre is a brass clip designed for marching band players. Theoretically, it clips around the shank of the mouthpiece and holds a sheet of music at eye level. Somehow, it hadn't been top of my kit list when I set out.

'No.'

'Don't worry, I've got a spare.' He delved into his case and pulled out a twisted museum piece that hadn't seen the light of day since the French Revolution. 'Does it fit?'

We slipped it over my mouthpiece and screwed it tight. It stood there for a second, then toppled over apologetically.

'No.'

'Try the slide.'

We tried it on the slide. It fitted. With a ghastly smile, I clipped a sheet of music into place. It stayed put. Jean-Yves slapped me on the back and hurried over to the podium to get the rehearsal started. I went back to my seat, dreading what was to come. He announced the first piece. Music rustled. I slipped the A4 sheet into the lyre: another unknown master-piece. He gave the up-beat. We started playing. My slide shot in and out. The lyre, firmly attached, whizzed up and down before my eyes. The music waved to and fro like a palm in a hurricane. My eyeballs did aerobics trying to follow musical dots that were leaping about like interference on a TV screen. I was still half-way through the first phrase when the rest of the band finished.

'Excellent!' Jean-Yves beamed. 'Now let's go outside and practise doing that while we're marching!'

I'm not even going to try and describe it. It was all of the above, plus walking in step and trying not to stab the clari-nettist in front of me with my slide. I gave up even trying to sight-read, and concentrated on improvising convincingly. It got some funny looks from Jean-Yves, who was walking back-wards ahead of us playing the trumpet and conducting, but he was too wise to comment. You can do a lot of damage with a well-aimed trombone.

I'm in for a fun weekend, I thought drearily as we shambled back to the band room. I was just contemplating slinking out when a sax player launched into *In the Mood*. It's the first big band piece I ever played, and it still hits me like an electric shock. Before I knew it my trombone was up and blasting out the answering arpeggio. Next second a trumpet scream ploughed a furrow through my hair as Jean-Yves took the bait. The drummer hurled himself onto his kit. Alain and two more saxes joined in. Suddenly the band-room was rocking. The windows shook. Our bass drummer, a generously-built nurse called Melanie, grabbed a mike from a shelf and started impro-vising vocals *à la* Ella Fitzgerald. Then *au* Louis Armstrong. Alain and I danced around one another, still playing. Jean-Yves clambered onto a chair and conducted one-handed. The entire sax section started swinging their instruments with near-perfect choreography. A sixty-year-old clarinettist grabbed one of the teenagers and started jiving. Stands and music went flying. We didn't care. By the time Jean-Yves seared up to the last top C we were so high we were in orbit. Around Mars.

It was going to be a good weekend.

Jazz is a drug. And, like all drugs, its effect varies from person to person. Some people are occasional users. They get a mild kick from playing, but they can take it or leave it alone. Others need a fix just to get through the week, and they don't care how they get it. Musicians are anarchists at the best of times, but put a bunch of jazz addicts together with a few instruments and you're talking revolution.

There were a lot of jazz addicts in le Mont-Dore, and it showed.

The official programme ran as follows: Saturday afternoon, unveiling of a commemorative plaque by the Belgian Consul. Short parade. Saturday evening, ball. Sunday, grand parade commemorating the visit of the Princess of Flanders to the Auvergne in 1899. We were the keystone of the local musical effort. A small jazz band had come down from Liege to provide the evening's entertainment. Another arrived from Namur, for fun. Thirty jazz addicts in a town used to two or three . . .

The unveiling went well. The Consul spoke with commendable brevity. The local mayor did not. Jean-Yves said a short piece thanking the newcomers to the band (five of us had been drafted in to cover the gaps left by holiday-makers). We played assorted fanfares without too much irreverent embellishment, though Jacques the drummer started whistling *Colonel Bogey* as we marched away to the beat of his snare drum and got most of the rear rank to join in. Alain provided a running commentary on the speeches for the edification of all those in ear-shot, while Melanie hissed 'Your flies are undone!' just as Jean-Yves turned to face the audience, provoking the desired reaction. On the whole, we were very well behaved.

Things deteriorated in the evening. To pass the time before the party, we went for another march, circling clockwise through the town. Unfortunately the guys from Namur had had the same idea, and were circling anti-clockwise. Le Mont-Dore isn't a very big town. We met them outside the Casino supermarket. They were playing *Take Five* as we played *Hello Dolly*. It made an interesting combination. We let them march by, reformed ranks and kept going. Ten minutes later we met them again just outside the thermal baths: *Under the Double Eagle* against the *Saint Louis Blues*. This time they gave way. Ten minutes after that they were back outside the supermarket treating an appreciative audience to *Running Wild* as we marched up to the strains of *Chattanooga Choo-Choo*. They promptly took off ahead of us, wiggling their rears provocatively. We followed them for almost a minute before succumbing to laughter.

The ball took place in a marquee in the park. Waiters in Belle-Epoque costume hurried back and forth with huge trays of *moules-frites* and Belgian beer: the Belgians had heard of French cuisine and wanted no part of it. We sat at trestle tables around the dance-floor and gorged while the official band played high-class blues. After two numbers the boys from Namur occupied the next table. They were dressed in clown costumes, still carrying their instruments. Their leader was the spitting image of Hercule Poirot. Their drummer began a surreptitious beat on the table with his fingers. Jacques joined in. They held a happy dialogue in demi-semi-quavers while the rest of us swapped anecdotes. It was great to hear the Walloon accent again. I sat listening through a haze of four-month-old nostalgia.

Sudden shouting interrupted us. It was 11 o'clock, and the official band was retiring to vast disapproval. 'Play!' someone shouted from the dance-floor. 'We want to dance!' Others took up the shout from all over the marquee, clapping and stamping. 'We want to dance! We want to dance!' The band leader waved regretfully and switched off his mike. Poirot stretched out a lazy hand for his saxophone and looked at his cohort.

'*Allons, mes enfants.*'

My trombone was leaning against my knee. Jean-Yves' trumpet lay between the mussel-shells. We looked at each other. A spark began dancing in his eyes.

'*On y va?*' he suggested, picking up the trumpet and wiggling the valves.

'*On y va,*' I agreed. As the Belgians picked up their instruments and looked towards the dance-floor he leant back, aimed at the chandelier and tore into *When the Saints*.

The official show was over, and the real party began.

My memories of that night are hazy. My veins were aswim with alcohol, my ears battered by applause. We'd never played as an ensemble before, so we had to stick to the standards, and the audience loved it. The marquee was supposed to be empty by midnight. We were still playing at one in the morning. We stood in the centre of the dance-floor hurling bits of improvision from player to player. The dancers whirled around us shivering the floor-boards. Jean-Yves swung into the *Marseillaise*. Suddenly everyone was singing. I had to retaliate. As breathless silence fell I whirled into a Highland fling. Four bars' astounded silence disintegrated as every dancer in the place started jumping. Poirot answered with a piece of his own. I'd never heard it, but I was the only one there who hadn't. The singing shook the night. Anarchy reigned. We only stopped playing when our lips threatened to collapse. Even then the dancers wanted more.

'Tomorrow!' we promised them, and called it a night.

Sunday was memorable. I'm not sure how much our impromptu concert had had to do with it, but the town buzzed with irreverent humour. Not even the parade organizers were taking it seriously. We were ready at 11 o'clock. The organizers asked us to march into position opposite the thermal baths, then decided we'd be better off further up the street. There wasn't room to turn round, so we marched in reverse. Alain tried playing something backwards, but it didn't quite work. A Belgian woman dressed as the Princess' lady-in-waiting shouted at us to behave. As soon as her back was turned Jean-Yves played a ribald ditty, to which the entire band sang the words, 'You're not wearing knickers!'

'Oh yes I am!' she shouted, and swept up her skirts to show us. Alain promptly played the first phrase of the *Can-Can*, which sounded most unusual on the tuba. Jean-Yves joined in. She stormed up to him with blazing eyes, snatched his trumpet away, and gave him the most ferocious stage kiss of his career. As he reeled she flounced away, shouting 'That took your breath away!' The band cheered.

The parade began. We were wedged in between the Ambassador of the Belgian Congo (resplendent in leopard skins and a feather headdress), walking arm in arm with the Princess' Equerry, and a group of fashionable ladies in parasols. Alain turned round and blew the *Can-Can* at them. The front rank immediately started dancing. The lady-in-waiting was not amused. She shrieked orders in a voice worthy of a Gestapo sergeant. 'You're not wearing knickers!' came a voice from the band, so she proved it again.

We marched on. Jacques started whistling *Colonel Bogey*. Others joined in. As we swung along the street a low murmur began, ''Itler 'as only gone one balle . . .' International culture. Suddenly a motor roared and the Princess' Baby shot into view: a fifteen-stone rugby player in a fetching bonnet, mounted on a quad-bike heavily disguised as a pram. 'Need a pee-pee!' he squeaked, and sprayed us liberally with a small water-cannon. As he swept past the Congolese Ambassador one burly arm plucked an ostrich feather. The Ambassador yelled with rage and sprinted after him, waving his assegai. Baby kept just out of range, shooting water everywhere. 'Still need a pee-pee!' he cried.

The Equerry watched, then yawned. The excitement was too

much for him. Her looked thoughtfully at the road. Then he lay down, spread his handkerchief over his face and fell asleep. Jean-Yves stood to attention by the body and started playing the *Last Post*. Alain added the *Funeral March*. 'No!' shouted the lady-in-waiting, and swept up, puckering her lips. Jean-Yves lowered his trumpet and ran. The last we saw of our illustrious leader was a flurry of vengeful skirts pursuing him down an alley.

'He has that effect on me, too,' sighed his wife, and carried on marching.

It was a triumphant afternoon. There were grinning faces all over town as events moved to their ceremonious conclusion with another round of speeches, musical interjections, thunderous kisses and cries of 'still need a pee-pee!' God knows what the Belgian Consul thought, but the grass-roots voters loved it. Scattered groups were still enjoying themselves as we made our way back to the band room. They had another rehearsal, and it was time for me to go. There were a couple of hours of daylight left, and I wanted to watch the sunset from the ridge above town. We said an affectionate farewell, and I headed back down the stairs as they started warming up.

I could still hear them at sunset. I'd reached the heights, and in the clear mountain air the faint music carried for miles. Slowly the lights went on and the music died away. As the last note faded a lorry let out a colossal honk in completely the wrong key. On the whole, it was a fitting end.

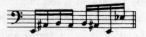

In the first week of August I came out of the mountains and headed eastwards towards Le Puy-en-Velay. Since Guy had mentioned it I'd checked my maps and worked out that it was as near as dammit to the half-way point of my walk: a fitting place to take a week off. Fifty miles from the town I stopped to visit a tenth-century chapel perched on a cliff-face. It was hotter than ever and there wasn't much shade: by the time I reached the top I was gasping. I made a quick circuit of the church, admiring the fortress-like battlements and red-tiled roof, but there was no way in and the blank walls were more defensive than decorative. As I swung down the slope towards the town I saw a girl coming towards me: young, pretty, and labouring under a colossal rucksack. My heart warmed to her. I'd like to say that it was simply because she was a fellow-sufferer, but after four months' effective isolation I would have felt the same if she'd climbed the hill in a jeep.

She came to a halt below me and rested with her hands on her knees, breathing hard. She shot me an ironic look.

'I thought I was crazy . . .'

I stopped and leant on my poles. 'You are. I'm crazier.'

She grinned and slumped against a wall. 'So why are you still alive?'

'Practice.' I dumped my sack and sat on it. Her eyebrows raised.

'How much practice?'

'Four months.'

'You're right. You're crazier.'

She introduced herself as Anne, a twenty-nine-year-old university librarian from Brussels. It was her first ever walking holiday, and she was planning to head westwards into the Cantal massif, southernmost of the Auvergne ranges. My heart sank. Just for once, I thought I'd found some company. After a while she pulled out her map and asked me for advice. She hadn't had much experience of navigation, and she wanted to know what route to take. I looked at the map, and sat up suddenly. It was the new edition. There was her route climbing the Plomb du Cantal. There was mine, the road southeast to St Flour and Le Puy. And there, linking the Cantal and St Flour, was a path that my map didn't mention.

I thought about it for at least a second. Was it sensible? No. Did I care?

No.

'Just a thought: can I accompany you as far as the Cantal?'
She stared at me. 'But you're going east . . .'

I showed her the linking path. 'It's not much out of my
way,' (like a whole day's walk), 'and it'd be nice to have the
company.'

She threw me a beaming smile. 'Wonderful! *On y va?*'

And on y went.

It was wonderful. I hadn't walked with anyone since Luxembourg, and though Chris has many sterling qualities, he's no
pretty girl: we walked through summer-scented pine woods
winding up past sheer escarpments, and as far as I was con-
cerned, it was paradise. She was a woman of a thousand inter-
ests, music, literature, art history, politics and many more: only
lack of breath stopped us talking for long. Noon came before
we knew it. We picnicked in a shady field full of flies, then
made our leisurely way towards the hills. Instead of the ten-mile
downhill walk I'd planned, I was going fourteen miles uphill,
and I didn't mind at all. I was captivated. If I hadn't been
wearing shorts I would have flung myself on my knees before
her, begging for more company, but the stones of the Auvergne
are hard and jagged and they'd cost me enough skin already.
Instead I laughed and prattled like an idiot. Imagine a pretty
girl taking a large, excitable dog for a walk and you'll get the
picture. Beauty's a drug, and I was hooked.

Just before sunset we reached the mountain hostel where
Anne had booked her bed and board. The evening breeze had
cooled my ardour, and I was just starting to wonder how much
I'd embarrassed myself when she turned to me and said, 'Can I
buy you a meal?' It was so unexpected I reeled. She immediately
thought she'd offended me and started apologizing, so I apolo-
gized in return, and she said no, it was her fault, and we'd
probably still be there now if a cold blast hadn't warned us a
storm was coming. We ran for shelter, and reached the warden
just in time to book an extra meal. Three courses and several

glasses of wine later we were *still* talking, slumped in front of a cheerful fire dissecting the inter-racial tensions in Brussels. She was almost asleep when I took the plunge.

'Why don't we walk together for a few more days?' It would take me in completely the wrong direction, but what did that matter? Le Puy was only a town. This was a pretty girl!

She thought about it, then shook her head regretfully. 'I don't think so. I really wanted some time alone.'

I took it bravely. 'Oh well. Happy walking, anyway.'

'Sorry, Ben.'

'*C'est la vie.*' I forced a grin. 'At least I'll see Le Puy.'

Next morning she treated me to breakfast. Auvergne hostel wardens take their culinary duties seriously: this one had laid on five sorts of cereal, six jams, three sorts of milk and enough toast for an army. I tried to dull the ache in my heart with an overdose of muesli. It didn't work. Making friends, losing friends . . . We said an uncomfortable goodbye, and I set off alone.

The walking did what the fool hadn't. After less than a kilometre a cold mist rose, shutting me off from the world. Alone and bitter, I started swearing. What had possessed me to abandon my friends for this lunatic mission? I found myself quoting the bloodier bits of Shakespeare, ranting at the wind. When they ran out I followed with Kipling's *If.* Suddenly I began to feel better. From Kipling I went on to Flanders and Swann's *Song of the Weather*, and by the time that was over I was back on form. I swung on singing war-songs and scaring the cattle. I'd covered eighteen miles and St Flour was already in sight when the phone rang.

'Ben, it's Anne.' Eh? 'I'm still in the refuge. I was thinking about what you said. Why don't you come back and join me for a week?'

'Errm . . .'

'Where are you?'

I had to laugh. It was that or scream. 'Thirty kilometres away.'

'Ah.' Long pause. 'Can you make it by this evening?'

'Thirty kilometres *downhill*.' Who did she think I was?

'Oh.' The irony hit her and she laughed helplessly. 'Oh *merde
. . . Bon voyage, mon ami.*'

'*Et toi. Au revoir.*'

I rang off and walked on, shaking my head. Guy was right. There must be a God. Fate didn't have that much humour.

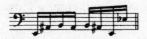

Two days later, I'd run out of laughter. It was three in the afternoon, the air was jungle-hot and jungle-sticky, I'd lost my map, my hip was aching, and I was beaten. The path had petered out at St Flour. Since then I'd been on tarmac, shaking my joints to pieces. The region seemed to specialize in savage dogs and homicidal truckers. I'd had two near misses that morning on a road that switch-backed over endless ridges. As I blundered up to another crest a third juggernaut came within an ace of flattening me. Right, I thought. I staggered off the road and slumped with my back to a pine-tree. I quit. I'm not moving until Christmas. Where am I, anyway?

I glanced around wearily. Something white stood by the roadside. I looked at it without much interest. Some French highway marking . . . Then my subconscious started jumping up and down, screaming. I looked again.

'Le Puy-en-V. 20 km'.

Twenty kilometres! That was almost close! No, said my limbs, don't be stupid. You can do it tomorrow. Le Puy! cried my mind. A youth hostel, a warm bed, hot showers! No more walking for a week! Very slowly I climbed to my feet and staggered towards the kilometre-stone. It was just below the ridge. Beyond it, the road dropped down arrow-straight towards a distant plain. Right on the edge of sight was another bluff, another drop. Beyond it, my mind's eye could already see the pinnacles of Le Puy. It's downhill all the way, whispered the voice of temptation. *Hot showers!*

Every aching fibre in my body told me not to. Hard-garnered walking experience echoed the message. *Don't do it!* It'll hurt ... I looked at my watch. Three o'clock. Twenty kilometres downhill. Even with rests, I should be there by eight ... Don't! screamed my body. Hot showers! clamoured my brain.

I sat down. I pulled my emergency chocolate-bar from my rucksack, looked at it for a second, then ate it. I knocked it back with half a pint of luke-warm water. I sat completely still for another five minutes, breathing deeply.

Then I went for it.

The first kilometre-stone went by after nine minutes, the second after seventeen. Raw chocolate pumped through my veins like rocket fuel. I swung on my sticks as if they were crutches, pushing myself faster. The slope ran down for four kilometres. I left it after thirty-seven minutes and scorched into the flats. Stubbled fields whipped by on either side. My feet were throbbing inside my boots. After an hour I forced myself to rest and drink. I stopped for less than three minutes. I'd started a sugar rush. I had to ride it until it, or I, burned out.

At 6 o'clock I reached the edge of the plain and saw the main road sweep down before me into a broad ravine. Below was another valley, much lower, and at the end was an urban darkness hazed with fumes. I stopped to breathe, looked back, and shouted. The western horizon was black. Lightning flickered along the Cantal ridges. Clouds were boiling up out of the mountains with terrifying speed. Better get moving, said my inner voice, or you're going to get very, very wet.

The clouds were like an explosion of coal-dust, deep black with a strange luminosity behind them, rolling across the sky. I pulled my hat down over my ears and tried to speed up. Ten minutes later, the rain began. There was no warning. One second I was dry, the next a lake crashed down around me and exploded. Cars crawled by, up to their hub-caps in water.

Lightning strobe-lit the landscape. In ten seconds I was soaked, Gore-Tex and all. I threw back my head and yelled, too elated to be scared. It was a fireworks show and a water-fight all together. It was superb.

I pelted down the hill. The road was streaming with yellow-brown water. It sloshed over my ankles and into my boots. I was too wet to care. At least it was cool! The kilometres swept by. Eight minutes, nine minutes, eight again, I couldn't believe the speed I was making. Before I knew it I was wading down the last hill and the vale of Le Puy opened up ahead of me.

'That's outrageous!' I yelled. Lightning flashed behind the town, and for the briefest second I saw the panorama in black-and-white glory: statues and spires rearing above the town on pinnacles like sharpened stakes. Hollywood would be ashamed to use shots like that. I accelerated, singing at the top of my voice, barely audible in the chaos. The streets were running rivers and there was nobody there to see as I plunged on into the town centre and swung up the hill to the Cathedral.

There's no other building like it in France. Built at the top of an almost-sheer slope, its Romanesque façade towers over the town, supported on colossal pillars like a giant's gateway. To climb the steps towards it is like walking slowly to heaven. As I climbed the thunder boomed overhead. I couldn't believe I was there. Halfway already? I'd only just set off . . . Tourists sheltering under the portico looked at me curiously. I ignored them, and went on up to the iron gates. Triumph burst inside me. I was there! I'd beaten my weariness, I'd beaten the storm, I was halfway to my goal. The emotion was too great to contain. As thunder cracked again I laughed. If this was the halfway point, how would it feel to arrive?

Suddenly I went cold. Arrive? I'd never thought about arriving. It had always seemed too far away. The halfway point had crept up on me almost unawares. Where had the time gone? From here on, the end would be drawing nearer. It was a grim thought. I swallowed my laughter abruptly. End my walk? I couldn't do it.

Then the lightning flashed again, blinding the world beyond the black archway, and I laughed anyway. What an arrival! I couldn't have done it better if I'd planned it. The first half had been exhilarating. The second would be even better. I could hardly wait! But there was a promise to keep first . . .

And I went back out into the pouring rain in search of a hot shower.

PART 7

The *Midi*

'If you can force your heart and nerve and sinew
To serve your turn long after they are gone,
And so hold on, when there is nothing in you
Except the will that says to them, Hold on! . . .'
Rudyard Kipling, *If*

The more I saw of Le Puy, the more I liked it, and not just because the youth hostel showers were every bit as good as I'd hoped. I've always had a soft spot for rampant exhibitionism in music, art and architecture (opposites attract, presumably), and Le Puy was my kind of town. Like Chatel-Guyon, it's built upon a cluster of volcanic pinnacles, but where Chatel's summit is crowned by a tastefully understated park and war memorial, Le Puy's architects went for the ecclesiastical look. The smallest pinnacle stabs up from the valley floor like the tip of a sharpened pencil. On its top perches a tenth-century chapel illuminated with red and white stone mosaics inspired by the great mosques of Arabic Spain, and if the medieval builders hadn't hacked a staircase out of the solid rock you'd need a helicopter to get to it. Even with the stairs, the priest of St Michel d'Aiguilhe must be the fittest clergyman in Europe. Perhaps it's just as well that the climb weeds out all but the most dedicated devotees. The chapel occupies the whole summit, and it's still only about the size of a squash court.

The largest pinnacle isn't much larger, but it's much less steep, and therein lies the problem: everyone can climb it, and in the Middle Ages everyone did. The current cathedral was started in the late tenth century, just after the Bishop of Le Puy had become the first non-Spaniard to make the trek to Santiago, and within a generation it became a pilgrim centre of such international importance that it couldn't hold all the visitors. It was enlarged twice in the next century, and then the architects ran out of hill-top. Another expansion was urgently needed. So, with a pragmatism bordering on insanity, they decided that since they couldn't move the cathedral down to the plain, they'd have to bring the plain up to the cathedral.

They did.

The cathedral of Le Puy-en-Veley is simply the most spectacular church I've ever seen. The best approach is from the west, up a hillside so steep that even the road is divided into steps. It leads to a broad staircase funnelling up under a towering archway, its pillars six foot across. Above them is a frowning façade also covered in red-and-white mosaics. Under the dark vault the steps run on, flanked by dwindling pillars, the walls decorated with gilded medieval frescoes. Triple doors block the way, carved with Arabic script by craftsmen imported from Spain; the central pillars are red porphyry survivors of the Roman temple that once stood here. Beyond them, shallow steps lead up into the nave. Climb them, and turn round. Behind you stands the ponderous magnificence of the cathedral, sharp-edged grey granite reflecting the light. Duck, and you look back down through the archway to red roofs and white walls gleaming in the sun. That's when you realize that the entire length of that massive nave rests on the pillars below. Half a cathedral perched over the abyss: it takes the breath away.

I spent a lot of time sitting on the stairway. Le Puy's been a centre of pilgrimage for more than a millennium, and the mere fact that we stood at the end of the Secular Century wasn't about to alter the traditions. Every morning at 8 o'clock there's a Pilgrims' Mass in the cathedral, followed by a blessing for all those about to depart, and then a little flood of rucksack-wearing wanderers trickles out down the stairs, hesitates under the archway, and sets off purposefully downhill. Many carry staves as tall as they are, simple branches or works of art as elaborate as Guy's; others have aluminium walking-poles like mine. Most carry a cockleshell tied to their rucksack or strung around their neck. Every day that week I was there on the steps to watch them go, wondering at the sheer variety: individuals, couples, groups, teenagers and pensioners, men and women from all over Europe. The youth hostel warden told me that a group of Belgian young offenders had come through that week, each with their own probation counsellor; before that he'd seen a young German in full medieval costume, a team of Japanese nuns, a Swedish couple who'd met on the way twenty years before and were celebrating their anniversary there, an English couple who'd met there the year before and had brought their baby in a papoose, so that he could take his first steps on the 'camino'. The cathedral staff were bursting with stories. That year the feast of St James (25 July) was on a Sunday, so it was a jubilee year in Santiago, and the pilgrims had been arriving in droves. A hundred thousand had reached Santiago already, and astonishing stories were filtering back: hostels crowded to overflowing, armies of tents springing up around towns, entire villages emptied of provisions. I'd expected to be alone in Spain. When I said so, the staff laughed pityingly.

I spent five days in the youth hostel, and for the first time since Luxembourg I felt part of a community. Everyone there was a traveller of some sort: two Welsh lads looking for summer jobs with whom I watched the legendary August Eclipse, a Japanese student trying to improve his English (in France!), a group of newly-qualified teachers from Clermont-Ferrand, a pharmacist from Lyon who'd just completed the first two hundred kilometres of the pilgrimage and was going to do more the following year. She was young, pretty and friendly, so I should have been hooked, but even her charms couldn't distract me from the most interesting guest: a bone-thin thirty-something Frenchman with flowing black hair and glowing eyes, dressed in a white tracksuit and sandals. His name was Pierre-Géraud. He'd been a civil engineer once, until he tired of twentieth-century materialism; now he was a part-time astrologer and herbalist, and a full-time pilgrim. Every spring he set off from his home in Normandy, and walked until winter came. He'd been to Santiago and back three times, gone on to Fatima, Gibraltar, the Atlas mountains, walked to Lourdes, Rome and Assisi. His hobby was retracing lost pilgrim routes to half-forgotten shrines all over France. When I told him I wanted to cross the Cévennes and the Pyrenees rather than following the traditional route to the border he grabbed a note-book and sketched in three alternate pilgrim roads. We spent a whole evening talking about all we'd seen and done on our travels. By the end of it we'd reduced all our philosophies to one basic truth: most people are nice, and there's no better way to spend your life than meeting them. He knew. He was doing it. All the next day I found myself whistling 'Oo-be-doo, I wanna be like you . . .' One pilgrimage simply wasn't enough.

Nice people abounded that week, and they weren't all strangers. Four different friends rang me in the space of twenty-four hours and asked if there was a chance of meeting up. Em wanted to come out in the last week of August, Dad and my twin sister Rachel both hoped to catch me in Carcassonne at the beginning of September, and Tom, another friend from Raleigh, volunteered to join me in the Pyrenees for the last fortnight of September. I jumped at all the offers with delight. Company on the way! Only one thing could have improved matters, and that would have been looking at a map *before* I agreed to meet them all. When I did so later, my heart sank. There was an awful lot of ground to cover. August might not be as relaxing as I'd hoped.

I spent my last night in Le Puy in one of the official pilgrim hostels, a refurbished house just behind the cathedral complete with a fully-equipped kitchen and a wide, walled patio hung with honeysuckle. There I received my official 'credential', a stamped passport certifying that I was indeed a pilgrim, and spent a happy evening chatting with my fellow-guests. We were an odd group: half a dozen retired women from Paris, two German student girls whose white T-shirts were belted with rosaries, a Dutch couple in their fifties who'd walked from Utrecht, and I. Only the Dutch pair were planning to go all the way to Santiago: the others were here to do the two-hundred-kilometre walk to Conques, coming back for more next year. One by one they voiced the fears I'd had: will it be difficult, am I doing the right thing, what do I do if . . . ? Time and again the Dutch and I were asked how far we walked each day, whether we thought this or that piece of equipment would be useful, how much we were carrying. Weight was everyone's biggest concern. We sat around the kitchen table cheerfully discussing exhaustion, shoulder and knee injuries, heart conditions and spinal damage. Chaucer never wrote this, I thought, as the younger German whispered to me that she'd started her period that day, and asked if she should carry less as a result. Oddly, everyone felt better by the time we turned in. I was sorry I wouldn't be joining them on the road.

We all went to the pilgrims' blessing before we left. I hadn't been quite sure if I'd be welcome, not being a Christian, but the priest at St Michel d'Aiguilhe had said that it wouldn't be a problem, so as dawn played grey and cold upon the granite pillars I found myself clustered with friends and newcomers before a fifteenth-century statue of St James and a late-twentieth-century bishop, being sanctified. It was a peculiar ceremony. His Reverence went solemnly round the group, asking each of us where we were from, passing an appropriate comment and handing out little silver medallions of the Virgin of Le Puy. The comments were an intriguing insight into the episcopal mind: 'Holland? Do they have Catholics there?' 'Ireland? We'll say a prayer for peace.' 'Lyon? Ah, I was at university with the bishop . . .' When he came to me he asked where I'd started.

'Canterbury.'

Short pause.

'Did you walk across the Channel?'

It didn't seem the time and place to claim that I'm the Messiah. 'I'm a diver.'

He looked confused and moved swiftly onwards.

As soon as the introductions were done, he lost interest. The blessing itself was perfunctory, pronounced with all the sympathy and personal meaning of an answerphone message. As he walked out in a swish of robes we stood uncertainly, looking at one another. Slowly we filtered towards the stairs. Below us the town swam in mist. The towers of the cathedral shone faint and gold through trailing veils. It was set to be a scorcher of a day, and I was planning to walk right through it.

'Nimmo, you're mad,' I muttered, and set off downhill.

There were no footpaths heading in the direction I wanted, so I found myself on country lanes again, climbing between dusty cornfields into the green hills of the Upper Loire. The harvest was already in, and the scents of stubble and dust filled the air, getting into my clothes and rucksack and almost drowning out the essential reek of sweaty pilgrim. August was well on its way, and the heat and humidity were murderous. Within hour of leaving Le Puy I was longing for the winter. The beneficial effects or a week's rest vanished like the morning mist.

The land rose to a high plateau criss-crossed with roads lined with plane-trees, rose again to a wooded ridge, and quite

suddenly I was in the south. One slope was thick with beech-
and oak-trees looking back to the corn-fields; the other was
black with pines, carpeted with needles, redolent with the warm
scents of resin and heather, the unmistakeable breath of the
Mediterranean. As I crossed the ridge the horizon opened up
before me, and I beheld the blue-hazed ranges of the Cévennes,
lapped in a sea of blooming heather. Only then did it sink in
that I was truly in the *Midi*, the land against the noonday sun.
Had I walked that far? I pulled out my map of Europe, and
stared. There was Le Puy, there the hills. A finger's width below
them was the Mediterranean. I couldn't believe it. My last chill
paddle in the North Sea off Ostend might have been a lifetime
away. I couldn't even imagine being cold.

The heat increased. Every step became an ordeal. I'd been
on the road for over four months, and the strain on emotions,
body and equipment was starting to tell. The frame of my pack
had ripped from its sockets, and the full weight pulled at my
shoulders and made my neck crack as I walked. Day after Bad
Sack Day the effort grew harder, and not all the good moments
quite relieved the burden.

Five days out of Le Puy, I found myself following a narrow
road along a limestone gorge thick with orchards and vineyards. The day before had been the anniversary of the last time
I ever saw Anna, and the memories were thick and vivid. Just
after my noonday halt a dog slid from the shadows at my side.
I gripped my sticks tighter and prepared to sell my life dearly,
but he threw me a lopsided grin and went on past with a
curious sideways gait. I stopped. He stopped, looking back
with his tongue hanging out, waiting. Sudden warmth filled
me. Someone actually wanted to join me! I would have gone
down on my knees and hugged him if he'd been in range. He
clicked on ahead of me, a beautiful brindled farm-dog with a
collie's fine lines. I was so happy I started whistling. It was the
first time in days.

It was a full hour before reality hit. Was I really thinking of adopting a stray? Feeding him, sheltering him, taking him across the mountains onto the pilgrim road? And then leaving him in quarantine in a cold, strange land? It says something for the state of my emotions that I seriously considered it. It took another hour of furious internal debate before I decided that the kindest thing would be to drive him away now. I stopped, shouted, raised my sticks menacingly. He shot me a look so desolate I hadn't the heart to finish the job. We walked on. Half an hour later, desperate, I tried again. This time he turned and ran. I watched him go and felt like a traitor.

That evening I camped beside a tiny twelfth-century granite chapel on an outcrop above the gorge. I was sitting on the doorstep stirring my pasta and watching the stars come out when the phone rang.

'Ben? It's Ant.'

'Ant!' He was one of my best friends among the Raleigh volunteers. Hearing him just then was like a drink in the desert.

'Where are you, fella?' he asked.

'France.'

'No shit, Sherlock!' It's great to see the respect we staff got from the volunteers. 'Where?'

I checked the map. 'Just north of Villefort.'

'Hang on.' A map rustled. 'Excellent! I'm working in a holiday camp in the Ardèche. It's not far and the manager says you'd be welcome. Why don't you drop by? You can get a bus easily enough.'

I did.

The bus ride eastwards was one of the more unsettling moments of the voyage. For months I'd been dealing with farmers, pilgrims, priests and walkers, lost in my own special world utterly removed from everyday life. Suddenly I was in holiday territory, and the roads were crammed with cars and caravans. The car-park where Ant picked me up swarmed with holiday-makers: sandals, T-shirts, sun-hats, screams and shouts and whoops of laughter. Ice-cream vans lined the roadside like wreckage on a reef. Tourists swarmed around them like beach-combers. I sat, stared and felt like an alien.

Ant arrived in the official mini-van just before sunset, a short and muscular young man with a disgustingly deep tan, a huge grin and eyes that didn't seem to be quite focused. He gave me an enormous bear-hug. His breath was like a Polish distillery on New Year's Eve.

'How you doing, fella?'

'Excellent!' All worries had left me at the sight of a friendly face. 'How about you?'

He laughed, all flashing blue eyes and white teeth, and I remembered that he'd been the heart-throb of half the expedition. 'Pissed. First day off in a month, we've been drinking since this morning.'

Fortunately, he wasn't the driver.

We sat and chatted as the van jolted out of town and onto a rutted track through a wilderness of twisted holm-oaks: the *garrigue*, the haunt of boars, hunters, rebels and outlaws since time immemorial. Ant had been working at the centre for almost two months, helping British visitors to have a laugh-a-minute holiday rock-climbing, kayaking and playing silly games. He wasn't particularly coherent, but I picked up the fact that he was loving it. I sank back into the seat and let my aches melt away. I didn't talk much. I was too happy just relaxing.

'It's a big disorganized!' he shouted. 'Everyone's celebrating the day off!'

'I can imagine!' I'd worked in the adventure-holiday industry, and I knew its philosophy: work hard, play hard, die of cirrhosis . . . 'When do the next guests arrive?'

'Dawn tomorrow!'

'Ah.' It's considered good manners to be sober for the clients, and if they'd been drinking since ten . . . 'Won't the manager mind?'

140

'He passed out at lunchtime!'

Leadership by example.

The centre was far out in the *garrigue*, a huge old farmhouse near the Ardèche gorge. The mini-bus wound its way past stands of heavy blue canvas tents into a courtyard that looked like a war zone. Laughing figures with red-gold tans and bleached hair ran round bombarding each other with buckets of water; more were clustered around a set of low tables in one corner, playing skittles with empty bottles. Casualties scattered the ground, groaning. As I watched, a reeling disciple of Bacchus bent over a recumbent corpse, hiccupped and rolled the sufferer into recovery position, then spun round and threw up. I was among professionals. A lone figure in a red T-shirt, sandals and nothing else sat happily on the bar, swinging his legs and other organs. Ant looked at him and swore.

'How did he get up?' Then, turning to me, 'Come and meet the boss.'

All eyes that could still focus turned towards us as we crossed the yard. 'Get 'em off, Ant!' yelled a charming young lady in a pink tinsel wig. The mob took up the cry, 'Get your kit off!', sung to the approximate tune of *Bread of Heaven*. Ant turned towards them, spinning the drawstring of his shorts and wiggling, *Full Monty* style; someone started roaring out *The Stripper*. A drunken chorus of cheers and catcalls followed us across the yard.

The manager slid along the bar and pulled a couple of bottles of beer off a shelf. Somehow he avoided serious friction burns: evidently a man of impressive parts. He looked down a long nose at us and held out the beverages.

'Ant,' he said consideringly, 'you're a bastard.'

'Cheers, Stanley.' Ant took a swig. 'This is Ben, who walked here from England. I told you about him.'

Hazel eyes swooped round to hover on my face. 'Ah yes. The mad fucker. Ben,' he told me solemnly, 'you're a mad fucker.'

I decided I liked him.

'That's the most honest welcome I've had in months,' I told him. 'Cheers.'

'Of course it is!' He held up a declamatory finger. 'We pride ourselves on our professionalism, our . . .' The finger stopped. A puzzled look crossed his face. Then he looked at us and said, 'Gentlemen, I mean bastards, I believe I just sat on a splinter.'

We left him to his problems and went to join the crowd.

It was a glorious evening. A friendly welcome, irreverent English banter, and an industry I understood: I felt that I'd come home. I spent an hour chatting with a girl who was planning to buy an ice-cream van and travel across Europe with it, shared a bottle of wine with a kayaking instructor who was the double of one of my diving friends, swapped anecdotes of the year with Ant, and contrived to be incoherently drunk by about 10 o'clock. I hadn't touched alcohol since the Auvergne, and it showed. As the last dregs of consciousness started draining from my vision Ant led me to a tent among the trees, tipped me into a creaking metal bed, put a bottle of water beside my hand and left me to snore: the perfect host.

'Incoming!'

The bellow jerked me awake a few minutes after dawn. The air throbbed to the noise of engines. Running footsteps pounded through the trees. God, I thought, it's the invasion! I was halfway out of my sleeping-bag when my brain caught up. What invasion? I peered out of the tent and was nearly decapitated by a running girl. She looked odd without the wig. The woods were alive with hurrying shapes: one stopped to retch against a tree, then ran on, clapping artificially. Behind the farm-house a horn sounded. High voices approached the yard like the war-cries of a Zulu *impi*. Not far from me two of Ant's friends were sobering themselves up by hurling glasses of water into their faces. Then a stereo boomed into life, and I jumped. I knew those chords!

Ten seconds later I was in the yard watching a beaming staff team lead a couple of bus-loads of bewildered school-kids through 'Bend over, let me see you shake your tail-feather'. They had to be hung over, but it didn't show. My respect for their professionalism increased.

A day which starts like that can only get better, and it did. The manager (fresh-faced, smiling and barely green at the gills at all) had given Ant the day off, and together we battled our way through the *garrigue* and went exploring in the gorge. The joy of walking without the Pack From Hell was unbelievable. I spent half an hour raving about how good it felt. Then, since there was obviously something on his mind, I asked how he was, and spent a happy couple of hours listening to the sort of confused love-life that only an attractive twenty-year-old with the gift of the gab can weave. He'd just finished his first year at physio school, and had evidently had rather more hands-on experience than most ... After so many months of talking about the pilgrimage and about Europe, it was wonderfully domestic to gossip. I could have listened for days. We strolled along the river-bank, skimming stones across the water and watching canoes full of screaming tourists shooting the rapids, and I felt better than I had in weeks.

I'd been invited to do a spot of tromboning that evening to entertain the masses, but there was time to spare first. Ant led me up a thigh-crippling path to the lip of the gorge, and we sat sunning ourselves and taking in the view. It was a staggering sight: mile after mile of *garrigue*-covered plateau split and gouged by the river hundreds of metres below, the canoes as small and distant as floating leaves. It was one of those warm, still, peaceful afternoons when time stops and the soft song of the birds seems to come from a different planet: a good time to sit and talk in quiet voices about things that matter. I could feel the happiness growing inside me, demanding expression.

After a while I set up the trombone, and as Ant sat and hummed along I started to jam.

I'd never played so well in my life. *Summertime*, *Danny Boy*, *Misty*, the slow movement of Tchaikovsky's fifth symphony, favourite after favourite came flooding out in a torrent of improvised magic. The echoes drifted down the gorge and back in chords and antiphonal responses, as though a trombonist stood above every curve of the river. I've no idea where the music came from: it was *there*, falling under my hand and my lip. The sun was going down behind me: I turned and serenaded it with *Tipperary*, then woke the echoes with a final *Last Post*. Faint cheers rose up from the river as I finished, and there was silence for a long time.

After a while Ant put his hand on my shoulder.

'Well played, fella. Let's go and do the gig.'

By the time it started, everybody knew what I was doing. For some reason the tourists hadn't expected to hear a trombonist in the wilderness, and the staff had been only too happy to tell my story: anything to keep the little treasures quiet for a minute. All of a sudden I was in demand. But, rightly judging that a trombone recital wouldn't hold the infants' attention for more than about ten seconds, the staff had put their aching heads together and come up with something rather more exotic in the entertainments line.

I was perfectly-placed to see the action. They'd put me on a pedestal (it happens all the time) in the middle of the yard, and I felt like the eye of the storm. Staff members in silly costumes stood in each corner; others were hidden around the site. The visitors were divided into teams, whose job seemed to be running around screaming. Now and then staff members would give them messages for other staff members, such as 'Go and throw a bucket of water over Stanley.' When the splashing started I feared for my safety. Standing on a platform above a water-fight is not a survival strategy. But my hosts were the soul of courtesy. Wave after wave of excited infants poured up to me and said, 'X says will you play us a tune *please* . . .' It wasn't easy. More than half my audience seemed to be larval music critics, though only one group had the nerve to whine 'Can't you play some techno?' I did my best with the *Pink Panther*, *Bare Necessities*, and *When the Saints*, which they at least recognized, but somehow the subtleties of Dixieland improvisation were lost on them.

Things warmed up in the finale. Apparently there had been an intricate intellectual detective game going on the whole time, and the kids were supposed to have worked out who murdered the entire staff team. (Was it safe to give them ideas?) Not entirely surprisingly, they hadn't, so the staff decided to act out the drama for them. I sat and watched entranced as they paraded before a cheering audience: Miss GBH (her normal nickname – you have been warned), Ace Instructor (in wetsuit, buoyancy jacket and shades), Cook (apron and cleaver), Nurse (in drag), the Queen (likewise in drag, with tinsel wig), and the Manager (a wine bottle in each hand). Miss GBH narrated, making the story up as she went along while the rest of the cast tried desperately to act it out. I'm not sure how it worked, and nor, by the look of it, was anyone else, but given the number of water-fights, sneak attacks with shaving cream, and kick-boxing matches between the Queen and Ace Instructor, it was the kind of plot that would have given Agatha Christie nightmares. The play ended with GBH standing alone amidst a heap of sniggering corpses, who then proceeded to grab her and dump her in a water-butt. Somehow that led to a chorus of the National Anthem, while the Queen danced the *Can-Can* and blew kisses to the pretty girls. Then it was the children's bed-time. Laughing and joking, the staff herded them towards their tents, hurling insults and water at the slowest movers (getting wet seemed to be a prime purpose of the holiday). Then we retired to the bar.

It was like watching evolution in reverse. As the team sat down they slumped like so many jellyfish.

'God I hurt,' groaned Ace Instructor, pulling off his shades. His eyes glowed traffic-light red.

Miss GBH lay back with her head in his lap and whimpered. 'Has anyone got some aspirin?'

The Queen pulled off his wig. 'How hot is that thing? I thought my head was going to explode!'

'Somebody pass me a beer.' The cook hadn't even made it to the table. He was flat on his back in the courtyard. 'Nobody's watching, are they?'

Truly a professional outfit.

Ant was duty staff member that night. After a while I went to join him in the office, and we sat and picked up the gossip where we'd left off. We talked until far into the night, about the things we'd been through together and the dreams we had for the future. Thoughts that I'd been treasuring for four months bubbled to the surface: other trips, other adventures, new worlds and experiences waiting round every corner. The more I talked, the more enthusiastic I became. I told him about Pierre-Géraud, about Bart, about Guy. We talked about Anna, and how much she'd meant to me. 'She'd be proud to see you now,' he said.

I went back to my tent some time after midnight. He was on duty until dawn. He woke me when he came off shift, and we shared a quick breakfast, sitting on the wall watching the sun come up. Then it was time to catch the bus back to Villefort. One bear-hug from Ant, waves and hugs from the staff team, and I swung into the minibus and jolted back down the track out of the *garrigue* and back towards life as I knew it.

It was back to heat, and fatigue, and loneliness, but not all the difficulties could blind me to the beauty of the Cévennes. I climbed stubbornly from Villefort into the hills, and three days running my diary records the simple comment: 'best walking yet'. I was on the threshold of the south, and it welcomed me with open, shining skies. Day after day passed in a blaze of imperial heather and a frenzy of blackberry-scrumping as the blue ridges drew in on either side and the sun blazed down. I ground my way along high ridges scented with pine and thyme, gazing out across a sea of hills. I passed the headwaters of the River Tarn, shining blue and silver against the sky, and camped beside a thundering fall where the spray threw rainbows across the banks. I met walkers following the steps of Robert Louis Stevenson, many of them recreating his voyage with a donkey in tow. Once the track ran out in a new motorway cutting and I spent a hair-raising half-hour contouring my way across a sheer cliff-face with traffic snarling and hooting below. Then the ground rose again in wave after wave of hills, and I picked up the GR7 and turned west to the might Mont Aigoual, the highest summit in the range.

I was slogging up the hill in the morning heat, gasping out a defiant marching song to the tune of the *Battle Hymn of the Republic*, when I rounded a hairpin bend between the pines and tripped over a hairy pair of legs. Only my sticks saved me from going headlong, and as I recovered he drew in his legs and looked me up and down slowly: a stocky, grinning Frenchman in his late thirties sitting on a rucksack, his neck swathed in an enormous silk scarf.

'Hear that?' he said.

'What?'

He raised a finger. 'The birdsong.' And, as I looked at him in complete bewilderment, he added, 'If you can't stop to listen to the little birds, you're doing something wrong.' He shifted himself into a more comfortable sprawl. 'Sit down for a second and listen.'

I swung my pack off, dropped onto it and opened my ears.

The wind was blowing gently like surf between the pines. Somewhere above us sheep-bells rang sleepily. A human voice called out. The air was warm, and a ray of sunlight falling on a bare rock seemed to crackle with the heat. There weren't any birds that I could hear.

'Hear them?' he asked softly.

'No.'

He grinned. 'If you listen long enough, maybe you will.' It sounded like Confucius.

Thus I met Charles, poet, philosopher and modern-day Renaissance man. When he was eighteen he was a biker and part-time drug dealer. One day he unwisely decided to combine his pleasures, and drove his Yamaha under a ten-tonne truck. After a month in hospital he was a changed man. Driven by sheer determination, he finished his studies, won a place at a prestigious university and qualified as an architect. For ten years he worked 'like a demented ant', putting in ludicrous hours and watching the bank-balance bloom. Hooked on success in all its forms, he also seduced a colleague's wife. Unfortunately, the colleague was a man of his hands, and proved it by cutting Charles' throat one summer's night in a Marseilles bar. Charles survived by driving himself to hospital while a friend sat behind him, plugging the wounds with his fingers. The silk scarf hid a scar running half-way round his neck. Another month in hospital brought enlightenment.

'What did you do?' I asked. We'd started walking together, climbing towards the summit.

'I stopped taking work seriously. I'd made so much money, I didn't need more. These days I work for seven months of the year, then spend five months on holiday. I'm doing this walk to prepare myself for the GR20, and I'm doing that to get myself fit for my big holiday. I'm off to Peru in December to walk some of the old ways through the Andes.'

'How long for?' I was glowing a fetching shade of green.

'Oh, two or three months.'

The green intensified.

'And then?'

'Oh, I'll come back and work for a bit, but I want to keep fit. I'm going up Mount Kenya next spring.'

I tried to remind myself that his life wasn't *that* much more exciting than mine, but it wasn't easy.

148

'So where are you going now?'

He shrugged, and his rucksack almost slipped off. He never used the hip-belt. '*Merde!* I don't know exactly. I thought of following the GR7 south.'

My heart jumped. 'So did I,' I said casually, and he grinned. 'Want some company?'

'Do I!'

I'm still trying to work out if it was a mistake. Charles is a man of many talents. Unfortunately, one of them is to be bloody irritating. It's ironic that after so many months' searching for someone to share my journey, I ended up with him. Of all the legs in all the world, I had to stumble over his ... I knew how Bogart felt.

We spent two days together. On the first we crossed the summit of Mont Aigoual (true to French form, it had a weather station, a car park and a large restaurant at the top), and dropped down into the scented forests beyond, talking the whole while. The first doubt set in when we reached an unexpected track junction. I was certain that the main trail was off to our right. Charles was equally certain that if we cut straight ahead through the bush we'd rejoin it, saving ourselves a detour. This involved bashing our way up a steep slope littered with brambles.

'Are you sure?' I hate going off-piste when there's a perfectly good track available, but I didn't want to appear less intrepid than he was. False pride's going to get me into trouble one of these days.

'Of course! Come on!' And he took off like a jet.

We hacked our way up the slope, laying about like Crusaders with our walking-poles. After about five minutes Charles paused and looked around surreptitiously.

'We must be almost there,' he told me with distinctly forced cheer.

I didn't answer. It's never very encouraging when the navigator looks lost.

'I said we must be almost there,' he repeated, louder.

'I believe you,' I replied as mildly as I could. A bramble had just torn a long rent in my beloved trousers and still more beloved knee, but I was learning self-control.

We ploughed on, Charles leading. Almost at once he began angling to the right. I said nothing. Right we went, and further right, as he told me again that we were almost there. Sure enough, within a few minutes we saw golden sunlight ahead. He accelerated, and in no time at all we crashed out of the bush through a ditch and onto a forestry road.

'There you are, I knew we'd find it,' he told me. 'Told you it'd work, didn't I?'

'Yes,' I said – still mildly – and bowed to him to lead the way. As soon as his back was turned I looked to the right. The track we'd left was about fifty yards away. A splendid short-cut.

I let it go. He was still good company. He spent the next hour pointing out mushrooms by the track, throwing out recipe after recipe for frying, baking, stuffing, casseroling and season-ing a bewildering variety of lethal-looking fungi. He went off into a long digression on the evils of the mushroom-poaching industry, heartless citizens of the southern plains driving up into the woods at the dead of night to plunder the mushroom-beds. Irresistibly the image crept into my mind of black-clad commandos stealing through the forests with wicker baskets ... He denounced the government for not protecting the environment, the scenery and the old ways of life (such as mushroom-poaching, though I didn't mention that). He stamped along waving his arms passionately as he damned all Parisian bureaucrats. If I hadn't kept an eye on our direction he would have ended up in Germany.

That night we camped on a limestone ridge overlooking the Mediterranean plain. I hadn't planned to be there, but Charles had scorched past the two sites I'd planned, saying that there were still hours of daylight left, so why stop? – then run out of steam in the middle of a dry and featureless hillside and tried to convince me that it made a sensible place to camp. I grabbed my patience hard and told him that I'd rather sleep near a water supply. When I kept going he followed me, calling out that we wouldn't need more than the litre we had. For cooking, washing and drinking. Half an hour later we found a stream at the foot of the ridge, and he became all smiles. He offered to cook. I sat watching the sunset. The view was sublime. To one side the sun was going down in crimson splendour. Opposite the full moon was rising, dusted with gold, and straight ahead on the edge of sight was the faintest of white lines where Europe met the sea. Slowly the light died, the horizon deepened to an eye-caressing blue. Along the coastline the lighthouses awoke, flashing in regular patterns. All across the plain the lights were coming on, the great roads like strings of jewels, the cities clusters of fire. I sat enthralled, marvelling at how far I'd come. The end of France was in sight already. It was indescribably beautiful. I sat, listening as Charles had taught me, and let the peace wash over me.

Feet swished through the bush, and Charles came up behind me and farted like a howitzer. 'Dinner time,' he said unselfconsciously, and dropped a full mess-tin with a clatter. He was an excellent cook. Shame about his waiting skills.

I woke up early the next day, and lay wrapped in my sleeping-bag watching the sunrise. The plain was quiet, the air cool, the faintest of bird-songs drifted down the hillside, and a series of farts and belches rose from the next tent like the aftershocks of an earthquake.

'Morning, Charles,' I said wearily.

'Morning!' he said enthusiastically. A tousled head popped out of his tent. 'How did you sleep? I slept really well. I knew this tent would be comfortable. Didn't I say it would be comfortable? (He hadn't.) Lying on heather makes a great mattress. I've still got loads of water left, too, do you really think we needed to come this far? Isn't it a great view from up here?'

I'm never at my best first thing in the morning. 'Charles?'
'Oui?'
'I'm watching the sunrise.'
'Oh.' He withdrew with an offended sniff and a thunderous fart, and left me listening to the birds.

Again I warmed to him during the day. He was a wonderful talker, and made the hours pass with lightning speed as we dropped down the stony track and out of the Cévennes. He lived in Toulon, he told me, where the National Front had recently won a shock victory in the local elections with almost 50 per cent of the vote. Everyone he knew professed to be horrified by the result, but he was morally certain that at least half of them had voted for the Front. It started us talking about the whole history of intolerance, racism and collaboration. He knew more about it than most. His family came from Alsace. When that unhappy province was handed back to the Germans in 1940 his father and uncle joined the resistance. His uncle was betrayed by a collaborator, arrested in the family home, and shot. Charles went to school with the son of the informant. He never did know how to treat him.

We walked fast and happily, the disagreements of the day before all but forgotten. Just after lunch we reached Le Vigan, a delightful town clustered along the banks of a gentle river, blazing in the sun. I'd been planning to stop there, but Charles was all for pushing on. Twenty kilometres further on was the Cirque de Navacelles, France's answer to the Grand Canyon, and he'd set his heart on camping on the edge of the gorge in the moonlight. 'Why don't we go for it?'

Because it's bloody stupid, I almost said. The temperature had just broken the thirty-degree barrier, the sun was thumping down, and from all I knew of limestone country it would be like walking through a furnace.

'Can't you do it?' he asked cheekily.

The heat must have got to my brain. I took the dare.

We filled our water bottles from a public tap and crossed

152

the river at three o'clock. From there the track climbed two hundred metres sheer through sultry oak-woods to the lip of the plateau, a punishing climb in crippling heat. By the time we reached the top Charles was scarlet. 'Why are we doing this?' he panted, and I resisted the urge to hit him.

'You suggested it,' I told him, and kept going. I'm not at my best in the afternoons either.

We stamped along in sulky silence. Within an hour his morale was disintegrating. Why don't we stop here? We don't have to make it tonight. Why don't we take a breather? I agreed to that, and gave him all the water I could spare: his bottle was already empty. Why not camp? he said irritably. We'll never make it. We should never have started. I looked around at the baking wilderness. It was a nightmare of thorn-trees and shattered limestone. Camping was not an option. I waited. He groaned to his feet with theatrical slowness. I offered to carry some of his heavier gear. He accepted with alacrity.

The last hour was a race against the sun. After twenty minutes Charles stopped grumbling, set his teeth and picked up the pace. I was proud of him. We thundered our way across country, picked up a minor road and swung onto it without slackening speed. His breath was coming in hoarse gasps. Sweat streamed down my face. The western sky was fading from pink to grey, the east bright with the rising moon. The land rose before us, barred with bushes like twisted skeletons. All of a sudden it fell away again, and before we realized it we were there, standing on the edge of a wall of limestone barred black and white in the moonlight. To right and left an immense sweep of rock curved round in an arc sixteen hundred metres wide and four hundred metres deep. Tiny lights twinkled in the black emptiness below: the village of Navacelles. Somewhere a river roared, and far away across the canyon a car's lights swooped and jabbed along an invisible road. We stood there on the edge of nothing, grinning at each other in triumph.

'I knew we'd make it,' said Charles, and belched.

He left me the next morning, setting off in the dawn light, and I watched him go with nothing but relief. He was the first walker I'd spent more than a day with in over five months, and for all his enlightening stories solitude would have been better. I wasn't in the mood for strangers. Mont Aigoual marked the beginning of the hardest phase of the whole walk, and as day after murderous day dragged on I would have become impatient with the Archangel Gabriel.

There were three reasons for it. First was the heat. I never function well in hot weather, and that August was brutal. Day after day saw cloudless skies and searing temperatures, and my body reacted with grinding headaches and gritty eyes, burning throat and cracked lips. My head felt stuffed with feathers, and even simple decisions became agony. Second, I was exhausted. In the thirteen days since leaving Le Puy I'd taken one day off, visiting Ant, and I couldn't afford another. Even pushing myself hard, it was touch and go whether I'd make the rendezvous with Em. Every climb hurt. Every joint ached. None of my traditional remedies worked, not even condensed milk. My reserves were gone, and only a long rest would be able to put things right.

Third, and worst, were the memories. It was late August, and exactly a year before I'd been on Coco Plum Cay waiting for news of Anna. Anniversaries are always hard, and I wasn't in a state to handle it. Every night I dreamt of Belize, and they weren't good dreams. The philosophy I'd learnt in five months of walking deserted me. I prayed for something to happen, someone to attack me and give me a chance for revenge. Nobody appeared. The people were as welcoming as ever, but their friendship couldn't reach me. You might as well pour water on a volcano. For four days I stormed south-westwards looking for trouble. I was lucky it didn't come.

Salvation came on a bus from Montpellier airport, in the shape of a beautiful artist bringing gifts beyond price: a pile of letters from expedition friends, new trousers to replace my tattered wrecks, new boots, a kilo of Kendal Mint Cake, and one of her special hugs. Any one of them would have made my week; in the circumstances, the combination made my millennium. We met in the fabulously-named Lamalou les Bains, a town made up almost exclusively of rehabilitation clinics for the seriously injured, and headed straight up into the hills. Autumn was just around the corner, and we walked under boughs groaning under the weight of fruit: apples, chestnuts, pears, and more blackberries than even I could eat (and I'm a specialist). Birdsong filled the trees. So did the occasional crack of a boar-hunter's rifle. The stony path ran between pillars of light and shade. For the first time in days I was out of the sun, and the air was pleasantly cool. We climbed between wooded bluffs like scowling foreheads, zigzagging across the contours towards the high ridges, looking down sheer slopes onto the roofs of arms and hamlets, many of them sagging and gaping. It was a desperately poor land, sheer and savage and ploughed by shouting rivers, but it was beautiful, and I loved it.

For me, it was a holiday. For Em, who hadn't been walking since Belize, it ... wasn't. There's much to be said for the Espinouse area, but it's not kind to unfit walkers. If we hadn't taken a short-cut along a main road on the first day we'd never have reached the campsite I'd planned. After that I halved the distances and doubled the time, and rediscovered the joys of leisure. We ambled comfortably from ridge to valley and from valley to ridge, catching up on five months' of gossip, and our hearts were light even if our packs were heavy. I spent a lot of the time that first day complaining about how hard the preceding fortnight had been, and when I awoke the next day the world felt right again. I still ached, but I didn't care any more.

At lunchtime on the third day we dropped down a precipitous path and found ourselves on a riverbank opposite a tiny village. Stone houses with tiled roofs huddled together under stands of fig-trees, so old and haphazard and covered in ferns that they looked more grown than made. Below us the river ran through a series of great stone basins, spilling from one to the next in bright arcs of light; a peacock drank from the lowest pool, its reflection a brilliant splash of colour. The first house in the village bore a hand-carved wooden sign, 'Restaurant de Bardou.' Beyond it an overgrown archway led into the crooked streets.

'How about exploring?' Em asked, dropping her rucksack by the roadside with relief. I hesitated. The Carcassonne deadline still itched at the back of my mind. Then we both stopped, frozen. From a squat cottage halfway up the village the sound of a solo cello drifted across the valley.

'Good idea,' I said, and dumped my pack beside hers.

The streets were cold and shady, lined with chestnuts and vines, ferns grew between the cobblestones. This was a true medieval village, houses and courtyards blending into one another with no coherent plan; the main street was no more than six feet wide. Cats dripped and circled from the shadows, eyeing us superciliously, and another peacock screamed from a rooftop. Through it all ran the lilting first theme of Elgar's cello concerto. We climbed a flight of dented steps onto a brand-new tiled patio and looked around. There was nobody in sight. The phantom cellist started practising scales. We looked at each other in bewilderment as a chamber orchestra struck up with Mozart forty. This seldom happens in mountain hamlets.

'Hello!' The voice made us jump. A door had opened soundlessly behind us, and a tall woman with thick white hair stood looking at us. Her arms were full of papers. 'Can I help you?' Her accent was pure American.

'We heard the music and came to explore,' I said. 'What's happening?'

She laughed and set the papers down on an age-blackened wooden table. 'They're good, aren't they? It's a German group, they come here every summer for a three weeks' residential course. They're doing a concert in Saint Pons at the end of the week, if you're interested.'

'Er . . . Do you often get orchestras here?'

She laughed warmly.

'This is a residential centre. We get visitors all the time.' She took pity on our bewilderment. 'Why don't you sit down?'

We sat on a low bench looking out over the valley and listening to Mozart as she explained. Her name's Jean, an American who came over to Europe to study, married a German, and stayed. They worked hard at their respective jobs, until they took a walking holiday in the Montagne Noire in the sixties and discovered the remains of this village, Bardou. Somehow the dream was born to rebuild the village and live the life they wanted. Helped by friends and working on a shoestring budget, they made one house habitable, and started on the others. The money was almost gone when a film company discovered them and decided that Bardou was the perfect location for a Bolivian drama. The fees from a six-week production run provided the couple with a water catchment system and the materials for two more houses. Gradually word of their creation spread. Musicians, artists, yoga groups and writers all realized that Bardou was the perfect sanctuary, two hours' walk from the Orb valley and the nearest tarmac, and came flooding in. As Jean began to run the village as a rural retreat, Klaus started breeding sheep in the hills above. Both businesses flourished. Slowly they expanded the village, improved the water system, took in more visitors. In 1997 they finally bowed to modernity and paid for electricity. They'd lived without it for thirty years.

'Have you got any rooms left?' asked Em innocently, not meeting my eyes. Jean shook her head.

'I'm sorry, we're all full at the moment. You could camp at the back if you've got a tent, it's only fifty francs.'

Em shot me an appealing glance, as only a beautiful woman can. It was wasted on me. Not that I'm not susceptible, but

I'd already decided that dynamite wouldn't shift me from this haven of peace.

'Can we go and pitch now?' I asked, and was rewarded with two beaming smiles.

We couldn't have chosen a better place to take a day off. The sun shone, the birds sang, the river splashed across the stones, the breeze whispered in the trees. The twentieth century seemed a forgotten nightmare. We pitched my tent behind the last house in the village, then Em sat down on a low wall and started sketching. I sprawled under a fig-tree and got to work. I stripped and cleaned my stove, mended my sleeping-bag liner for the ninth time, sharpened my pen-knife on a stone, tried in vain to force my broken rucksack frame back into shape, thought vaguely about writing a few letters, then decided that a day like that was a heaven-sent opportunity to get the washing done. Soon the trees around the camp were festooned with dripping clothing. A spring-cleaning frenzy seized me. I swept out my tent, turned my rucksack inside out in a shower of dirt and leaf-mould, scoured all my cooking gear, and hung my sleeping-bag out to air. Em watched with amusement.

'You never did that at home.'

'I did, you just didn't notice.'

It was good to be with a friend.

Neither of us wanted to leave Bardou, but we both had deadlines: I was still a long way from Carcassonne, and Em was further still from Montpellier. In the morning cool we packed up and set off down the valley, our feet crunching on fallen chestnuts, the stream chuckling to itself on our right. An hour's walk brought us out into the vineyards of the Cotes de Languedoc, the vines heavy with great blue clusters of ripening grapes: we cut bunches from the outermost plants and munched them as we walked, our chins red and sticky like vegetarian vampires. The Orb flowed like liquid light in its bed below us, and ahead was the main road. It was a shock to be back in the world of tarmac and fumes. Both of us longed for the hills, but the time had come. We waited at the bus stop together, chatting about inconsequentials: home improvements, the evils of being a school-teacher, the joys of French wine. Far too soon the bus swept up with a roar and stink of diesel. Em jumped aboard, waved, and was gone. I watched the bus go with a lump in my throat, then turned and walked on up the valley.

Three days later I climbed the last ridge of the Montagne Noire and looked past a nest of wind generators to the towers of Carcassonne, looming like a heavyweight fairy-tale over endless rows of vines. For two days a September storm had flayed the hills, and it had been like coming home. The colder it got, the happier I became. Dropping back down to the sweaty heat of the plains was an instant disappointment. The landscape fell, the temperature rose, and my mood dropped. I toyed with the idea of camping early and walking into the town the next day, but it was easier to plug on than to stop. The slate-blue roofs of the medieval towers gleamed in the late sunlight, the golden walls were touched with fire. I slogged on towards them, hell-bent on arriving, too busy sweating to take much delight in the view of France's most spectacular fortress. By sunset I was on the old town bridge, looking up at towers and battlements straight out of the Brothers Grimm. The road wound up past tourist coaches and a vast car-park to the double gate of the ancient citadel, perched on its hillside overlooking the town. Even in the shade of the gatehouse the air was thick and muggy, full of the sounds and scents of tourists. Beyond the arch were narrow cobbled streets lined with souvenir boutiques, offering for sale medieval costumes, two-handed swords, badges and toys and gimmicks. The tourists were everywhere, wall to wall. I ploughed through them leaving a trail of cross exclamations (never stand in the way of a five-stone rucksack) and went in search of the youth hostel.

Dad was there waiting for me, grinning and tanned and wearing the same cloth cap he'd had on in Canterbury. Five minutes later Rachel came to join us with boyfriend in tow and a brand-new rucksack slung over one arm to replace my poor, torn wreck. Soon we were sitting in a medieval tavern digging into the local speciality of *cassoulet* (a stew of white beans, goose, duck, pork and sausages cooked in goose jelly) and red wine, while an Irishman played traditional French melodies on an old guitar and a Scots waitress bustled about.

'How long are you staying?' Dad asked eventually.

'A week at least,' I replied, and poured myself another glass of wine.

PART 8

The Pyrenees

'Halt sunt li pui e li val tenebrus . . .' (*La Chanson de Roland*)

South of Carcassonne lie the dry limestone heights of the Corbieres, topped with ruined castles, wild expanses of thorns and scrub, and (most likely) the bleached skeletons of hapless walkers seeking for water in vain. I left Carcassonne late one muggy morning, and almost immediately regretted it. The hills are high and almost bare of cover, the ground a treacherous tangle of shattered limestone, and the waymarked path is almost non-existent. I hacked my way through bush and briar, sweating like any mammal you care to name, and within an hour my nice new boots had given me the finest blister I've ever endured.

It grew worse that day, and the next morning it was so bad that I abandoned the trail entirely and thrashed my way down into the valley. There, at least, I found water, shade and endless fields of vines ripe for plundering (which I did), but nothing could relieve the pain. Blisters sound like a trivial complaint until you've tried to walk on them. I tried, and it was crippling. By the time I found a campsite I could hardly hobble. When I lanced the bubble a jet of fluid shot half a metre across the grass. Coming so soon after a week off, it was heart-breaking. Suddenly Santiago seemed a long way away.

I was sitting gloomily by my tent above the medieval beauties of the town of Lagrasse, wondering if I'd ever make it, when the phone rang.

'Ben? It's Tine.'

'Tine!' It was a month since I'd heard from my god-daughter's mother. 'How are you?'

'We're fine. We're in Foix. Where are you?'

'You're in Foix?' I flung myself on my map and let out a small howl as my abused heel hit the gravel. Mobile technology has a lot to answer for. 'I'm in Lagrasse!'

'Can we come and see you tomorrow?'

Silly question.

At four the next afternoon they swept into the campsite in a huge dusty car: Bart, Tine, baby Manou, Bart's sister Els, and Els' daughter Eveline. We were talking nineteen to the dozen before they'd even got out of the car: what I'd been up to, cooing over Manou, what they'd been up to, cooing over Manou, what we were all planning, cooing over Manou ... My god-daughter (my god-daughter!) was as beautiful as Bart had said. She was five months old, with brilliant blue eyes that melted my heart every time she gurgled at me, a sunny disposition, and a deep fascination with life. She only cried if we put her down out of sight of the action. She slept like a dribbly angel as we sat in the shade and chatted in English, French and Spanish (the whole family was as polyglot as I was becoming), then woke up just in time to come to a restaurant. I ate while they played with her, then the roles were reversed. She loved being tossed in the air. Halfway through one throw Bart snapped a photo; the picture hangs on their kitchen wall. Honour comes no higher.

They left the next morning to drive back to Flanders. I made for the Pyrenees. Bart had told me the best places to stay and the best views to see, and I was determined to sample the lot. Bandaged and iodined, my heel barely even tickled. All of a sudden I felt that the punishing summer was over. Ahead of

me were the snowy heights of the Pyrenees, the cold winds of
Autumn, and a meeting with Tom. For all that the worst climbs
were still ahead, I felt that the real work was done.

If I'd wanted confirmation that the pilgrim's life is full of nice
surprises, it came three days later in the shadow of the chateau
at Peyrepertuse. There can be few more bewitching locations
for a wayside meeting than the long dinosaur-backed spine of
limestone crags glaring towards the Mediterranean plain,
fleeced with holm-oak forests and topped with a double fortress
like a vast ship. The cliffs rise three hundred metres sheer above
the valley, facing the first true ramparts of the Pyrenees and
the dizzying eyrie of the chateau of Quéribus. Below them
nestle a few scattered houses, the inevitable vines, a single
petrol station-cum-general store, and a pay-phone. I'd just rung
Tom to check the details of his arrival (we were to meet the
following day, my twenty-seventh birthday) and was standing
outside the box pondering whether to call Em when a polite
voice broke into my thoughts.

'*Pardon, monsieur, mais – merde alors!*'

I spun on my heel. That voice! . . . Glowing eyes, wild black
hair, white tracksuit, sandals. Pierre-Géraud! We hugged one
another in the middle of the pavement, laughing and asking
questions without waiting for an answer. How are you? What
are you doing here? Where are you going? How was the walk?
We hurried into the filling-station for a can of coke, then sat
on a low wall outside, chatting. He'd spent a few days with a
friend in the next valley, and was walking back northwards to
catch up with another friend in Béziers. We swapped anecdotes,
experiences, lessons. We talked far too fast, semi-coherently.
There was so much to say, and the daylight was fading. We
were laughing and waving as we set off in opposite directions.
He'd invited me to come back to his friend's house, but I

wanted to sleep in the castle that night. I regretted my impatience as soon as he rounded the corner; but only until I reached the fortress.

The climb was the hardest I'd ever done. There was no water on the summit, so I'd refilled all my bottles in the village: six litres of water added to three days' food, and I'd swear my pack was half my body-weight. The climb was a brutal slog up a near-vertical cliff face, but it was worth it for the view. The inner keep loomed over the castle like a supertanker's bridge, staring eastwards to the sea and south to the heights. I sat there for a long time watching the sun set and the moon rise. It was full that night, and I serenaded it, low and soulful, until the dogs started howling in the valley far below. I slept lightly, and was up before dawn to watch the sun rise through a crimson keyhole in the clouds: my birthday. It was a good way to start another year.

It got better.

I met Tom off the bus in Axat, a long thin mountain village spread along the valley between towering cliffs, with a bright rushing river carving the place in two. It was a joyous meeting. The last time I'd seen him had been in Belize. We looked at one another for a moment, then met in a crashing hug (complete with rucksacks), and picked up the friendship where we'd left off.

We met in Belize during the first expedition of 1998, when he was the expedition trekking leader, and spent three whole months failing to have a decent conversation without quite knowing why. We instinctively liked one another, but whenever we met we were afflicted by a curious tongue-tied paralysis. It wasn't until the very last day that we went off for a walk together and discovered the cause: we had so much to talk about that we couldn't even start unless we had a whole day for the conversation. Our lives were eerily parallel. While I was on a year out in New Zealand, he was in Nepal. As I grappled with the intricacies of medieval epic, he was studying philosophy. We both left academic careers to take up outdoor pursuits: Tom qualified as a British Mountaineering Council Mountain Leader at the same time as I became a diving instructor. We started working for Raleigh at the same time, and remained in Belize for both expeditions. We shared the same enthusiasms, the same dreams, the same way of thinking, even fancied the same girls. It says a lot for the friendship that we were quite happy to discuss the women we were both chasing. The only difference between us is our style. I oscillate between wild enthusiasm and fits of gloom. Tom is so languid I occasionally want to check for vital signs. Tall, fair-skinned and slightly stooped, with a rich BBC accent, he looks like the hero of a Saki short story. It's deceptive.

We spent the first night in a *gîte* in Axat, a converted watermill with a stone-flagged kitchen, an enormous scarred wooden table, a bizarre assortment of cooking utensils (three garlic presses but no spoons) and a heavy-beamed dormitory full of rusty bunk-beds. I'd been shopping to welcome my guest, and regaled him with tinned *cassoulet*, grapes and potted puddings: stylish to the last. Afterwards we sat in the light of a flickering fluorescent strip, sipping wine and playing with Tom's new short-wave radio. There was something deeply poignant about sitting in a Pyrenean mill and hearing the voice declare, 'this is London'. I felt like a scion of the Empire.

We set off walking at dawn, two ragged children of Britannia. The murderous summer heat was already a distant memory: the sky was blue, scattered with golden clouds, but in the shadowed valley we could see our breath steaming, and our hands were cold. Tom had firmly relieved me of half my load, and I felt wonderfully light as we climbed through dripping beech-woods and out into a sunny mountain pasture. We were heading roughly west towards the castle of Montségur, famed as a heretics' stronghold and the home of the Holy Grail; from there the plan was to turn south and intercept the GR10, following it westwards along the flank of the Pyrenees. My memories of the scenery are limited to snapshots: a golden meadow full of feather-seeded, dripping grass; the Joucou gorge, a narrow road carved out of a sheer rock wall, impossibly dark and winding; the plateau above Joucou looking south to snow-tipped peaks, the sky purple and gold with the touch of sunset. We were too busy talking to look around much. Not even the nagging ache in my blistered heel distracted me – unfortunately.

The conversation went round the world and back. Halfway through a perfectly normal discussion of the evening's menu Tom stopped, looked thoughtful and asked, 'Do you think Britain deserves the name Great?' An hour later, as the track petered out above a sheer river-bluff, he startled me with, 'Should we bring back National Service?' Pitching his tent on a grassy knoll, he asked me, 'Is Buddhism an explanation of the world or a way of regulating human behaviour?'

As the sun went down in splendour over the glowing heights, we sat and discussed Nirvana. The spirit that built the Empire . . .

We were five miles short of Montségur when things went pear-shaped. Around us wooded hills frowned over the narrow valley, as sheer as ramparts. Ahead, blocking the horizon like a great cork, was the round back of *le Pog*, the peak of Montségur, the castle on its summit dwarfed by distance. We were marching along a narrow road between fields full of goats when my heel started to throb. I ignored it. The pain increased. I still ignored it. Six months' walking had made me bloody-minded. We'll stop at Montségur, I told myself. Still the pain increased. Fiery darts were stabbing up my ankle. It was too much.

'Hang on,' I told Tom, and sank down on the roadside, wrenching at my boot. Suddenly I was sweating.

'What's wrong?'

'Blister,' I answered through gritted teeth. As I pulled the boot off a burst of pain seared my foot like a flash fire, there and gone. I tore off my sock. The plaster on my heel came with it. 'Christ I'm turning into a rhododendron!'

The heel was green. Pulsating red veins ran across my foot and up my ankle. I won't say how the wound smelled, but I choked as I bent to examine it. The blister that I'd burst before Lagrasse had filled again, and not with iodine.

'Are you okay?'

'Possibly.' It was a mess. Nightmare scenarios flashed before my eyes: gangrene, blood poisoning, abandoning the walk. Not a chance! I reached for my sewing scissors and drenched them in iodine, then turned to Tom. 'Minor flesh wound.' Before he could reply I was cutting away.

It wasn't pretty. Roadside surgery is not a hobby I'd recommend, but I was in a hurry. Walking the five miles to Montségur with that heel didn't seem like a wise option. As I opened the wound, I realized that I was lucky. The infection was wide, but not deep, and once I'd exposed the area and swabbed the whole lot down with disinfectant, I knew there wasn't much to worry about. Tom lent me his sandals, and soon we were limping onwards. The heel alternately burned and throbbed viciously, and despite my best efforts the sandal strap kept catching the plaster and making me swear. Tom took yet more from my pack and kept me distracted with a conversation that ranged from a discussion of his career options via a socio-political analysis of James Bond to an in-depth assessment of our favourite Bond girls. No medicine could have cheered me as much as the thought of Sophie Marceau. Boys will be boys.

We reached Montségur village just before sunset, and made straight for the local *gîte*: we'd been planning to camp, but there are times when a soft bed and a wood fire are worth their weight in Internet shares. The town is a bare strip of houses huddled below the shoulder of the hill, considerably smaller than the coach park just above it, and the few inhabitants making their living from the hordes of tourists who come every summer to see the legendary site. In the thirteenth century, Montségur was a stronghold of the Cathars, a sect which believed: in the holiness of the spirit; that everything of the flesh was evil; in the practice of poverty and charity; and that the Pope was the Antichrist. Not perhaps wholly surprisingly, the Catholic church declared a crusade against them. In 1243, with the whole County of Toulouse laid waste and subjugated to the King of France, the crusaders besieged Montségur. After a siege that lasted all winter, the defenders capitulated, and all those who refused to abjure the Cathar faith were burned at the stake in the meadow below the castle: two hundred men and women, including twenty new converts who'd been impressed by the Cathars' behaviour during the siege. Legends have grown thick and fast ever since: that three defenders escaped at the last moment with the Church's treasures, that they took the Holy Grail and the spear of Longinus, that the architecture of the castle was a replica of the Temple of Solomon in Jerusalem. Despite all the efforts of local tour guides to emphasize the other millennium of the site's history, Montségur is synonymous with the Cathar suppression. Romance-ridden tourists flock there in droves.

Tom and I had the *gîte* to ourselves that night, and profited from the solitude to chat until the small hours and drink far more wine than was good for us. The next day my foot was greatly improved, despite being a mottled pink-and-brown from an excess of iodine, but our heads weren't. We decided to stay. The landlord warned us that we'd have company: a group of twelve walkers from Toulouse.

'Do you think they're women?' asked Tom when he was gone. There was a mad gleam in his eyes.

'Definitely! A dozen beautiful single women who love an English accent.'

He rubbed his hands gleefully. 'Yes, yes, I can see them now. A dozen nubile sixth form beauties, trainee dancers . . .'

'Models . . .' My specs were steaming up.

'Geishas! That's it, they're trainee geishas from the famous French geisha school in Toulouse. It's very famous.'

'Very famous. Are they rich?'

'Of course! And scared of the dark.'

'Aha! They'll need a strong protector in the night.'

He looked at me, completely straight-faced, and replied in coolly measured BBC tones, 'No, I just think they'll be really horny.'

They arrived that evening: a dozen women from Toulouse, fit, healthy, friendly, and every one of them sixty if she was a day. They never did work out why we burst out laughing as they walked in.

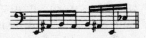

Tom's a fine mountaineer. He proved it the following day when we left Montségur and made our assault on the first great peak in that part of the Pyrenees: the Pic St Barthélémy, a towering outrider of the main ranges. It was a beautiful day as we zig-zagged up the grassy slope, discussing the power of the Vatican while the hill of Montségur dwindled in the distance behind us. We needed no skill to follow the summit path: it was a question of muscle and stubbornness as our legs grew heavier and heavier and the slopes swept away above us for ever. After an hour we stopped for a mint cake break, then charged on refreshed, rounded a shoulder of the mountain, and walked slap into a gale.

It was a terrifying moment. One second we were sweating in the sunshine. The next we'd rounded a high rock and were knocked sideways by the blast. Tom stumbled and almost fell. I staggered, caught myself, and was spun round as the wind caught my rucksack and bowled me over. My pack-cover boomed like a sail, and with a rip and a roar the orange sign that I'd written so long before tore away and went sailing down the wind, with Tom gambolling behind it like a gangly St Bernard. I lay sprawled in the heather and watched the flashing speck dwindle in the distance with a lump in my throat. It was like losing a friend.

There wasn't time to linger. The wind was bitterly cold, and the track led straight up the back of a razor-sharp ridge with no shelter at all. As I tried to stand the wind knocked me sideways again. The straps of my rucksack whipped my face. I had to roll over to my knees and push myself upright with my sticks. Tom came running back, stumbling as the gale buffeted him.

'What do you want to do?' he asked breathlessly. I was glad to see he was out of breath. I'd been gasping like a whale all morning. What I wanted to do was get out of the wind, but that would have meant retreating and doing it all again the next day. Some things are inconceivable.

I checked the map. I didn't look good. The path led straight to the summit, then dropped down another knife-edged ridge towards the village of Appy, a kilometre below. Attempting that in a high wind was not a good idea. Tom looked at me sharply as I started to shiver.

'Get your jacket on,' he said, and for once his voice wasn't languid. 'We'll head up to that stand of trees there' – he pointed – 'and see how things look.'

His confidence steadied me, and I stopped panicking about risks and started thinking again. 'We can always contour round below the summit,' I said, pointing to the map. He nodded.

'Let's get to the trees first.'

He helped me to my feet, and we struggled into the wind together. We'd been two friends out for a stroll; now he was the boss. He led the way, keeping up-wind of me to make my walk easier, looking about at the bleak green-brown scenery.

We were high above the surrounding hills. I could see clearly back to the plain of Toulouse and the haze of Carcassonne. Sheer below us in a sweep of scree lay a tarn like a cold black eye. Everywhere rocks protruded from the hillsides. It was like the Lake District, but a hundred times bigger and wilder. I was glad I wasn't alone.

We sheltered under the trees and listened to the wind roar, sitting together in his survival bag. Tom was infectiously cool and calm: my ears burned and my head ached from the constant battering air, but we hadn't come close to losing our footing again, and I began to trust that we wouldn't. We pinned the map under two water bottles and decided to contour round the slope. I could see that Tom was aching to break for the summit, but he nobly swallowed his inclinations and bowed to my nerves. We set off before we could lose more body heat, angling off the track and wading through the heather.

Abruptly the wind dropped.

We looked at one another, then up to the summit. Tom said nothing. He was waiting, tense as a gun-dog.

I grinned. It wasn't that far.

'Go?'

His face lit up. 'Go!'

We went for it, straight up the mountainside in the hollow between two ridges. Heather tugged at our boot-laces and the weight of our packs shook our legs, but we were full of mint cake and something more: a mad delight in doing something crazy. We didn't know if the wind would rise again, if we'd get caught exposed on the descent, if we even had the energy to reach the summit; and we didn't care. We raced the last few metres, gasping with laughter as we scrambled over tumbled stones onto the summit, and looked south across the valley to the towering main ranges.

It was a triumphant moment. Tom jumped on the highest rock and stood with his arms outstretched. I dragged my trombone from my rucksack and scrambled up beside him. All around the land fell away in great sweeping empty curves. The wind scoured through the heather. I stood and played right into the teeth of it, *Jerusalem*, fortissimo furioso, then switched into *Danny Boy*, jaunty and raucous and as full of my heart as I could make it. Tom grabbed my camera and ran around taking pictures, punctuating the music with cries of 'Left a bit! Bell up! There!'. It was a great victory. I wouldn't have managed it alone, but Tom had been a pillar of strength. I learned a lot that day. I still feared the mountains, but I knew better what I could achieve. It stood me in good stead in the weeks to come.

The next day we went shopping, and trouble began. Tom's a gourmet, and has raised camp cooking to an art form. I'm greedy. Both of us are very bad at disagreements. It's a dangerous combination. We went to the supermarket in Appy, and the dialogue ran thus:

'How about some meat with the pasta?'

'Good idea. What?'

Tom ran a finger along a shelf of tins. 'Pheasant paté?'

'Sounds good!'

'Are you hungry?'

'Always.'

Two large tins of potted pheasant clattered into the basket.

'Something else? Let's see, chillis, tomato purée, garlic,' – bottles fell among the tins – 'that'll do for starters. How about one of these fruit cakes for lunch?'

'Better make it two. Do we want some snacks as well?' I was already holding bags of dried figs, raisins and chocolate chips.

'Good idea.' He heaved the load up onto the counter gravely, and the shopkeeper stared and decided that Heaven had come to him. We spent a week's budget on two days' food.

Then we were off along the valley, groaning under the renewed weight (tins of potted pheasant are not light), and climbed through a bright, mossy beech-wood out onto the mountain-tops. In a narrow valley we cut across the GR10, and turned right up the hillside, Tom moving with swift elegance, I following with the grace of an elephant. With arthritis. The climb seemed to last for ever, passing through bracken to heather and out onto short-cropped grass that smelt of cows, and then we were on the back of the ridge, and to the north – across the valley – lightning flickered around the Pic St Barthélémy. A cold mist was pooling slowly in a valley to the south, whipping up into sudden streamers above the crest and spilling down the northern slope. High on a bare-backed col, a tin mountain-hut strained against its retaining wires with an eerie whistling moan. Inside the hut were foam mattresses on a concrete bed, stubs of candles pooling on a graffitied wooden shelf, a bag of hazel-nuts hanging from a nail and a twenty-kilo sack of rock salt: a shepherd's home for four months of the year. We sat on the doorstep in the last of the daylight and brewed our luxury tea, looking out across the world. There were no traffic noises here, no voices save the wind, no sense of time or hurry. We stretched our legs out in front of us and ate in companionable silence, then took the empties down to the spring below the saddle to wash up.

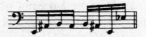

Ever since Tom joined me, we'd been skirting the edge of the true Pyrenees, crossing the tails of the great northward-reaching ridges to move from valley to valley. From that day on, we were in the real mountains, and we loved it. There's not much wilderness left in Europe, but the Pyrenees between Montségur and the great spa town of Luchon come close. September was on the way out and the tourist season was over: in the week that followed we didn't see a single walker, only the occasional shepherd still watching his charges in the high pastures. To our surprise, there were young men amongst them.

They all complained that the old way of life was dying, but it's not dead yet.

The scenery was sublime. The eleventh-century French *Song of Roland* claims 'high are the peaks and the valleys are in shadow', and the millennium that followed has yet to produce a better description. Nothing I'd yet seen came close to the majesty that surrounded us from dawn to dusk. Valleys with sheer walls a kilometre high drove dark clefts between sweeping corries gleaming with snow. At sunset the light streamed in blinding mist across canyons where night had already fallen, the interface as sharp as the hand of a clock, slowly rising. Cold breezes swept down from the heights on wings the width of a county. Clouds studded the sky above and hid the valleys beneath our feet. Vultures circled at dawn, swallows swooped past our ankles at sunset. They only emphasized the emptiness. This was a land where human concerns and human time-scales seemed irrelevant. It was captivating. One day, I promised Tom, I'm going to spend a year up here with a bivvy-bag, stove and camera.

He looked at me sideways. 'You really mean it, don't you?'

'There are worse dreams.' The truth was that I was addicted. The further I walked, the more I dreamt of other voyages.

'Word to the wise?'

I looked at him quizzically. He was wearing his contemplative face, the sure sign that a wind-up was on the way.

'Hire a Sherpa next time.'

We had our first proper argument after five days together. We'd spent the night in a shepherd's hut which Bart had recommended, a dizzying eyrie perched on the very edge of a plunging valley, and woken to find ourselves in the clouds. The descent was hair-raising, a zig-zag path across damp slick stones with the precipice yawning beside us, and the climb back up the far side was cripplingly steep. For a while we kept ourselves happy talking about expeditions we dreamt of organizing, but soon shortness of breath took its toll, and we climbed in silence. Halfway up the hill I stopped for a breather.

'Two minutes,' said Tom jokingly, but there was an edge in his voice. He wanted to keep climbing. Instant resentment filled me.

'Well I won't bloody stop at all, then!' Before he could protest I'd pushed past him and was stomping onwards. At least the anger gave my legs energy.

'Sorry,' he called behind me. I kept on going.

Ten minutes later we climbed above the clouds and looked back on a sea of sun-touched gold, the peaks black and glorious beyond. Automatically I stopped and reached for my camera. Tom let out an exasperated sigh.

'What?' I snarled, still focusing.

'Bloody hell, Ben . . .'

'*What?*'

'Oh, nothing.'

We ploughed on, both hot with anger, round a rock pinnacle which I photo'd out of sheer bloody-mindedness, and down another precipitous slope into a valley just tipped with the sun. It was early afternoon. Broad grassy meadows shone warm and inviting, and the water glittered and sang. A mountain refuge snuggled up against the beech-woods. Beyond it the path climbed yet another near-vertical valley wall. An hour uphill, I knew, was another hut; an hour above that was a col, with a *gîte* in the valley beyond. I'd set my heart on reaching the next hut. Tom took one look at the sunny valley, and dropped his rucksack.

'I'm tired. I'd like to stop here,' he said formally.

I didn't say anything, but my irritation must have showed. 'Can you tell me what you're thinking?' he asked, so carefully that I almost laughed. There speaks a man who's worked in youth development!

'I wanted to get to the second hut. I don't want to have to start tomorrow with that climb.'

'I know, but what's the point? It's nice here, and even if we go up we've still got more climbing to do. Why not stay here and relax?'

'I thought you were in a hurry!'

For once he started to lose it. 'Well, if I hadn't been we'd never even have got this far!'

'Listen, pal!' It's always a bad sign when I call someone pal. 'I'm knackered, all right?'

'So why not stop?' We weren't quite shouting, but we weren't far off it. There's no point repeating the discussion that followed. Tom wanted to stay. I wanted to go on. There didn't seem much room for compromise.

'All right!' I snapped at last. 'We'll stay, then!' And as I flung my rucksack down the anger left me and I started feeling embarrassed. By way of apology I said, 'It's a shame we can't just go on to the *gîte* and have done with it . . .'

There was a sudden thoughtful silence.

We looked at our watches.

We looked at each other.

Tom began to grin.

'It would be insane,' he said neutrally.

'Demented,' I agreed. 'Do we care?'

He looked around thoughtfully. The sun was clipping the ridge, and darkness seemed to flow out of the valley walls. 'Nope.'

It was four o'clock.

We reached the middle cabin a few minutes before five, sweating and muddy. The track had led straight to the foot of a brand-new landslide, and we'd been forced to hop between earth and boulders that slipped and grated under our feet. Dun cattle watched our acrobatics curiously from the flower-studded pastures above. The blade of the darkness rose ahead of us steadily and appallingly fast; never before had I understood the phrase 'racing the sunset' so clearly. At the hut we stopped for a two-minute pant and a long drink, and then we were off again. Hostility was forgotten. We laughed at one another as we filled our bottles from a shining spring. The sky was deep blue, beautiful and warm, cut off in an abrupt sweep by the blackness of the ridge.

Sugar-shock hit me ten minutes later. Suddenly my legs were shaking and my head spun. I hadn't eaten enough that day, and my fuel reserves had burned out.

'Two minutes,' I gasped to Tom. He took one look at me and understood.

'Sugar?'

'Got some.' I sat down on my rucksack, wolfed a bar of mint cake, slugged back a couple of mouthfuls of water, and sat with my head between my legs, watching pretty red patterns swirl across my vision. Tom leant on his staff, waiting. Neither of us was worried. We'd both been through this before, and we knew what Kendal Mint Cake can do.

Within five minutes my blood-stream began to fizz. Mint cake has only half the calories of chocolate, but it's pure sugar: I'd swear it starts digesting before it even hits your stomach. I looked up and felt my vision clear. Tom was waiting patiently.

'*On y va?*' I asked.

He nodded. '*Vamos.*'

Sugar coursed through my veins, and I felt as if I could fly. The mountain was an enemy, the sinking sun a defiance: we threw ourselves at the hill like lunatics, storming straight up the slope. To my own astonishment I found myself singing, though God only knows where I got the breath from: a song of pure machismo to the tune of *Battle Hymn of the Republic*. We stormed up the slope like idiots, leaving a smoking trail in the turf, and reached the col in forty-five minutes flat. It was a triumphant moment. Below us lay the *gîte*, smoke drifting from the chimney, the last of the sunlight slowly fading from the sky. I turned round in triumph and sang a final verse:

'And now we've reached the mountain-top, our bodies
   racked with pain,
There's nothing more we've got to lose, there's no more
   height to gain,
So sleep, you mighty mountains, 'til I sing for you
   again,
And we go walking on!'

I turned to grin at Tom. Arguments and stress were forgotten.
He looked at me thoughtfully, and I waited for some quiet
acknowledgement of what we'd just achieved.

'I think it's shocking that America still has capital punish-
ment, don't you?' he said.

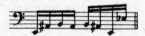

It was a beautiful *gîte*, a converted farmhouse with wooden
floors and stairs, an enormous fire-place and wonderful luxurious bunks. As soon as we saw it we decided to take the day
off there. We were just spreading our kit around the largest
possible area when the owner came in. He'd seen the lights
come on from his house further down the valley.

He looked at us quizzically, then turned to me and said, 'Are
you Ben?'

I gaped. Tom had to answer for me.

'Yes, he's the famous Ben.'

The owner's face lit up, and he shook my unresisting hand.
'*Splendide!* A friend of mine warned me you'd be coming. He
left you that.'

He pointed to the mantelpiece. A thick white envelope leant
against a stuffed owl. I took it and opened it cautiously, aware
of the bright eyes watching me expectantly. Half a dozen
photos fell out, wrapped in a sheet of paper: copies of the
photos Bart had taken in Lagrasse.

'He sent them last week,' said our host as I unfolded the

letter. 'He told me that he'd pay for your stay here. What food can I bring you?'

The letter was a poem in my honour, in French, 'written by Manou and translated by her father.' The postscript was in English: 'I've named the garden pond Lake Ben Nimmo. There are little green frogs living there.' I left Tom to order the food and stood staring into nothing, grinning like an idiot.

'I'll bring the wine,' said our host tactfully, and left us.

The next day's walking brought the greatest triumph so far. The track left the gîte in yet another shatteringly steep climb, this time winding beside a shouting stream between brilliant green ferns, passed abandoned mine-workings and reservoirs, and dropped into one more deep-bottomed valley; and on the far side of the valley was Spain. The border bends abruptly northwards as the GR10 curves south, and for one moment they touch by the village of Fos. We sat on the hillside in the last of the daylight looking down on an old customs house. Beyond it the road snaked up over a low col and into a different country. It was a moment to treasure. I still found it strange to think that the hill I was sitting on and the hill I was looking at belonged to different countries, different laws, that people there spoke different languages and used different currency. I switched my mobile phone on: for the first time it picked up a Spanish network. It dawned on me that I'd just walked diagonally across the whole of France. I'd crossed a country on foot! How many travellers can claim that in this day and age? We weren't planning to enter Spain there. I'd set my heart on crossing further west, in Roncesvalles, where the *Song of Roland* was set; but still, it seemed like the end of an era. We sat looking across the valley for a long time.

'Well done,' Tom said.

'Thanks,' I said. 'What's for tea?'
'Special occasion. Pasta and wild boar paté.'
We'd earned it.

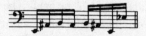

After two weeks together, we dropped out of the hills to
Luchon, a bustling spa town sprawled across the valley floor.
There we found a campsite with its own restaurant (where
Tom risked restarting the Hundred Years' War by sending back
his steak because it was undercooked), pitched under a horse
chestnut tree, took one look at the scattered seed-cases all
around us and scandalised the other guests by ceremoniously
conducting a conker fight. That night a heavy dew fell, and in
the dawn light I accompanied Tom to the railway station. We
almost missed his train, and as he pulled away I wished that
we had. It was hard to walk back to the campsite alone, trying
to remember the skills of solitude. From Luchon it was a solid
fortnight's walk across the High Pyrenees to the pass of Roncesvalles, and everyone I met assured me that I'd be the only
walker up there. Some spoke direly of early snow, others of
sub-zero temperatures. If I hadn't conquered so many tough
climbs with Tom I might have concluded that the risks were
too great, and taken the easy route over the hills to Spain; but
I'd learned. When I set off the following morning I took the
GR10 straight westwards, back into the heights.

It was heavenly. The tourist season was gone, and the hills
were empty. Even the shepherds had moved back down to the
winter pastures, and only a few hunters remained, lean men
and women with dogs and guns, tracking down anything that
moved. I had the mountains to myself in all the blaze of their
autumn glory, the forests golden and crimson, the heights
streaked with white. It snowed three times in the two weeks I
was alone there, a glittering dust across the bare stones, and
every night the frost grew heavier. I crossed the highest point

of my walk on a glorious sunny afternoon, then spent the night shivering in a shepherd's cabin as the temperature dropped to minus ten. I spent two days snug in the annex of a summer refuge waiting for a storm to blow itself out, and was rewarded for my patience with the finest view of the walk: the cloven Pic du Midi d'Ossau reflected in the dark waters of the Lac d'Ayous. I camped above the 2000 metre line so often that it bored me, and came back down into the populous valleys with regret. I could have stayed up in the hills for ever; but the seasons were drawing on.

I dreamt of Anna once, just after crossing the highest point, a dream as warm and happy as her friendship had always been; but this time the awakening was easy. She'd smiled at me in the dream and said she was glad to see me, and that was all that mattered. All day I missed her and thought of her, but I knew she was gone. I knew she'd come and visit me sometimes in my dreams. It wasn't the way the world should be, but it was the way things were.

The climbs grew harder and harder. With the full weight of the Pack From Hell and the necessity of carrying days' worth of food at a time (half the shops had shut at the end of the summer, and supplies were always doubtful) every step was an effort on the stair-steep paths. Slowly and steadily, I went on. The highest point lay behind me; soon the longest climb did, too. The terrain began to change, the hills growing lower and the countryside greener as I drew nearer to the coast and the Basque country. The weather worsened. Few days went by without rain. I lived in my waterproofs and my woolly hat. Once I got the trombone out and played to the echoes for my own pleasure, but it was too cold to linger. I kept on going, and Roncesvalles drew nearer.

The Basques are a friendly people. The last three days of the walk took me into their territory, a lush country full of unpronounceable place-names, and more than once I was invited in to the farms I passed to share a heavy meal. One such family unwittingly gave me the scare of my life, just before I reached St Jean-Pied-de-Port and the pass into Spain.

'Watch out,' the father of the family said seriously. He had an enormous grey beard, a deep tan and smiling eyes, and looked like a minor prophet. 'Someone saw the bear near here last week.'

I raised my eyebrows politely. I'd heard tales of the last bear living on the French side of the Pyrenees, but they sounded too romantic to be true.

'It's true!' protested the farmer instantly. 'Isn't it?' He appealed to his wife, a silent grim-faced woman. She nodded vigorously, and the children chimed in. Oh yes, it was true, he was often seen in those parts ... I left them with warnings ringing in my ears, convinced that they were winding me up.

That night I slept once more in a mountain hut, a low stone cabin with a rusty iron door. The nights were drawing in: it was dark by the time I'd brewed and eaten my tea (pasta and venison paté, Tom had corrupted me). I decided to leave the pot to soak and wash it in the morning. I tipped a little water in and stood it outside the door.

I was just getting ready for bed when something growled outside.

I'm a romantic. I know it. I've got a good imagination and a natural talent for exaggeration – but I'm a musician, and I can recognize a deep note when I hear one. I don't know what was standing outside the door and rattling at my cooking-pot, but it had a throat like an organ-pipe.

Twenty thousand years of civilization vanished. In one second I reverted from calm superiority to troglodyte terror. *It's big, it's hungry, it's outside the door!* Before I knew it I'd shoved the table across the door (which had no latch) and was sitting on top of it thinking heavy thoughts and sweating. My ears roared with panic. *It's outside the door!* I'd never realized how it feels to be a cave-man before. The terror struck straight into my bowels. My brain bolted around my skull looking for a way out. There wasn't one. I sat on that table and panicked.

Ten minutes later I still hadn't been eaten, and the twentieth century crept up on me again. I started to feel embarrassed. What was I playing at? Of course it wasn't a bear! My ears still carried the note of that appalling contrabass growl, but I ignored them. Stress reaction. Imagination. Influenced by the farmers' stories, naturally. I was so convinced and so embarrassed that I pulled the table aside and stepped out into the darkness with my torch to look.

I'd taken six steps when the growl came again – behind the hut.

Not even Tom and Jerry could get into a house and slam the door as fast as I did. It would have made a great video. Table and chairs scraped across the floor and crashed against the door, my rucksack thudded on top of them, I wedged my poles against the door handle. Nothing moved outside. The night was as silent as the grave. I sat there quivering for a long time. Then I climbed the ladder into the sleeping-loft, pulled it up behind me and tried to get to sleep. It took a long time.

Next day I looked all round the hut for tracks. There was nothing to be seen. Had it all been imagination? Yes, said my mind, laughing at me; but my ears still resonated to that growl. In my heart of hearts I'm convinced. There's a bear in the French Pyrenees, and I've met him.

And at last, after six and a half months on the road, I walked into St Jean-Pied-de-Port and climbed the hill towards the pilgrims' welcome centre. As always after a long stretch, I was hungry, dirty, and determined not to move again for a week. This time, however, there was a difference. The Pyrenees lay behind me, and the greatest physical challenge was over. From here on, barring accidents, I knew I'd make it to Santiago for the Millennium.

The welcome centre was in a beautiful red stone house just below the ruins of the castle. French windows led into a small office. I had to open both doors to squeeze through with my rucksack. A middle-aged lady looked up sharply, and her eyes widened.

'That rucksack's too large!'

There didn't seem much to say. I concentrated on negotiating the door without breaking anything. A small, pretty girl and a large man hidden by a beard watched with interest.

'Did you carry that all the way from the station?' my interrogator went on.

'No,' I said shortly. 'From England.'

She looked at me as if I were stupid. 'I meant on foot!'

So did I!'

There was a short silence. Then she rallied.

'Ah, but you've got to cross the Pyrenees now!'

I smiled politely. 'I just have. Lengthways. Checkmate, madame.'

Thus I joined the pilgrim road.

PART 9

The Camino:
Roncesvalles to Helena

'If music be the food of love, play on . . .' (*Twelfth Night*, I, i, 1)

The pilgrim hostel in St Jean Pied-de-Port had sixteen beds. When I arrived, late in the evening of October the twenty-fourth, there were fifteen pilgrims there. So much for solitude.

The housekeeper met me at the door with a pop-eyed '*Mon Dieu!*' and flew into a frenzy of hospitality: a little wrinkled Basque woman with a maternal streak the width of the English channel. She showed me my bunk in a tiny green-walled room like a prison cell, introduced me proudly to the inmates, showed me the other dormitory, the shower and the kitchen, introduced me again, told me that the office staff were far too unwelcoming, added that my pack was far too heavy, and swept off, leaving me standing in the kitchen feeling like a bit of driftwood caught in a hurricane.

Four pairs of eyes stared at me in awe.

'Did you really walk from England?' A pair of Americans were sitting at the table holding hands: fresh faces, perfect teeth, an air of wide-eyed enthusiasm. They looked about twelve. 'That's awesome!'

'What did he say?' asked a small Frenchman with an aggress-ive moustache.

'Excuse me, what did you say?' the Americans asked him politely.

'I'm going for a shower,' I told them, and fled.

Scrubbed, shaved, and dressed in the only clean shirt I had left, I felt brave enough to face the United Nations. I went back down to the kitchen (it was in the cellar, a stone-flagged room with an enormous chimney) and discovered that I was expected. Half the pilgrims in the hostel had come down to see the one who'd walked from England. Joe and Jane (their real names!) were there; so was the Frenchman, bristling with challenges ('How many kilometres do you do a day? Hah! We did more than that when I was in the desert army!'). I christened him Laurent of Arabia. They'd been joined by two of my room-mates, a Finnish mother and her nineteen-year-old son who'd seen a TV documentary on the Santiago pilgrimage and decided to attempt it before he was snapped up by national service. Anne, the pretty girl I'd seen in the welcome centre, was there too, watching from a corner with quiet eyes. Three Spaniards were sitting on the stairs, smoking and chatting loudly.

It was a heady evening. Anne had walked from Le Puy. All the others were starting in St Jean Pied-de-Port, and they were even more nervous than I'd been in Canterbury. They wanted to know everything: what will it be like, what do we need to take, will the people be friendly, how far should we walk each day, what time should we set off? I answered as well as I could, jumping from French to English and back until my brain ached, soothing the Americans' nerves and trying not to let Laurent annoy me too much. He was more nervous than any of them, and comforted himself by arguing with everything I said. After a while Jane asked me to help them pack. We went up to their dorm – an infinitely more appealing room than mine – and they showed me their rucksacks, lumpen misshapen things with plastic bags tied on at all angles. Laurent wandered up to offer advice and criticism as we went through the luggage item by item. Waterproof poncho, yes. Three-kilo camera tripod, no. Mess tin and spoon, yes. China plates and bowls, no. Have you got a torch? I asked. They looked blank. I dug my spare out of my rucksack and gave it to them. Their faces lit up like the Times Square Christmas tree. Laurent sniffed. 'When I was in the desert army we all had torches.' I hope it made him feel better.

Later I sat talking with Anne. The others had retired at nine o'clock, vowing to leave at six the next morning (it wasn't light until eight), but she was a veteran pilgrim, and it showed: she wasn't going to hurry. To my surprise, she was full of questions too: what do you think about when you walk? Why are you doing the Camino? (She'd come to a full stop in her career as a dancer and was hoping to find enlightenment on the way.) Do you miss twentieth-century society? Is it worth doing what you're doing? More than anything in the world, I told her. Friendship, freedom, the feeling that as long as I have food and shelter nothing else was worth worrying about ... Her eyes lit up. 'That's how it is for me!' We were still talking philosophy at midnight.

I saw them off the next day, little nervous groups hurrying down the cobbled street by starlight, then moved all my kit into the other dorm and went back to bed for the rest of the morning. I was still there when the day's pilgrims started trickling in: a thin, nervous Parisian, two more Spaniards, a pair of students from Quebec with Art Garfunkel hair, a Brazilian executive in a ski jacket and Ray-Bans. They chose their bunks and wandered off uneasily. I got up and showered, and was just contemplating going back to bed for the afternoon when a fresh group arrived, chatting merrily. Two were on foot, one was pushing a laden mountain-bike, and something about their air of utter confidence told me that they'd been travelling for a while.

Sandra is a short, dark Dutch architect with sharp eyes and

a sharper intellect. She'd been touring southern France by bike for a month. Bastian is a tall and ludicrously handsome Swiss landscape architect: golden hair, golden skin, blue eyes, immense smile. He'd walked from Lausanne. Liesbeth is a tall, shapely Dutchwoman who doesn't look a day over forty. She's sixty-two, and she'd just walked from Holland.

'You must be Ben,' they said. 'Want a cup of tea?'

My kind of people.

We spent the whole afternoon chatting: the people we'd met, the things we'd seen, the places nobody should miss, the endless surprises of being on the way. All three were aglow with faith in human nature. Between us we'd travelled over six thousand kilometres to get there, and nothing had happened to shake that faith. Who would have thought it in this day and age?

We set off together the next day. Sandra rode off towards the highway, promising to meet us in Roncesvalles. The three of us made for the hills. We'd hardly passed the town walls when we saw a black speck on the road ahead, barely moving. We swung on with long, comfortable strides, chatting easily. The climb from St Jean Pied-de-Port to the Spanish border is dreaded by pilgrims everywhere, an eight hundred metre ascent over ten kilometres, but we were more in training than most ... The figure ahead wasn't. He'd climb a hundred metres, stop and lean on his staff for a minute, climb another hundred, stop again. None of us said anything, but all three grew suddenly alert. It wasn't long before we caught him: a fifty-something Québecois with flowing black hair, a thick beard and an enormous belly, his face streaming with sweat. His rucksack swung lopsided across his back, dragged sideways by the weight of a folding chair. His breath came in shuddering rasps. We looked at one another.

'*Ca va, pelerin?*' asked Bastian cheerfully. Yvain grinned ruefully.

'*Tabernac*'!' True Canadian swearing. '*Oui, ça va.*'

188

We swung in on either side of him and slowed down to his pace.

The Camino – the traditional route of pilgrimage – is many things to many people. Sandra was there for the architecture, Bastian was lost in life and wanted inspiration, Liesbeth was walking for peace, Yvain was there to rediscover himself. Others we met on the way were looking for inner tranquillity, weight loss, forgiveness of sins, beautiful scenery, love. But one of the classic sayings of the Camino is that it doesn't matter what people are looking for. What they'll find is an experience that will enlarge their spirit.

Ours started right there, with Yvain.

He was over fifty years old, and well over fifteen stone. He managed a burger bar in St Jérome in Quebec, liked beer and chips, and had never done a day's exercise in his life. He'd been divorced and gone through a long period of counselling, and just when he was starting to rediscover his self-confidence he saw a TV documentary on the Camino. Like so many other pilgrims, he realized it was the answer to a question he hadn't known he was asking: a holiday with a meaning, a chance to find himself. A flight and a train journey later he was in St Jean Pied-de-Port, wondering how he got there. He set off at dawn. By the time we found him an hour later he was more exhausted than he would have believed possible.

He was indomitable. I'd thought I was mentally tough after all I'd been through, but I bow to Yvain. He plugged on up the hill, gasping so badly that I started rehearsing resuscitation techniques in my mind, stopping every fifty seconds for a breather, but when Bastian shyly suggested that it might make sense for him to hitch a ride over the mountains and start again on the plains he replied in terms that only a Quebec peasant could know. We couldn't just leave him there, so we crawled on at his pace. After an hour he could barely walk. At that point we convinced him to let us carry his rucksack. When I mooted the question of hitching a lift (the pilgrim trail followed a back road all the way to the border) he gave me a glare that could have pierced armour plate, and staggered on.

'Listen, boys. I'll do it if I can just go at my own pace. This bloody mountain isn't going to beat me!' And on he went, swearing and spitting. Bastian and I shrugged helplessly; Liesbeth smiled and strolled on. The sky was a brilliant blue, and V-formations of cranes laced the heavens, battling a stiff breeze as they flew south for the winter. All around were the hills, green and rolling and covered in pigeon-hunters. Down to our right was Valcarlos, the steep-sided pass into Spain that had been a road and a battleground since Roman times. Somewhere in that valley Basque guerrillas had massacred the rearguard of Charlemagne's army in AD 778, a minor skirmish in an endless series of border battles. In the centuries that followed the story grew to become the tale of the death of Roland, Charlemagne's nephew, and of the Twelve Peers of France: the most magnificent epic ever written in French. I'd loved it since I was twelve. I couldn't believe I was actually there.

Yvain slogged on. If any of Charlemagne's heroes had seen him then, they would have taken him for one of their own. He looked on the verge of collapse, staggering and gasping, but somehow he kept going, and as the slope grew more gentle and the end of the climb came into sight he even found the breath to tell us his own philosophy. 'You can only be beaten if you say "I give up". (Gasp, gasp.) As long as you believe you can do it, you will. (Gasp, gasp.) Like yourself. Tell yourself "God, I'm good!" (Spit.) When I get to that top I'm going to say, "Yvain, you're a hero!" and give myself a hug . . .'

He did, too.

We reached the border at three o'clock, a wooden gate across a muddy path between stunted mossy oaks with a great standing stone beyond. The trees roared with the wind, and in the distance the cranes were calling. I was leaving France at last. The others sat in the shelter of the trees, and I unshipped the trombone and blasted the breeze: *Danny Boy*, *Tipperary*, and a new piece that Bastian had taught me, *Ultreia*, a medieval pilgrims' song which he'd learned in Conques cathedral. Then I turned and blew a *Last Post* down the valley. According to the legend, Roland died blowing his horn to summon help, and it seemed churlish not to leave him a tribute . . . Anna was in there too. She was worth a little mountain music.

As I packed away I saw something white lying in the mud. I picked it up: a little ivory elephant with a tiny length of chain still attached.

'A gift from the Camino,' said Yvain. 'Keep it. You've earned it.'

It was too cold to linger. We set off again, for one final climb through the woods to a low saddle. There before us stretched the valley of Roncesvalles, broad and flat and patched with forest. Low hills rose beyond the plain, and on the edge of sight was a dark smudge that might have been a city: Pamplona. We stood looking for a second.

'Is that the last climb?' Yvain asked.

'Yes.'

'Damn, I'm good!'

He set off ahead of us, swinging his staff jauntily. We could only follow in awe.

We slept in a stone-cold monastery that night, full of the music of creaking beds and snoring pilgrims. Sandra had been there to meet us, and we'd mugged a passing pilgrim to take photos of us all: a bewildered-looking Austrian girl in a woolly orange jumper. We ate the pilgrim menu (fish and chips) in a local restaurant for the princely sum of four pounds including wine, and praised Yvain until he blushed. For sheer determination in the face of excruciating pain, I'd never seen anything to match it. Next morning we set off in a group, chatting and hurling cheerful Québecois obscenities at the weather, which lashed us with icy rain. We shared a hostel that night – an official municipal *refugio*, hot water, a kitchen and a bed for two pounds a head on presentation of the pilgrim's credential – and Bastian astonished us all by cooking a superlative pasta sauce and following it up with chestnut cake. That was when he told us shyly that he'd been a fighter pilot before becoming a landscape designer, and did we have any suggestions as to what he could do next? We thought about it for a second at least, and chorused, 'Cook!'. He thought we were joking.

We were a family. Yvain was the father, and Bastian, eternally shy, his admiring son: they walked together, discussing life, relationships and dirty jokes. Liesbeth was our mother, talking with whoever was lonely, watching over us, setting off serenely alone when she needed time to herself. A silver-haired Frenchman named Yves joined us as the favourite uncle: he was a financier with a heart of gold, and kept us laughing for hours with tales of the business world, a feat I wouldn't have believed possible. Sandra and I were somehow a couple, the new in-laws: she had a boyfriend at home, and I'd made and said goodbye to too many friends along the way to risk getting close to anyone, but anyone who didn't know that probably wouldn't have guessed it. Every day she'd head off on her bicycle. Every evening we'd meet up again, and sit chatting until far too late, until I found myself looking forward to the sight of her bike locked outside the *refugio* even more than the showers. When Liesbeth's daughter came to join us for a few days, taking time off from her regular job of organizing a Russian circus in Barcelona, the family was complete.

Every hostel was full. Even so late in the year, the flood of the faithful continued, terrifying in their enthusiasm. Some were walking in trainers, a few in sandals, many in boots they'd bought the day before setting off: any surgeon wanting to specialize in blisters need look no further than the Camino de Santiago. Rucksacks varied from brand-new luxury items to school satchels festooned with plastic bags; I spent entire evenings helping the weary adjust their magic adjustable ruck-sack frames from the Darth Vader fitting back to normal size. Waterproofs ranged from Gore-Tex salopettes with fur lining to bin-bags joined with gaffer tape. Their maps were nothing more than inefficient sketches without scale or orientation, but then, so were mine: Spain does have excellent topographical maps, but nobody sells them. As a veteran of the British hills, I was appalled. As an observer of human nature, I was elated. These inexperienced, untrained city-dwellers were putting themselves through utter physical misery, and coming out smil-ing at the end of the day. In two months on the Camino I only heard of one pilgrim dropping out.

After four days of long conversations and late nights, we reached Pamplona. There the family separated. Liesbeth and Bastian were eager to go on. Yvain wanted a rest, but he preferred to stay with them. Not having taken anything like enough time to rebuild my strength after the GR10, I was exhausted again. To my delight, Sandra wanted to take a day off as well. We agreed to separate for the day and meet in the evening, bumped into each other at lunchtime, went for a quick coffee and were still talking four hours later, swapping anec-dotes of the road and the one grumble we had in common: the overdose of pilgrims. Pilgrims walk the pilgrim road between pilgrim hostels, eat the pilgrim menu in pilgrim restaurants, follow the pilgrim waymark (a yellow arrow) and talk about the pilgrimage. It's a unique situation, but where, we asked, were the locals?

'It's nice to get away from the pilgrims for a bit,' she said to me eventually. We were sitting on a sunny bench in one of Pamplona's many squares, watching Spain go by and suf-ficiently charmed with each other's company that we didn't even spot the irony. Female pilgrim tells male pilgrim how nice it is to escape from pilgrims and see Spain – in English. An immensely tall and immensely pretty girl walked past, stopped, and then came towards us.

'Excuse me, are you pilgrims?' she asked in American-accented English.

We laughed. Some days you can't win.

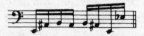

Sandra left the next day. It was a wrench to see her go, but I knew my body needed rest. I told her I'd follow in a couple of days. In fact I spent a week there. As soon as I stopped, the accumulated fatigue of seven months' walking hit me, and I collapsed. I spent two days in a *pension* on the edge of town doing nothing but sleeping and eating potato tortillas. As I recovered I started a little gentle exploration, getting used to a new country: language, food, opening times, styles. Pamplona was full of well-dressed women and smart teenagers, and every street had a chestnut-seller on the corner, so my first experience of urban Spain was the scent of charcoal fires mingling with Chanel and petrol vapour. At first it was terrifying. Gradually, as the language grew more familiar and I worked out where the food-shops were, I began to relax and enjoy myself. I missed my pilgrim family dreadfully, but I'd been missing people for so long that it was almost familiar. Not long now, I told myself. New Year's not far off.

The week that followed was a testing time. Something within me changed in Pamplona. Whether it was knowing that I'd passed the barrier of the Pyrenees or the result of two thousand miles on foot I'm not sure, but the effect was to rob me of all energy. In the Pyrenees I'd zipped up half-mile ascents as if they weren't there. Leaving Pamplona, the two hundred metre climb to the Alto del Perdon almost killed me. In Burgundy I'd managed to walk thirty-five kilometres a day. After Pamplona I never did more than twenty. I'd lost the ability to force myself onwards. All I could do was plod.

It was heartbreaking. All around me were other pilgrims, with friendly faces, warm hearts, captivating stories, and an eager desire to hammer on at forty kilometres a day. I felt like the underdog in every fairy story that's ever been told, watching the fit and happy stream past and knowing I couldn't keep up. I made a dozen friends that week, and said goodbye to the lot. The good ones spent a day with me. The very best spent two. After that their own timetables kicked in, limited holiday time or limited patience, and they were gone in a cloud of dust. I plodded on across vast stony fields like a Thomas Hardy nightmare, scrambled past olive-trees glowing silver in the winter light, the olives on the branches as bright as stars, and wished I were as tough as Yvain. I could make myself keep going, but I couldn't force my spirits up. Messages started appearing for me in the *refugio* guest-books, from Bastian, Sandra and others: where are you, how are you, when will you catch us up? I wished I could answer them, but there was nothing left inside me to push me faster.

I reached the town of Estella late on a blustery afternoon, dropping down between olive groves to a glorious medieval town littered with beautiful churches: Estella was a thriving hub of Camino life when the Conqueror crossed the Channel, and it has the monuments to prove it. It also has an *hospitalero* renowned along the Camino: Carlos of the bushy moustache and sad eyes, the kindest soul in Navarra. Sandra had passed through the hostel two days before I did, leaving me a long message, and she'd warned Carlos about me. I was welcomed in with a huge hug, a glass of wine and a 'You must be the mad one!'. Fame indeed . . .

The Jubilee Year had been a nightmare for the *hospitaleros*. Estella had seen more than two hundred sleeping there in a single night. The word from the last *refugios* before Santiago was even worse, with up to a thousand people per hostel. Roncesvalles had become a sea of Army tents. There had been fights over bed-space, death threats against snorers (quite right too), blisters, tendonitis, heart problems, dehydration, attempted bribery, attempted rape, deaths from heart-attack and deaths on the roads. To balance it there had been astonishing demonstrations of selflessness. An eighty-year-old pilgrim had arrived in Estella one night; four separate guests had offered him their bunks. Pilgrims had turned up without even the money to pay for a bed; others had bought them accommodation and food, given them clothing and equipment. Everyone looked after their friends; a dozen times a day Carlos heard the question, 'Have you seen so-and-so yet?'. The guest-book in his hostel was a vast tome four inches thick, and it was full of letters and messages, everything from 'Juan, I made it, where are you?' to a two-page description of the meaning of divine love in shaky Portuguese. Carlos had seen Yvain and Bastian, still together, infecting everyone they met with the 'Damn, I'm good!' philosophy. Liesbeth had passed a day later, alone, as serene as ever. Sandra had spent two days there, sketching and chatting, her two favourite hobbies. It was good to hear their news.

That evening a familiar face arrived: a girl from Quebec whom I'd seen in the last three hostels, a small, quiet young lady with a voluminous sketch-book. We'd done no more than say hello in passing, but two syllables can communicate a great deal, and we both knew we were potentially friends. As the sunlight faded we found one another in the communal dormitory, and on the spur of the moment I asked if she fancied joining me for a stroll. (Not even Pamplona had crushed the chasing-pretty-girls reflex.) We crossed the river by a splendid medieval bridge and climbed to one of the many churches, exchanging potted autobiographies. Her name was Mélanie, and she was twenty-two and an unemployed actress. She'd been backpacking around Europe with her boyfriend. Somehow the constant travelling and sight-seeing hadn't satisfied them. They were sitting grumbling in a youth hostel in Rome when someone mentioned the Camino. There and then they decided to walk to Santiago, separately, Mélanie by the classic route, Eloi by the *Camino del Norte*, the road along the coast: wilder, less organized, less popular.

'How will you meet up again?' I asked, intrigued. She laughed, and it's the first time I've really understood the phrase 'a bell-like laugh'.

'Oh, whoever gets there first will wait. We'll manage somehow.'

'Isn't it a bit hard on the relationship?'

'It's good to have some time apart. I think we needed it. He'll be there.'

I could only admire the confidence, and hope she was right.

We strolled from church to church, admiring Gothic sculptures and the sunset sky, and she asked me about my walk. It all came out: my feelings when I set off, the slow rebirth of trust, the astonishing generosity at every turn, the loneliness, the happiness, the addiction. I said 'There are worse lives than this,' and meant that I couldn't imagine a better one. Her eyes shone as I talked, which is never a bad thing to see. Night fell, and we sat and stared at the street-lights reflected in the windows. I was happy again, despite all the weariness.

'Thank you,' she said, when I finally shut up. Once I get passionate about something I tend to lose track of time. 'I'm really glad I met you.'

It was so unexpected words failed me. Wonders will never cease.

We set off together the next day. Just outside Estella is one of the legends of the Camino: the Iratxe vineyard, where the drinking-fountains run with wine. We stopped for a quick sample, and I decided to visit the neighbouring monastery. She wanted to go on, so we separated with a cheerful 'See you later.' But we didn't. She wasn't in the hotel that night, and I didn't see her the next day. The *hospitaleros* told me she'd passed by and kept on going. She was going at thirty kilometres a day. Yet again I found myself wishing I could walk faster, and knew that it was impossible. Suddenly I hated the Camino. Why had I ever left the mountains? Solitude was easy when I was on my own. It was the saying goodbye that hurt.

I plodded on. Compared with the Pyrenees the landscape was almost flat, broken only by low tumbled hills and river-bluffs, the trail a stony path marked with the eternal yellow arrows. Autumn had leached all brightness away, and the world was a symphony of browns and greys, earth and sky as dull as rusting iron. Sometimes the Camino followed the road, and the bright metallic colours of the cars hurtling by were like fluorescent dots on a black-and-white picture. Often it passed through little towns, huddled as if for warmth round a church. Even the shops seemed muted, little dark houses with *chorizo* sausages hanging from the beams and every kind of household goods cluttered on crazy shelves, a million miles removed from the gleaming supermarkets of France. I hardly dared to wear my bright yellow Gore-Tex jacket when I saw the locals in their brown and black coats. It would have been like shouting in a library.

On 10 November I reached Logroño. The *refugio* there was a palatial affair, as shining and new as a German youth hostel, and just as efficient: when I arrived the *hospitalero* handed me a piece of paper with my bed number written on it, and inti-mated in no uncertain tones that if I took any other bed the Lord might have mercy on my soul, but he certainly wouldn't. Other pilgrims trickled in and looked around in bewilderment, trying to find their beds. Soon eight of us were jammed together in one corner of a forty-bed room. A German pilgrim walked in, looked around, made an unflattering comment about con-centration camps and dumped his rucksack in completely the wrong place. Instant revolution erupted. Before long the dorm was a chaotic wreck of scattered equipment, scrunched-up bed allocations, and happy pilgrims. The *hospitalero* looked in, drew back in horror, and left us to it, his faith in pilgrims shattered.

The German's name was Joachim, a tall, thin, smiling man of about my age. We fell to talking that evening – the *hospitalero*'s attitude bred fellow-feeling – and within half an hour we were friends. The Camino's like that. He was a jazz fan, a trumpeter and a philosopher. He was on the Camino looking for inspiration, like so many others. He'd left a girl-friend at home whom he missed dreadfully, but he, like Mélanie, was willing to trust the strength of the relationship. Again, I marvelled at the courage. I wasn't sure if I could do that . . . As always, he asked me about my motivation, and as always, I told him. We talked about life and death, and how to deal with both. A Spanish girl overheard us and joined in: Beatriz from Madrid, twenty years old, pretty, lively and yet another philosopher. We talked about solitude and the courage that it takes to face it; about the need for human company, for joy, for time, for love; about the blessings and curses of modern society; about the survival of goodwill and charity. ('Does it still exist?' asked Beatriz, and received a resounding 'Yes!'.) Other pilgrims chipped in as they passed, and it says something about the Camino that they weren't surprised to hear us baring our souls in the common-room, and we weren't worried when they joined in. By the time we went to bed – late *again* – our friendship was assured.

I should have known better. Separation came at once. The next day I was determined to go busking. They were determined to go on. We went for breakfast in a café near the *refugio*, picking up the conversation where we'd left off. One coffee took us over two hours. It was a good chat. Beatriz paid for all three of us, and started walking. Joachim accompanied me to the Cathedral square and watched me set up and busk. After two numbers the donations were gratifyingly generous, and my morale was blooming. He came towards me with an anguished expression.

'Ben, I've got to keep going. I don't know why, but I can't stop here.' You hear that a lot on the Camino. 'Can you join me?'

'I wish I could.' With all my heart, but I'd come here to busk for charity, and it wouldn't have been right to stop. 'I'll follow you tomorrow.'

199

'Will you catch up?'

I knew how fast he walked. 'I doubt it,' I said sadly. He understood.

'*Buen camino, peregrino.*' Safe journey, pilgrim. We hugged each other there in the town square, and got on with what we had to do. The busking went well, but I still wished I'd gone with him. All afternoon I played with an aching lip and a heavy heart, and slept uncomfortably in a flea-ridden *pension*; nobody was allowed more than one night in the *refugio*. The next morning I set off alone, and swore never to get close to anyone on the Camino ever again.

One day later my luck changed.

It was about 11 o'clock when I saw a pilgrim coming back down the trail towards me, a little black speck against the vast sweep of the fields. It wasn't an unusual occurrence – I'd already seen a few veterans who'd made it to Santiago and were happily walking home – but every touch of human warmth was welcome. He came nearer, a short young Frenchman in a Breton beret. Then he stopped, looked me up and down, and grinned.

'You're Ben.'

I was used to it. The Pack From Hell was famous.

'I've got a letter for you.' He held out a crumpled paper. 'From Mélanie. And there's good wishes from Anne, Lisbeth and Sandra as well. Do you only talk with pretty girls?'

Harsh, but possibly fair . . .

I opened the letter eagerly. 'Hi Ben, I'm here in Heaven, in Santo Domingo. I'll be here until the thirteenth – hope you can catch up!' She hadn't even signed it.

'What's the date?' I asked him. He was watching in amusement.

'The twelfth.'

My heart leapt. 'And you left there this morning?'

'Yes.'

'Is it far?'

'No.'

'Excuse me,' I said exuberantly, 'I'm expected,' and took off in a shower of mud.

I reached Santo Domingo at noon. The hostel was closed until sunset, so I decided to visit the Cathedral and its legendary chickens, a monument to a local saint. Domingo was a twelfth-century boy who dedicated his life to helping pilgrims, and whose grave became a site of worship second only to Santiago. In the fourteenth century a German family passed through the town that sprang up around the shrine, and which still bears his name. The *hospitalero*'s daughter fell for the son of the family, was spurned, and in revenge accused him of theft, secreting a silver cup in his baggage with biblical cunning. The unfortunate boy was executed forthwith. His grieving parents continued the Camino, reached Santiago, and turned round to walk home. As they passed through Santo Domingo they found their offspring still on the gallows, merrily singing hymns and not at all harmed by three months' hanging around. They ran to the sheriff to tell him the news. He, being busy with dinner, retorted 'Your son is no more alive than these chickens I'm eating!', and the birds (a cock and a hen, as the chronicle states) sprang up and started singing. The boy was released, the chickens were placed in a cage in the cathedral, and Santo Domingo became the patron of the Camino and, presumably, poultry cooks. To this day, the Cathedral has maintained the tradition. It's blessed with eleventh-century stonework, four-teenth-century choir-stalls sporting some of the finest carvings in Spain, a colossal Renaissance altar-piece and a beautiful cloister, but it's the chickens that still draw the crowds. The Cathedral guides get really upset about that.

Mélanie's letter was enough to make me happy. Chickens and medieval art combined had me almost dancing. When I heard the music outside, I thought my joy was complete. It was the *quintadas*, a joint birthday party for everyone in the town who'd turned eighteen that year, with all the anarchy that concept implies. I joined the band just before one o'clock. We were still playing at six, and if I hadn't known that Mélanie was waiting I would have been there until midnight. I left the band with cheers ringing in my ears and an unprecedented spring in my step, collected my rucksack from the Cathedral and went on my way rejoicing, fuelled by happiness and more than a little *vino tinto*.

It was long after sunset when I reached the hostel. It was built into one side of an ancient church, up an echoing stone staircase that smelled of mice. Funny stairway to Heaven, I thought, remembering Mélanie's letter, as I stumbled through a door, and discovered that she was right.

It was like a sauna after a month in the cold. It was like a hug after a long separation, peace after fighting, music after silence. After seven and a half months on the road, it felt like coming home. A fire roared in a stone fire-place, lighting up the room. Around it were half a dozen arm-chairs, a bookshelf, a guitar, a small table laden with snacks. A teapot – a teapot! – stood on the hearth. Candles burned on the mantel-piece. Soft rugs were scattered on the wooden floor. Every chair was occupied. Voices chatted quietly. Somebody was singing. As I shut the door all heads turned towards me. I couldn't recognize a soul, my glasses had steamed up the instant I walked in.

'You must be Ben,' said a cheerful voice. 'Come in! Sit down! Have some tea, then tell me if you need anything. Any blisters, aches, pains?' A warm hand was slipped under my arm. 'I'm Sylvia, *hospitalera non officiale*.' All this in a strong Austrian accent. Then she called, 'Ben's here!' and stood back.

'Ben!' Mélanie's voice, ringing from a balcony above: the sleeping-area. 'Hey, Joachim, Beatriz, he's here!'

Feet clattered down the stairs. I pulled off my specs and saw all three of them hurtling towards me. Then I was wrapped in the biggest group hug of my life.

'We heard you were coming, so we waited,' Joachim told me, leading me to a comfy chair. 'How's it going, *amigo*?'

Mélanie was right. It was Heaven.

She left the next morning. I left my rucksack in the *refugio* and went with her, talking about the past and the future. She told me about her elder sister, born handicapped, and her own desire to work in the theatre with handicapped children. She told me about home, Montreal, and her desire to be there for Christmas with Eloi. She'd been away for two months, and it was enough; but she'd be back in Europe one day. I didn't know where I'd be, but I invited her to visit me anyway. She answered in kind. In the shelter of a church porch we swapped addresses. I gave her my last bar of chocolate as a farewell present (greater love hath no man . . .). Her face lit up and she hugged me. Then she walked on in the rain, and I turned round and walked back towards the *refugio*. Once more I was too tired to go on, and I'd promised myself a week's rest.

Half-way there I met Joachim and Beatriz, merrily singing and teaching one another phrases in their own languages. Beatriz looked divine in a green army poncho with plastic bags wrapped round her shapely legs, and thick white lip-balm all over her face. They greeted me with delight. I turned around and walked with them for another hour, listening to Beatriz' tales of her mother, a Mexican dancer. In the shelter of the same porch she gave us a demonstration of shamanic dancing, calling the sun. It didn't work. Again we hugged, again I watched them go, and for a second time I wandered home. Without the Pack From Hell on my shoulders I felt as light as air. Strangely, I didn't feel lonely. In twenty-four hours they'd shown me enough affection to keep me happy for a month.

That afternoon I did the washing in a little stone basin below the belfry, listening to the rain dripping through the roof. After a while Sylvia joined me, and we chatted and splashed in unison. She'd been there for a week already, having limped into the hostel with a dislocated toe and been instructed by the priest who ran the *refugio* to stay there as *hospitalera* as long as there were pilgrims who needed looking after. She was a nurse and an amateur chef, so she was good at it. The entire week before her arrival had only produced two pilgrims, so she doubted she'd stay long. As soon as she arrived they started pouring out of the woodwork. The priest couldn't believe it. He laughed, called her a stranded whale, and said the saint had sent her. He was that kind of priest.

'So now I'm a Whale Snail,' she added, laughing.

'Eh?'

'Big rucksack, I walk slowly, I call myself the Snail,' she said in the tones of one who'd explained it too many times before.

'We must be related,' I told her. When I told her my nickname she laughed out loud. There and then we instituted the League of Pilgrim Snails with a flourish of soapy water.

When the washing was dripping in the eaves we went back into the sitting-room and got to work. *El cura* had asked her to translate a Spanish vespers into German for him, and she'd been grappling with it for a week. My arrival with Spanish grammar and dictionary was a Godsend, or at least a saint-send. We sat with the dictionary and the priest's collection of international bibles, working our way through evensong in all the languages we had between us, and wondering if the saint would send us a few more pilgrims. Ten minutes later there came a thud at the door, and two middle-aged Spaniards stamped in, dripping. One was a tiny Menorcan with a leathery face and a permanent scowl. The other was a Catalan with the most magnificent twirled moustache I've ever seen. Sylvia launched into her 'welcome' speech – hello, I'm Sylvia, tea or coffee, any injuries? – and I sat and worshipped the moustache. They looked us up and down cheerfully, dumped their wet gear and made a bee-line for the fire, pooh-poohing all offers of assistance. It wasn't until they were buried in the armchairs steaming their socks that Twirly called back over his shoulder, 'There's another pilgrim behind us. German girl. Helena. Very tall,' and turned to lean closer to the flames. Sylvia went into the kitchen to water the soup. I got on with the translation.

I'd vowed to make no more friends on the way, and by God I was going to stick to it.

Helena arrived half an hour later in a flurry of stamping boots and flying spray while the gentlemen were unpacking upstairs. Busy with the intricacies of Spanish–French translation, I only looked up when she'd sidestepped Sylvia's hospitable bustle and was standing in the middle of the sitting-room. My eyes shot out on stalks. Six foot two of dreadlocked damsel looked down at me curiously.

'Hi. You must be Helena,' I managed, shocked into something like German. 'I'm Ben.'

She looked confused, which was fair enough.

'The other two told us you were coming.'

'Ah.' She looked around, noticed the fire, threw herself into an armchair with childish glee and forgot me completely. I turned back to my work, determined to ignore her too. It was a good intention.

Twirly and the Dwarf looked down from the balcony, saw her, and came thundering down to say hello. I gritted my teeth over a recalcitrant subjunctive and tried to ignore the sound of three voices pouring out machine-gun Spanish. Then my brain caught up with my ears, and I looked up. There was Helena, declaiming passionately in fluent Latin American. The speech was way beyond my comprehension, but I understood enough to recognize a linguist when I heard one.

'Where did you learn your Spanish?' I asked when she came over to the teapot.

'Bolivia,' she said simply. 'I spent a year there with a family when I was sixteen.'

As my jaw hit the table she turned back to her fellow-pilgrims.

It should have been a dilemma. With one sentence she'd convinced me that she was worth knowing, but I'd vowed not to spend time with transient pilgrims. Sadly, my self-control isn't what it might be. The dilemma died still-born. Twirly and the Dwarf had hardly left her when I went over and said, 'Would you tell me something about Bolivia?' in my best German. Not the kind of sentence you learn at GCSE.

She looked puzzled again. 'What do you want to know?'

I shrugged. 'Whatever you think is worth telling.'

An hour later I'd discovered that there was a river beneath the trees where she used to go swimming, that the people she'd stayed with were as dear to her as her own family, that she'd arranged the placement through a schools exchange scheme, that she spoke no Spanish when she got there, and that she hated machismo but loved cows. (Strange but true.) By my reckoning I was about ten seconds away from being completely bewitched. Lucky escape, I thought as self-preservation reasserted itself with a chill along my spine. How many times are you going to get yourself hurt? Don't do it again!

Yeah right.

I made sure I sat well away from her at tea, chatting determinedly with Sylvia. Afterwards I washed up, and tried to concentrate on knives and forks and ignore the fact that she was just round the corner. Twirly and the Dwarf were back by the fire, with Twirly blowing random noises on a battered descant recorder. I'd just wiped the last dish and was trying to convince myself that I really did want to stick to my vow when Sylvia looked into the kitchen and said, 'Do you want to play the trombone for us?'

'Do you want to listen?'

They wanted to listen.

I stood beside the fireplace and put the trombone together. Sylvia sat at the table, smoking a cigarette and blowing the smoke tactfully away from us. Twirly and Dwarf were in the most comfortable arm-chairs. Helena sat with her back to the wall just beside me, eyes shut. I blew a few quiet warm-up notes, then looked at my audience.

'What do you want to hear?'

Twirly waved an airy hand. 'Oh, something fun.'

I gave them my special version of *Waltzing Matilda*, staring slow and solemn and kicking into a fast Dixieland tempo for 'You'll come a-waltzing . . .', then decided that I was in the mood for tranquillity, and switched into *Summertime*. The Spaniards lost interest as soon as the tempo slowed. I was about to compensate with another fast number when I glanced at Helena. Her head was back, her eyes still shut, and she was swaying in time to the music, her shoulders jerking with every blue note I struck. Unless you're a musician who's used to fast-moving street audiences, you can't imagine the power of such a moment. My trombone is my passion and my music's my voice. Both mattered to her, so she mattered to me. I went round *Summertime* three times, improvising as well as I'd ever done in my life, and I would have gone round again; but Twirly shifted uneasily in his chair and I brought the piece to a reluctant close.

'Now play something fast,' he said. Possibly he meant it gratefully.

Helena shook her said. 'Play something slow.'

'Fast!' agreed the Dwarf, putting his feet up on the hearth.

I gave them *When the Saints* to keep them quiet, and then I played slow (*Georgia on my Mind*, I think), and that piece was for her. When I finished she smiled at me, eyes far away. I packed up, ignoring requests for more. As soon as I stopped playing I'd realized my peril. Friendship hurt, that was all there was to it. As they sat chatting I fled to bed. Remember the others! I told myself desperately. You can't go through all that again. Better to stay lonely than keep on saying goodbye! I was impressed with my own discipline. The fact that I knew exactly when she came up to the dorm, where she lay down and how many times she rolled over in the night was neither here nor there.

I got up deliberately late the next morning, hoping to avoid yet another parting. It worked, but not the way I'd expected. When I staggered down to breakfast the first thing I saw was

Helena sitting there with Sylvia, happily sipping tea. As I gaped she smiled at me and told me she'd decided to stay an extra day. There was no sign of Twirly and the Dwarf. The three of us had the hostel to ourselves.

There are two versions of what followed: mine and Sylvia's. It took me thirty hours to work out what I was feeling. Sylvia told me later that it took her thirty minutes. When I asked her how she knew she gave me a long-suffering look and said, 'It was the way I couldn't pry you apart with a crowbar.'

'Oh,' I said. I'm quick sometimes.

That morning we sat by the fire and chatted. Helena had picked up the guitar. She strummed the odd chord while we discussed this and that (I could never remember what), just as Marc had done in Belgium. Occasionally we sank into meditative silence, staring into the flames; after a while she'd start singing quietly. She had a beautiful voice. There were all kind of things I knew I should be getting on with – mending, letter-writing, more translation – and none of it mattered. As long as Helena was sitting there companionably, the rest of the world could take a hike.

Clue number one, I missed it completely.

Just before noon a trio of pilgrims crashed into the *refugio* calling excitedly for the priest. When they found he wasn't there they dumped their rucksacks upstairs and made for the fire like old regulars. Two – a Brazilian and his French girl-friend, as we discovered later – melted into a passionate embrace. The third, a small pretty Italian, sat down by us.

'Hi, I'm Elisabeta. Are you the one with the trombone?'

'Yes,' I said cautiously. Her smiled blossomed.

'I've heard about you from so many people! I've been wanting to meet you so much. Tell me, how long were you walking before you reached the Camino?'

I almost swallowed my tongue. Where did that come from? 'Er . . . seven months,' I croaked.

'Mamma mia!' She leaned closer, eyes alight. 'And how did

208

it feel to meet so many people after all that time alone?'

I swallowed the desire to tell her to sod off, and answered as honestly as I knew how. I didn't give a damn what she thought, but Helena was listening, and it was important that she heard the truth. Clue number two bounced off my head without even leaving a mark.

The three were on their way back from Santiago, and knew the hostel and the priest of old. They stayed for lunch, full of exciting stories about what they'd seen. I let it wash over me. I'd been enjoying a tranquil morning, and wasn't particularly happy about the invasion. After lunch I washed up again – a useful defence mechanism – and Helena sat by the fire singing and playing *House of the Rising Sun*. I could feel my fingers itching for the trombone, and it wasn't just bad detergent. After a while I collected the instrument from upstairs.

'Will it bother you if I play?' I asked her quietly. The others were still talking loudly at the table.

'*Quatsch!*' she replied, a wonderful word meaning 'Rubbish!' – I went into the church. A private door led from the *refugio* directly onto a balcony. I set up quickly, warmed up, and let rip into the soaring vault.

The stone walls rang, the statues sang. Somewhere on the other side of the wall I knew that a friend was listening, and I knew that before long she'd come down and join me, and all that mattered was making the best music I ever could for her. I played all the numbers I most loved, the slow, mellow, heart-felt ones, starting with *Ultreia* and moving on through *Stormy Weather*, Tchaikovsky's fifth and *Summertime*, and wherever my consciousness was, it wasn't behind my eyes. Some of me was in the music, rapt and dizzy. Some was in the acoustic. Some was lost in a creative dream, spinning out improvisations. Some was waiting for someone to come.

Then my eyes popped open, and she was there, standing silhouetted in the doorway, looking at me. Even though I'd known she would come I was so shocked I nearly swallowed my mouthpiece. I fluffed a note, recovered, played on, and somehow the magic wasn't broken. Quietly she stepped down onto the balcony, waited until I'd finished, then asked, 'Am I bothering you?'

'I hoped you'd come,' I answered. She walked down the steps into the nave, sat in a pew and folded her hands, listening. As I started to play I saw her dreadlocked head lift, straining towards the notes. Then my eyes closed again.

After a while the others joined us. The Latin Lovers stood in silence, hand in hand. Elisabeta put a gentle hand between my shoulder-blades, stepped back, started dancing. I couldn't have cared less. I was playing for a friend. It wasn't until I was empty, drained of strength and emotion, that I finally lowered the trombone and leant on it. Little sparks were flashing before my eyes. Silently Elisabeta came up, gave me an enormous hug and a kiss. The Latin Lovers touched me gently, one on each shoulder, eyes shining. I smiled wanly and watched them go. Slowly Helena stood, walked back up the stairs, came towards me, hugged me, and though the hug might not have lasted five minutes it certainly felt like it. My chin fitted nicely on her shoulder, I noticed in bemusement. It was a long time before we went back into the warmth.

Clue number three was starting to dawn.

I celebrated the best improvisation of my life by falling asleep at the table. Climbing mountains may be hard work, but it's nothing to a serious bit of jazz. Between them the others managed to wake me and steer me bedwards, and there I remained for a couple of hours, dead to the world. I awoke refreshed just before dark (the sign of a true jazz player), wandered down into the living room, and saw that Helena wasn't there.

She'll be in the chapel, I thought calmly; and she was. She was leaning on the balcony, looking down on the nave. She turned her head, and her face lightened, though she didn't smile.

'I was just going for a walk,' I said. 'Want to come along?'

Then she smiled. 'Okay.'

The breeze was cold, blowing strong over the endless fields. We stood staring westwards for a while, and again I've no idea what we were talking about. Suddenly she shivered. Without even thinking about it, and certainly without stopping to wonder whether it would be welcome, I put my arm round her. She leaned her head on my shoulder, and we stood there for a long time. Finally I let go. We walked on. A dozen paces later I reached out and took her hand, and this time my heart was in my mouth. Her fingers closed around mine. Our faces were too chilled to smile, but I saw how her eyes shone. It was a long while before we turned to the *refugio*. Before I turned in that night I moved my bedding onto the mattress next to hers. Again, I didn't even doubt it would be welcome. When she came up later she smiled and kissed my cheek. We fell asleep holding hands.

Clue number four. I was almost there.

The next day was hard. She'd decided to stay, but with every hour that passed she grew more restless. She'd only walked from Roncesvalles, and she was itching to push on, just as I'd been in my first month. The mere thought of parting made me miserable. I'd said goodbye so many times, and those farewells had been hard enough; what would this one be like? Within twenty-four hours she'd be gone, and I'd be missing her, but there was no choice. I'd never keep up.

It tormented me all day. I think she knew it. She vanished for most of the day, and when we did meet in the church the trust and comfort of yesterday were gone.

'There's a problem,' I said.

She looked at me warily.

'You're going tomorrow. I want to come with you, but I'm too tired to keep up. Could you do a few days at half speed?'

She shook her head, but in doubt, not negation.

'I don't know. I'm so restless at the moment, I just want to walk and walk. I'm sorry.'

'Okay,' I said quietly. It was a death-knell. 'Want to come for a walk?'

She shook her head again, and this time it was *no*. I left her there, and walked through the muddy streets alone, steeling myself for the goodbye.

When I came back she was sitting by the fire, playing a German pop song to herself, and a white-haired Spaniard was standing over her, lecturing her. She appeared to be listening with about half an ear. As soon as she saw me she threw me a smile. The speaker – short, burly, unshaven – kept on declaiming. Helena told me afterwards that it was a point-for-point analysis of the philosophy of Carlos Castaneda. My Spanish wasn't that fluent, and in any event he hardly seemed the most interesting person in the room. I leant on the mantel-piece. She leant over and hugged my leg. After a while Julio left us in peace and went to bother Sylvia. She smiled at him with the invincible friendliness of one whose Spanish was even more rudimentary than mine, and let it all flow over her.

There didn't seem to be much to say. Helena was leaving, and I was staying, and that was that. We sat in silence, enjoying the closeness. After a while my legs grew tired and I moved to the chair beside her. She reached for the guitar and started picking out the theme tune to *The Piano*, but every time she got so far she lost the melody. My notebook was lying on the table. Idly I reached out, tore off a sheet, sketched in a musical stave and started writing out the tune for her. When it was done I handed it over. She looked at it and smiled straight into my eyes. My heart did a backspring and I felt my own smile grow warm. At that moment a little messenger ran up my spine, knocked on the back of my conscious and handed a message to Mission Control.

It went like this: *legs to brain. Normal rules suspended. If she goes, we go.*

My smile grew warmer. Reality was dawning all over me, and telling me that whatever happened before, watching

Helena walk away and not breaking my back trying to keep up was not an option. Clue number five. Like I said, I'm quick sometimes.

PART 10

The Camino: Helena to Santiago

'‘Enceforward, evermore.’ (Kipling, *The Service Man*)

Helena's German. I'm British.

She was nineteen. I was twenty-seven.

She wanted to arrive before Christmas. I wanted to be there at New Year's Eve.

She was fit. I was knackered.

Sometimes it's best not to think too hard.

We walked together through muddy fields swept with rain and sleet, past little farming villages with concrete streets and choked gutters, with the ridge of the high plateau (the *meseta*) slowly shortening the horizon. Sometimes we went in silence, looking around at the cold winter scenery. From time to time out eyes met, and we smiled. There's no describing the effect of a smile like that; it made me feel like a god. Sometimes we talked the miles away. We discussed anything: travel and travellers, British attitudes to Germany ('What is it about 1966?' she asked), Bolivian attitudes to racism, the Hamlet adverts, children's fiction, Kipling, Goethe. The only thing we didn't discuss was the relationship. We knew that somewhere not so very far away, separation was looming. We had our own timetables to keep. Each day I woke up wondering: is it goodbye? And each day I answered myself: not yet.

The magic lasted ten days, from the fields of la Rioja over the back of the *meseta* and into the province of Leon, ninety-nine kilometres as the pilgrim staggers. In Burgos we were hit by a snow-storm, and spent two nights shivering in the coldest *refugio* I've ever suffered. We climbed into the *meseta* through ankle-deep snow, our feet sodden and aching, longing for hot water. None of the *refugios* was heated, few had kitchens, and half the villages we crossed seemed shut up for the winter: clusters of mud-brick houses shedding straw, doors and windows blinded with rolled steel shutters. If I hadn't had my camping stove with me it would have been unbearable. Helena came down with a cold. Just as she was shaking it off, I caught it. We lived for a week on lemons.

The trail was almost empty. Twice we met a small, incomprehensible Italian pilgrim who seemed eternally angry and ate so much garlic that even we smelled it: the Garlic Gnome. Once we met an English chef, walking back from Santiago. He was broke, so we bought him enough food for three, and he cooked us the best chilli of my life. Just short of Sahagun we came across another Italian, silver-haired and permanently smiling, with the worst blisters in history. He'd been laid up in the hostel for three days. As soon as he was fit he took off, vowing to cover forty kilometres that day. He managed it, and spent the next three days recovering. He'd been doing that since Roncesvalles. It wasn't the last time we saw him.

There were bad times. We were tired, we were cold, we were still half strangers: whole days went by when we hardly spoke a word and we both almost wished we were alone. There were good times, when the friendship and the smiles blossomed: sitting by a river watching the leaves drift downstream, building a snow-pilgrim in the blizzard in Burgos, joking about trivia, discussing philosophy and freedom. We went slowly, though she found it frustrating, and those who passed us brought news of Sylvia, making her slow way onwards a couple of days behind us. We left her messages in every guest-book we found,

'For Whale Snail from the Snailettes'. Sometimes there were letters for us from those further ahead: Bastian left me a note in Burgos, Mélanie and Beatriz in Sahagun, Sandra left several for me and Sylvia. (They'd met outside Pamplona.) The background to our love story was a community of seekers walking towards the west, leaving messages and love for one another. It was only background. One thing was important: being together while we could.

After ten days together we reached the town of Sahagun in the province of Leon, and stopped in the municipal hostel for lunch and to discuss our plans. There was another *refugio* six miles further on. She'd thrown off her cold and was raring to go. I was sniffling, feverish and drained of energy. We sat there trying not to argue, and it was almost as if we were enemies. She needed to go on, it was clear in ever line of her. I needed to stop. Quite suddenly I knew with cold clarity that it was time to say goodbye.

I fell silent, staring into nothing. She looked at me for what seemed like a long time, then said quietly, 'I think it's time for us to separate.'

I nodded, cold, ill, unhappy. 'I know. Can we go for a coffee before you head on?'

She nodded, warily, and led the way down the stairs. All the affection was gone, like shutting the door on a furnace. We walked down the street in silence, found a café, ordered a cocoa each. I knocked mine back and ordered another. I was chilled to the bone. She looked at me silently. I couldn't read her gaze. She opened her mouth to speak, shut it again. I waited. My brain was numb.

'What will you do?' she asked at last, awkwardly. I shrugged.

'Slow down. Rest when I can. Get to Santiago for New Year. You?'

She smiled sadly. 'Go fast. I want to be with my family in Frankfurt for Christmas.' And then, 'I'm really glad I met you. You're the first person I've spent so much time with since I set off travelling.' She'd been backpacking around since the summer.

A tiny corner of warmth grew in my heart. 'Me too. I can't work out if it was short or long, but – it was good being with you.'

She smiled, and a little more of my heart started to thaw.

'What will you do afterwards?' I asked. Very slowly, an idea was forming.

'I don't know. I want to travel some more, maybe go down to Athens, or maybe start studying in Berlin. I don't know. How about you?'

'Not sure. It all seems so far away. Back to London to start with. I've got friends there.' I paused, shrugged, crossed my fingers and took the plunge. 'And there are flights to Frankfurt, too.'

At that moment the juke-box came to life, and Whitney Houston started singing *I will always love you*.

She looked at me gently. 'You're too romantic. I might not be in Frankfurt. I might be in Berlin.'

Another shrug. 'There's flights to Berlin as well. Europe's small. I'll find you.'

And the warmth came back like a furnace door opening.

The rest of that afternoon was a happy daze. We wandered around Sahagun looking at the ruins of its Benedictine monastery, staring into bookshops, holding hands and laughing as though all our doubts had been resolved. Somehow there was no question of her going on that day. We walked back to the hostel, and bumped into Sylvia on the stairs. She'd hitch-hiked across the *meseta* to avoid the snow, and picked up two other pilgrims on the way: Phil from France, and Juan the Catalan. The reunion was so joyous we probably looked as though we were on drugs. We sat and chatted far into the night, catching up on ten days' gossip. When I went to bed the ladies were still talking, watching a mouse help itself to the remains of the day's bread.

Helena's rucksack was on the bunk next to mine. As she came to fetch her toothbrush I stopped her for a second.

'I've got a present for you.' I held it out to her: the little ivory elephant that I'd found in the mud above Roncesvalles. 'There's a saying in English: elephants never forget. This is just to remind you that I'll be thinking of you.' She folded her hand over mine and held it there for a long moment. Then she went to brush her teeth.

When she came back she looked down at me and said, 'I've got a present for you, too. I was in Portugal, wondering what to do. I decided to buy a mountain bike and ride home, but I couldn't find a bike shop. Then I had to go and meet a friend. While I was waiting at the bus stop I saw this on the pavement. It's my lucky charm. I want you to have it.' And she dropped a little gold heart into my hand. For a second I gaped. A heart? Did she mean it? Then she added, 'It's a heart. Sometimes I'm romantic too.'

She left early the next morning, having been too restless to sleep. I have her a hug on the *refugio* steps, croaked 'See you later' and watched her walk away, tall and buoyant. As she turned the corner she looked back and waved. I was still watching long after she was gone. Will I see her again? I wondered. The heart was hanging on a chain round my neck. I held it tight for comfort. Will I? There was no way of knowing.

I went back upstairs in time to see my entire week's food disappearing into Phil's rucksack. 'Oh,' he said. 'I thought you'd gone.'

'So I see.'

He had the grace to look embarrassed.

The four of us spent the day in Sahagun. For once it was sunny: I sat in a sheltered plaza, soaking up warmth and lemon-juice. Sylvia sat with me, occasionally vanishing, to return five minutes later beaming and carrying a cigarette. For a while Phil and Juan joined us, sipping beer. Juan was a small, neatly-built man with long dark hair, a sharp nose and bright eyes.

In the summer he worked as a mountain guide in the Pyrenees, and in the winter he went walking. Phil was short, shaggy and bloodshot, the most nervous character I've ever met. His fingers and straggly beard were stained with nicotine, his boots and socks were holed, he chewed his nails, and he had a permanent twitch. Sylvia had been with him for three days, and already her motto was '*Tranquilo*, Phil . . .' He'd walked from Le Puy. His money had run out in la Rioja, and he lived by begging. By a bizarre coincidence, Juan's money had also run out in la Rioja. When the church bells started ringing for Mass, and the burghers of Sahagun began to file past in their Sunday best (furs included), Phil and Juan stubbed out their cigarettes and made their way to the church door. They stood there like statues, holding out their cockle-shells, and as we watched in awe they made enough to live on for a week. Phil's first move was to buy us all a beer. He wouldn't take 'No' for an answer. I began to understand where the money had gone.

'I've never met a pilgrim beggar before,' I said to Sylvia, impressed. She gave me a funny look.

'Yes, you have.'

'Eh?'

'Where do you think my cigarettes came from?'

'Oh.' Calmly she told me that her money had run out before she even reached Roncesvalles. She'd been living on charity ever since. I'd never met anyone with literally no money before. Once, when I asked her if she had twenty-five pesetas (ten pence), she laughed at me. and yet, trusting to charity, she'd survived. I couldn't believe it in this day and age; but it was true.

She and I left together late the next morning. Phil and Juan had set off early, loudly psyching each other up. We ambled along a brand-new gravel path, laid specially for the Jubilee year, ludicrously white against the muted browns of the countryside. Soon after lunch we reached Bercianos, the next *refugio*, and by unspoken consent dropped our rucksacks and went inside. It was a beautiful old building standing at one end of a concrete village, next door to the crumbling ruins of an adobe church. I took one look at the deep, warm beds and decided to stay. I was just testing the mattresses when a scream rang out.

I shot from the room like a startled pheasant. 'What? What?'

Sylvia's head appeared round a door. 'Ben, there's a *bathtub*!' I've never seen such joy in a human face.

'I take it you're staying, then.'

'Silly question.'

She started rummaging in cupboards, looking for a gas-bottle to link to the boiler. I strolled to the village store and did the shopping: bread, *chorizo*, cheese, and (a rare luxury) half a dozen eggs. When I got back Sylvia was standing in the common-room, looking down at the guest book with a curious smile on her lips.

'Hello?'

She shoved the book towards me. I opened it with racing heart. The handwriting leapt out at me. '*Achtung! Snail mail!*' Helena had passed that way, and left a note to let us know she was thinking of us. She signed off: '*I'm writing slower and slower, hoping I'll see you come round the corner . . . ¡Hasta pronto!*'

I felt better than I had done all day.

December was almost upon us, and I could feel myself winding down. It was less than three hundred miles from Sahagun to Santiago, three hundred miles with barely a hill to climb. I knew that I could get there on New Year's Eve. Even going at a true snail's pace, I was going to make it. Somehow the knowledge set me apart from the other pilgrims. They arrived with steam billowing from their nostrils, all eager for the trail, left at the crack of dawn with cries of '*¡Ultreia!*', marched far into the night. Among them was Mister Blister, David the Italian, who joined us in Bercianos, shot off the next morning, and then spent yet another three days in Leon having his blisters treated. I couldn't be bothered any more. I'd been walking for eight months, and the end was in sight at last.

Meeting Sylvia was the best thing that could have happened. She was thirty-two, small and round-shouldered, with a neat, precise stride, tiny feet and a beautiful smile. While I was in Belize, she was working as a nurse in Vienna. Just after I came home, her boyfriend died of a heart attack in front of her. A month later her nursing unit was downsized, and she lost her job. She didn't give up. She went looking for work with the intensity of a shark in a swimming-pool, and found it. A month later *that* unit was downsized too. She attempted suicide. It didn't work. Most of her money went on health-care. By the time the dust settled she had no home, few friends, and no reason save stubbornness to go on living.

She packed her rucksack and hitch-hiked her way into France. Even if travel doesn't cure me, she thought, I can be depressed in different scenery. Somewhere in the Massif Central she heard about the Camino for the first time. The idea intrigued her, but she had her dog with her, and she doubted – rightly – whether he'd be welcome in the *refugios*. A week later the dog died. Two days after that, to her own surprise, she found herself in the archway of Roncesvalles abbey, just in time to take a team photo as I came down from the pass with the pilgrim family. A bewildered looking Austrian in an orange jumper? I knew she'd looked familiar.

She was the ideal walking partner. She liked going slowly. She liked the idea of reaching Santiago for New Year's Eve. She positively approved of spending hours each day sitting in cafés talking trivia. She didn't mind listening to me going on and on about Helena. She had a delightful grasp of languages (I still treasure her description of a Spanish baptism as '*chico con agua*'). She even helped me with my German. How many pilgrims manage to pick up an Austrian accent in Spain? The number just went up by one . . . It was astonishing how quickly we got used to one another. When we left Sahagun we agreed to spend 'a couple of days' together. It was a week before we even thought of discussing the situation. We decided to stay together a little longer. Christmas was looming before the question came up again. By then, there didn't seem much point in splitting up.

After a while, we found we were fashionable. Other pilgrims had seen the snail messages that Helena and I had left, and wanted to know what was happening. As soon as they heard of the League of Pilgrim Snails, they wanted to join. Snails started springing up in other hostel books, drawn by strange hands, sometimes even scratched in the roadside with the legend '¡Arriva los caracoles!' – 'Onward, snails!'. Somehow Sylvia didn't find the nickname Whale Snail very flattering; between us we fixed on the name Sister Snail. Helena, far ahead and still accelerating, became the Rocket Snail. We named Phil the Cannibal Snail (everyone knows what the French eat), Juan the Mountain Snail, David the Blister Snail. There was no end to our snailiness. It kept us happy for hours.

Another Snail joined the Club in Bercianos. His name was André, a French priest who'd walked from Switzerland. Sylvia and I were sitting with a cup of tea late in the afternoon when the door flew open and a tall, smiling madman threw his arms wide in greeting. Then he shut his eyes and *waltzed* into the room, humming a little tune. He was wearing blue Gore-Tex salopettes, a brown checked shirt and immense boots, which scattered mud all over the floor as he spin-turned towards us.

We exchanged a look.

'Hola,' said Sylvia with a somewhat strained smile. 'I'm Sylvia. And you are . . . ?'

'André.' He stood with his arms outstretched under the dark ceiling-lamp (it only came on when the street-lights did), eyes still closed, head back, then relaxed and turned a brilliant smile on us. 'Pleased to meet you.'

It's hard to reply to an introduction like that.

He spent three days with us. After one afternoon we loved him. We'd never met anyone so full of energy. After two more days I wanted to murder him. He jumped out of bed at six in the morning and walked around the *refugio* singing. If I'd been one scrap less weary I would have shot him. With a silencer. Luckily for us all, sleep was more important than homicide.

His theology was fascinating. He couldn't bear silence, so when the two of us had nothing to say he'd fill in the gaps with stories of his own – such as how he cheated in his university Hebrew exams, how he only really became a priest because it was more respectable than being a youth worker, and how he'd just been fired for extolling the merits of Buddhism in his Sunday school class. (Yet another pilgrim looking for his future on the Camino.) Sylvia had been brought up as a stern Protestant, and though she'd found her own version of spirituality long before, the knowledge lingered. She loved arguing with Catholics. I spent one afternoon listening in complete awe as they battled over the contrasting meanings of *agapa* and *eros* in 1 Corinthians. I suppose it was appropriate on the pilgrim trail.

Then we reached the city of Leon, swathed in Christmas decorations and ringing with piped carols (in English), and I stopped caring. Helena had passed through the *refugio* four days before, and left me a two-page letter so full of memories and shared jokes that I spent all evening laughing, to the utter bewilderment of all comers. André vanished into town, exploring. Sylvia and I breathed out a sigh of relief. Within half an hour he was back, bouncing like a Labrador puppy. He'd just been to phone home. He'd left his wallet in the phone-box. A '*bella chica*' had stood guard over it until he returned. She'd invited him to meet her in a tapas bar later that evening. He spent the next hour or so in the gents' showers, dancing and humming in front of the mirror, then dressed with exquisite care and went clattering off down the steps, singing at the top of his voice.

It was the last we saw of him. He didn't come back that night, and the next day we were gone. But we were to hear from him again. He reached Santiago before we did, and left us a letter in the pilgrims' office. It wasn't a long message: I made it, hope you did, *buen camino*. He signed it 'André – the Fiesta Snail.'

The strange thing about the League of Pilgrim Snails was that, no matter how popular it became in concept, very few pilgrims ever joined it in reality, for the simple reason that becoming a fully-fledged (fully-shelled?) snail meant *slowing down*. Somewhere deep in the subconscious of almost every pilgrim we met were burned the words 'Faster! Faster!'. The Blister Snail was a perfect example. Every three days with unfailing regularity we found him limping around a *refugio*, feet wrapped in a terrifying assortment of bandages. Two days thereafter he'd pass us in a cloud of dust, shouting strange Italian war-cries. On the third day we'd catch him, Sylvia would treat his blisters, and the merry cycle would begin all over again. There were many like him. Half the pilgrims we met seemed intent on breaking the record for the fastest transit to Santiago. Almost nobody seemed to appreciate the value of going slow.

We met the only exception just beyond Leon, in another huddled farming village half-shut down for the winter. The hostel was a beautiful old house with creaking wooden floorboards, an immense internal courtyard, and a well-equipped kitchen into which Sylvia flung herself with enthusiastic chirps. She talked to saucepans as most women talk to their pets: the lack of a dog was starting to tell. She was just telling a frying-pan what a fun time they were going to have together when we heard a diffident cough. There in the doorway was a pale-faced young man in tattered jeans, a suede-look jacket, and pumps.

'Excuse me, is this the *refugio*?' he asked in American-accented Spanish. Possibly he thought it was the madhouse.

'*Si, senor*,' we chorused. Our Spanish was improving. His face lit up, and he swung the smallest rucksack I've ever seen off his back and onto the floor. It was about the size of a margarine tub.

'Are you a pilgrim?' I asked in my best BBC Castilian. He grinned.

'Yep,' he answered in English. 'And boy, my feet are killing me. Mind if I sit down?'

He hadn't been on the Camino for long.

'Help yourself. Where did you start today?'

He sank into the chair and stretched out his legs with a sigh of relief. 'Damn, that's good! Set off from Leon, and I've never walked so far in my life. Spent a bit of time with a Spaniard, but he wanted to race. Does everyone on this damn' pilgrimage go so fast?'

Sylvia and I exchanged glances.

'Allow me to tell you about snails,' I said smoothly.

He didn't take much persuading.

His name was Jason, a twenty-year-old American Jew who was studying English in Washington State. He'd just spent a semester in Salamanca. The end-of-semester exams were due to start the following week, so as any true scholar would, he'd taken advantage of the revision leave to do a little exploring, and decided to walk a section of the Camino from Leon to the Galician border: the only pilgrim we ever met who wasn't intending to reach Santiago.

'I didn't realize you were supposed to arrive somewhere. Is it important?' he asked.

We thought about it.

'No, not really.'

He relaxed.

'Thought not.'

He was a Snail after my own heart. The next morning he stayed in bed until ten, shambled along with us to the next village (three miles at least), spotted a café and said 'I'll catch you up later.' It hardly seemed polite to abandon him so soon, so we joined him, and sat there gossiping until the early afternoon. We made eight miles that day, and again the next. On the third day we stretched ourselves and did almost twelve, a Herculean effort, arriving knock-kneed after a wicked fifty-metre climb, but we rewarded ourselves with an easy day the next day: a five-mile stroll took us to a tiny hostel in a village with one grass-grown street and a village green flooded with sunlight. We took one look at it and decided to stay. Ahead of us we could see the mountains of Leon looming, the very border of Galicia, and we were in no hurry to get there.

It was in that sunny hamlet that I heard my quote of the millennium. We'd been talking in English ever since Jason turned up, discussing everything from EU taxes to Monty Python humour, and the sheer joy of using my own language ran away with me. I was raving about the *refugio* where I'd met Helena and Sylvia. Suddenly my grasp of adjectives failed me. I could think of a dozen German ones and not a single English one, and I was damned if I was going to ask Sylvia to translate. At last light dawned.

'It was the dog's bollocks.'

Jason looked politely confused. 'The dog's what?'

'*Bollocks*. The dog's bollocks. It means, very good.' Short pause. 'You do know what bollocks are, don't you?'

Longer pause. 'Not as such . . .'

I explained. Sylvia was watching with interest.

'Ah.' He nodded thoughtfully. 'Ah.' Another pause. 'No. No, I'm afraid we don't have bollocks in the United States.'

It was worth walking two thousand miles just to hear it.

It took us a while to christen him. My suggestion of the

Bollockless Snail was firmly rejected, but nothing else seemed to fit until we looked at his rucksack, leaning between ours in yet another café. It looked like a joke.

'What kind of snail doesn't even have a house on its back?' asked Sylvia idly. She'd just cadged another cigarette, and was leaning against the wall in deep contentment.

Jason and I got it at the same moment. 'A slug!' we chorused; and the Pilgrim Slug was named.

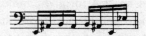

On our last day together we climbed from the town of Rabanal del Camino into the wind-torn heights of the mountains of Leon. I was in a better mood than I had been since Leon: there had been snail-mail in the *refugio*, and in the church that night we'd heard three monks singing a plain-song vespers. We took our time, pausing to look back over the endless plain, sheltering from the wind behind ruined walls. It was good to be back in the hills, but there was something heart-rending about it nonetheless. Village after village stood empty and gutted, skeletal roofs open to the sky. It wasn't hard to believe that Spain is the poor cousin of Europe. After an hour the mist closed in, shutting us off in a cold blind world. Slowly the slope grew more gentle. Sylvia and Jason were behind me, cracking jokes about the Holocaust as only Germans and Jews can. Suddenly a shape loomed out of the mist: a mound, an immense pole, a cross. We'd known it was near, but still it was a shock: the legendary *cruz de hierro*, the iron cross marking the highest point on the Camino in Spain, the most famous landmark on the way.

It was a disappointment. On one side of the mound was a car-park. On the other was a visitor centre, closed for the winter. A handful of tourists were scrambling on the mound, pointing video cameras at one another. As we hove into view, all lenses turned to record our ascent. The ground was foul with litter. It wasn't a place to linger. I stood on the mound and played a quick fanfare, but my heart wasn't in it. We hurried on. It was the most disappointing moment of the whole walk.

That night we slept in a restored farmhouse high up in the hills. There was no electricity. There was running water, but only in the stream outside. Warmth came from a wood-fired stove, and the hundred and one cats who crawled all over our bedding. The wind howled through chinks in the walls, and we sat by candle-light and listened to our host, who'd walked the Camino twenty years before, got this far, decided he liked it, and dedicated his life to serving pilgrims. It was the kind of night I'd had time and again in the past eight months. Suddenly I felt dizzy. It all felt so normal that I was astonished. I was sitting in a stone hut with a Spanish idealist as if I did this all the time. Well, I *did* do this all the time. It seemed more natural to be here than to think of myself back in Britain, surrounded by warmth and luxury. This was where I belonged, with these people, with these beliefs. This was my world.

I'd come a long way in eight months.

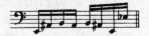

The mountains dropped down to a green plain full of rivers, and rose to the heights once more. Four days after passing the Iron Cross, Sylvia and I climbed wearily through a howling gale to the peak of O Cebreiro, the gateway into Galicia. From there the trail wound across snow-blind moors, down stony tracks lined with gorse, across verdant pastures, through stands of oak and gum-trees (a gift from the paper industry), and onwards to Santiago. It was a beautiful land, greener and hillier than anything I'd seen since the Pyrenees, enriched with scattered villages of stone and slate, sudden bright rivers, luxurious *refugios*, friendly faces. No matter how many pilgrims passed by – and the tales of the Jubilee Year were terrifying – the locals always had room for one more '¡Hola! ¡Buenos dias! ¡Buen camino!' Every day brought more pilgrims, Spaniards on short holidays hurrying the last hundred kilometres to Santiago. Every one of them had a story to tell. Every village we passed was a maze of temptations. Once, I would have spent a month exploring. Now, I went by in a daze. I'd been walking for almost nine months, and the end was drawing near.

The days went by as always, planning, shopping, walking and stopping. We met with friendship and generosity; we met with selfishness and spite. We met with a one-eyed pirate shop-keeper who asked me if I had a girlfriend, and when I answered 'Sort of' said, 'Go home and f**k her senseless, that's what women want.' Instead I thought about her, talked about her, wrote her a poem, rejoiced when I found her snail-mails, sulked and grumbled when I didn't. Business as usual; but behind it lay something new. The end of the walk was in sight. A stage of my life was almost over. It was time to look forwards, beyond Santiago, and it was time to look back, and remember. The other pilgrims weren't important any more. I needed the time for myself.

I'd changed. It was only when I started re-reading my diary that I realized how much. I left Canterbury nervous, paranoid, grief-stricken, neurotic, ready to cling to the slightest smile or attack the slightest threat. I didn't know if the walk was possible, if I'd survive physically and mentally, if I'd manage to make friends on the way, if I'd dare to carry on busking when it started going badly. As I looked over the map of my travels in the quiet of a refugio kitchen a hundred faces flashed before my eyes: Marc the harpist, my god-family in Leuven, the corpse in the Bruges-Ghent canal, the bands in Belfort and le Mont-Dore, Charles the Flatulent, Ant and his drunken crew, Em, Tom, Sylvia, the Snails – and Helena. Every face told me anew that I'd done it. I'd survived, and I'd left my fears behind me. When I looked back to the spring day I'd crossed the Channel with my merry band of smugglers, it seemed that three years had passed. I'd crammed the wealth of a lifetime into nine short months. I couldn't believe how rich I'd become.

I was hooked on the lifestyle I'd discovered. I didn't know what lay beyond Santiago, but it was going to be adventure. I'd lifted one corner of a curtain hiding the most fascinating continent on Earth. I wasn't going to stop until I'd seen it all. Throughout December a verse of Kipling's poetry had been rattling round my head:

> 'Tommy' you was when it began,
> But, now that it is o'er,
> You shall be called 'The Service Man'
> 'Enceforward, evermore.

I'd become someone new, and I was going to stay that way.

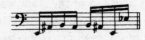

The miles unravelled behind us, and Santiago was in sight. I could feel the triumph growing inside me, but one question remained unanswered: what about Helena? Meeting her had been the greatest gift the walk had brought me. Would I ever see her again? Sometimes I thought of her smile, her touch, the messages she'd left me on the way, and thought 'Of course!' Sometimes I thought of the age gap, the distance, the practicalities of a long-range relationship, and thought 'No.' I rang her once on the German Christmas (24 December), and we chatted for an hour, as happy as could be. She said she'd call me before the New Year, and didn't. Paranoia struck. Had she, too, thought of the practicalities? Decided to end things now, before we both got hurt? Every day I waited for the phone to ring, twitching. Every day it rang, with messages from friends and family wishing me a grand finale. Some commented that I sounded odd. No, no, just tired, I assured them, put the phone down, and screamed. Sylvia tried to reassure me. It's just a bad connection, she said. She's staying with friends who don't have a phone. She's lost the number. *She's thinking of you, idiot!* It didn't sink in. Some things just don't.

On 30 December 1999, after nine months and two days on the road, I walked into Santiago de Compostela with Sylvia at my side.

It was the strangest moment of all. I'd been aiming for that city for what felt like a lifetime. I'd talked about it with every friend I'd made. Just as when I took the first step, I'd been expecting a sudden rush of triumph, exaltation, the breaking of some almighty barrier. Just as with the first step, there was nothing. It was one among six million. I couldn't believe I was there.

The Cathedral was buzzing. It's a vast building, towering over the city, but that day it was so crowded that it seemed tiny. We'd arrived on the feast of Santiago *el Menor*, Saint James the Lesser, whose relics were housed next to those of his fellow-Apostle, and the whole of Galicia seemed to have turned out to celebrate. Sylvia and I squeezed into the nave, elbowed and jostled by a thousand visitors, at least half of whom were wearing 'pilgrim' souvenirs, the hats, staves and cockleshells which have been the foundation of Santiago's economy for the last millennium. We watched with numb fascination as a phalanx of brilliantly-clad priests proceeded down the aisle behind the great reliquary. Every local dignitary north of Portugal had a speech to make, from the Archbishop of Santiago to the Prime Minister's spokesman. A team of seven burly priests hauled the legendary two-ton silver censer of Santiago aloft on a colossal pulley, started it swinging and heaved on the ropes until it roared down the nave like an aircraft crashing, gushing smoke and sparks. A quavering priest led the packed congregation through the Lord's prayer. Sylvia and I exchanged a glance and slipped out through a back door. It was way, way too much.

'What's that got to do with our Camino?' she asked, and I

agreed. The Camino was endless fields, long climbs, lonely *refugios*, a community of pilgrims. You could have put every pilgrim we'd met along the way into that nave and they would have been lost in the tumult.

We fled to the pilgrims' office. The streets of Santiago were alive with visitors. It was more massed humanity than I'd seen all year. Even the office was crowded. A dozen proud walkers had made the hundred-mile trek from the Galician border and had come to collect the certificate that proved it. We lined up behind them, still dazed, our credentials clasped in shaking hands. They were covered in stamps from all the hostels we'd visited.

'Next!' Sylvia went first. She handed over the paper. The receptionist looked, nodded, wrote down her name, handed her the certificate, and smiled: the first touch of warmth we'd seen on the production-line. Then it was my turn.

She looked at the credential curiously. I had three, stapled together: one from Canterbury, one from Le Puy, one which Carlos of Estella had given me as a souvenir. She didn't quite know what to make of it.

'Where did you start?'

'Canterbury.'

'On foot?'

'Yes.'

'*¡Madre mia!* How long did it take you?'

'Nine months.'

I heard Sylvia chuckle behind me, and wondered why. The receptionist smiled slowly, turned, and pulled a huge tome off a shelf.

'Would you like to write something in the pilgrims' book? We ask the unusual pilgrims to.'

I took it curiously, sat down, leafed through the pages. Familiar hand-writing leapt out at me, and I called Sylvia over. She put a hand on my shoulder and leant over me, and together we read the testimonies of Bastian, Liesbeth, David the Blister

Snail, André (quoting Buddhism again), and many other friends. They'd found the arrival difficult too. Somehow, that was comforting.

When I closed the book Sylvia pointed to the waiting-room. 'There's something you might want to see,' she said. I was so confused the receptionist had to remind me to take my certificate. Her eyes were kind. She'd seen it all before.

The waiting-room was a little whitewashed cell. Three leather armchairs and a crowded notice-board were its only furnishings. I looked around dopily, and my own name sprang to my eye. An envelope was pinned to the board. For a second my heart jumped, but it wasn't the hand I'd hoped. I took it slowly. More envelopes fell down. All were addressed to me, from Mélanie (I smiled), Joachim (the smile grew broader), André (Sylvia's eyebrows shot up); and, last of all, Helena.

The first letter was from Anne, with whom I'd spent the evening in St Jean Pied-de-Port. She wanted to let me know how her Camino had been, and how much she'd discovered about herself on the way. 'I thought of you often, but I didn't want to write,' she said, and I was touched. I read the others in order, smiling at their good wishes. They'd all felt as I did, somehow flat, disappointed, swallowed by the size and bustle of the city; except for Mélanie, who'd met Eloi and was content. When I'd read them I sat there, turning Helena's letter in shaking hands. I couldn't bring myself to open it. Even though we'd spoken after she wrote it, even though she'd been happy to hear me, I didn't know what to expect.

I'd never dreamed that it could be as good.

Scattered phrases jumped out at me:

I miss you. I thought of you a lot on the Camino . . . You left a hole behind you. But maybe that's the way it has to be, because it was so good to be with you. (And how could we see the light if there were no darkness?) . . . I admire you so much for what you've done. Just the

thought of you and what you're doing gave me strength on the way – that, and the knowledge that there are still great men in the world (greatness isn't always a matter of height...) ... Thank you. You're dear to me.
Helena.

When the shaking stopped, I read it again. It couldn't be true. Had she written all that? I read it for a third time. My heart lurched as I read *that's the way it has to be*. Was that goodbye? But there was laughter bubbling up inside me. I couldn't hold it in. My grin was cracking my face. Sylvia looked at me.

'Good news, then?'

I kissed the letter and jumped up, arms wide. 'Guess.'

It was the beginning.

The thirty-six hours that followed were, quite simply, the best I've ever had. Even though Helena didn't ring, even though I started to hate the sound of the phone going off, it was unbelievable. We left our gear in the pilgrim hostel. I remember the sky was full of seagulls crying, the first I'd heard since Ostend. We went to a restaurant with a pilgrim menu. There we bumped into a friend we'd last seen in Astorga, a Canadian actress and jazz singer, and walked through the streets humming improvised blues. We passed a saxophonist busking in front of the cathedral. Effervescent with happiness, I asked if I could join in. He agreed, allowed me to warm up and then said, 'Do you know *Summertime*?' The next three numbers he suggested were *When the Saints*, *Misty* and *Stormy Weather*, and my happiness as complete. Just as inspiration ran down another old friend passed, an *hospitalero* whom I'd met while walking with Helena. He instantly invited us to join him for a drink, and we sat in a bar by the cathedral for three hours sampling the local specialities of *vino tinto* and octopus. By the time we staggered back to the *refugio* it was very late, we were very drunk, and I was very happy.

The next morning I was still high. The sense of victory was

starting to fill me. I'd reached Santiago, and she'd left me a message! Some days you know you can't lose. I walked up to the Cathedral and asked if I could play the trombone there in between services. A priest passed me on to the organist. He looked surprised, but when I explained that I'd carried the thing four thousand kilometres nothing was too much to ask. He gave Sylvia and me a guided tour of the Cathedral, including the parts where no tourist was ever allowed, stationed me in the Musicians' Balcony above the Portal of Glory, and told me to play whatever I liked. I started with *Ultreia*, soft and mellow, and the echoes drifted around the cathedral like gold. Then I took a deep breath and started *Danny Boy*, Anna's piece, and I was so full of happiness that I had to fight to keep it solemn. Jazzing it up in the Cathedral didn't seem quite the thing . . . I hadn't warmed up. It wouldn't have been right in that atmosphere. All the way through the piece I was aware of the top G looming in the final phrase, the hardest note to hit cleanly on the trombone. I felt my stomach contract, my throat tighten. I can play this, I thought, and with a second to go I relaxed and felt my eyes smiling. I soared up to the note with never a hesitation, hung there for just a second as the echoes rolled and swelled, and in that second two faces flashed before my eyes, Anna and Helena. Both were smiling. I finished off with a simple *rallentando*, and walked out of the Cathedral with my head ten feet in the air.

Then we went back to the *refugio* and slept until the grand finale.

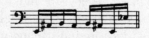

All day long the workers had been busy in the Cathedral square. While we dozed, a vast congregation gathered to watch the Archbishop bid the Holy Year farewell and seal up a small side door, the Holy Portal, until the next Jubilee in 2004. At the same time workmen were erecting stages all across the city, preparing fireworks on the Cathedral roof, building a vast bonfire in the square. TV crews were everywhere, big grey communications vans blocked every street, and the city centre bustled like an anthill.

By the time we arrived at quarter past eleven, the place was as quiet as a grave.

Sylvia and I looked at one another. Surely *mañana* couldn't apply to New Year's Eve? We wandered past enormous scaffolds, towering speaker-systems, batteries of cameras. The streets were empty. Nothing moved except a pair of paramedics, resignedly bending over a comatose drunkard still clutching his bottle of wine. At twenty past the silence was deafening. At twenty-five past the first figures began to appear, quiet, sober, making their way almost stealthily towards the square. Was there a fiesta or not?

At eleven thirty we heard drums.

Suddenly the street was full of dancers. Round the corner there came a whirling scrimmage of jumping figures, laughing and shouting. In their midst half a dozen young hippies stood facing one another, shaking heaven and earth with the music of bongo-drums. Behind them a flautist was playing with glaring ferocity, a guitarist was ripping chords from his instrument, someone was banging a tambourine. They were inaudible. The drums were thundering, voices yelled. The air crackled with electricity.

Then they saw the trombone.

It was Santo Domingo all over again, but louder and friendlier. Two dancers swept up and hugged me, almost making me drop the instrument. Sylvia grabbed the empty case before anyone could kick it, and I found myself in the circle of players with the beat pulsing right through to my bones. The flautist caught my eyes and nodded, mouthed something, and to my astonishment pushed in next to me and started playing *When the Saints* in my ear. I tore into it with raucous enthusiasm, and the dancers cheered. One of the drummers blew sweat off his nose and winked at me. Suddenly the beat changed and Dixieland was hijacked and turned into the *Mission: Impossible* theme. The dance broke down in screams and giggles. It's hard to dance in 5/4 unless you've got two and a half legs.

There wasn't time for more. It was quarter to midnight, and the streets were black with people hurrying towards the main square. We followed the flood, introducing ourselves as we went. The drummers were all students from northern Portugal who'd driven up for the party. When I told them why I was there they gaped. One, a small slim girl with flashing eyes, thrust a bottle into my hand and told me 'Portuguese celebration!': a bottle of Johnny Walker.

The square was packed. At one end a massive figure 1 with a curved base ticked back and forth; underneath it a politician stood making an incomprehensible speech. In the middle of the square firemen in full protective gear stood around the unlit bonfire with flaming torches, waiting for the word. A searchlight played on the Cathedral clock above us. Dark silhouettes moved on the Cathedral roof between ranks of fireworks. More revellers were pouring into the plaza behind us. Three different groups were singing three different tunes. One of the drummers started playing. The others joined in. Heads turned. The beat fit: I started a raucous *Scotland the Brave*. To my delight our entire corner of the plaza started jumping up and down. A TV crew shoved through the press and blinded us with their spotlights. My head was spinning. The words buzzed in my mind. *This is it, this it is, this is it!* I'd dreamed of being in Santiago for the Millennium. I'd sweated blood to do it; and I was there. Triumph fizzed inside me like champagne.

Suddenly silence fell.

'One minute!'

A few wavering voices cheered.

'Thirty seconds!'

Happy New Year! I thought to Helena, my grin growing wider. Hope it's good, wherever you are.

'Fifteen seconds!'

The countdown started.

At ten, it was deafening.

At five it shook the walls.

'Four!'

'Three!'

'Two!'

'One!'

'HAPPY NEW YEAR!!!'

Fireworks whooshed up from the Cathedral roof. Shouts and explosions split the sky. The 1 flipped over, became a 2. The bonfire roared into flame. Everyone was cheering, dancing, kissing. Six stoned drummers hugged me at once. 'Congratulations!' bellowed a voice in my ear. Sylvia was shouting to me, face alight. I couldn't hear the words. I flung my head back, whooped, hurled the trombone into the air, caught it, stood shaking it above my head as fireworks seared the sky behind. I'd done it! Nine months, two and a half thousand miles, and I'd done it! Those were *my* fireworks. That was *my* cheering. I yelled a war-cry that tore the lining off my throat and thrust my trombone skywards again. Victory! Smoke billowed across the square. A Galician piper stood on the Cathedral tower, lit by stabbing searchlights. Everyone was dancing. Sylvia gave me a rib-splitting hug. We stood there staring into each other's face and laughing. The drummers had started up again. Everywhere dark figures moved, spun, whirled against a backdrop of flames. The heat from the bonfire was incredible. The crowd pulled back. Without moving, we found ourselves on the edge of an open space. At once we came together, playing like demons. All around us the dance erupted again.

Slowly the square was emptying. On the far side of the Cathedral a band was starting up. We followed the crowd, dropped into a rolling beat. Reckless fireworks filled my mind. The *Pink Panther* fit that rhythm . . . I started to play. Suddenly the crowd slowed. All around us laughing Spaniards attempted the Pink Panther walk. Drunken voices sang along. We stopped on the Cathedral stairs. The drummers fanned out below me. A conga-line of Panther-dancers wound past, shouting the tune. I played until my ribs ached. The square below was a sea of faces looking up, laughing, cheering. Slowly the dance wound down. 'Encore!' they shouted. 'More! More!'

'More!' shouted the drummers. 'Play us a tune!'

There was only one tune. I hadn't played it since Belgium, but there are some pieces you can't forget. They recognized it the instant I started. The crowd cheered. The drums thundered. Sylvia threw back her head and laughed. The Cathedral walls shook to the sound of singing. A thousand Spanish voices joined in the chorus:

'I – did – it – myyyyyy wayyyyyy . . .'

That was *my* piece. I reckoned I'd earned it.

POSTSCRIPT

I spent four more days in Spain. Sylvia was with me. She'd decided to walk the Camino all the way back to Rome, but she wanted to see me off first.

I was flying to London. On 2 January I'd rung Helena. 'What's wrong with your phone?' she asked me at once. She'd been trying to get through all week, but somehow, it hadn't worked. It was good to know; but when I asked 'Can I come and see you?' she answered 'No. Not yet.'

'Later?'

'I don't know.'

It was a quiet few days. I spent most of my time writing postcards and talking with Sylvia in a hostel outside Santiago. There didn't seem any point in staying in the city. The place wasn't important. What mattered was that we'd arrived. We sat in the winter sunshine and talked about the things we'd seen, the ways we'd changed. We'd both found a new life on our travels. Neither of us could go back.

On the 5 January we caught a taxi to the airport. She gave me a quick hug and left me at the departure gate. I watched her walk away with the neat stride I knew so well, then went through to the lounge. It was shockingly clean, antiseptic and heartless. The aeroplane was worse. I felt that I was being kidnapped by aliens. My world was down below, the wide fields, the cold air, the people ... Two hours later I was in London, crowded in among rush-hour commuters. An hour after that I was ringing Sam and Martin's doorbell, and they came to meet me with nine months' worth of hugs. It was a long time before we even thought of going in. When we did, it was a shock. I looked around the luxuries of a London flat and felt like an alien myself. Was this the world I'd left?

I stayed there for a week, bewildered. Gradually reality asserted itself. I was back for a while at least, and there were things to do, friends to see, money to pay in (I'd raised five thousand pounds on the way), other trips to dream of, presents to buy. Soon it would be Helena's birthday. I scoured the shops looking for something suitable, something private, shared, important. After crossing half the city, I found it in a bookshop two doors down from the flat: two of the children's books we'd discussed as we walked.

I phoned her on her birthday. She seemed to like them.

'Do you want to meet up soon?' I asked.

Her tone of voice said it all.

I stayed in London. There were loose ends to tie up, phone calls to make, people to see. It's not easy, picking up the threads after nine months away.

I waited until everything was sorted.

And *then* I flew to Frankfurt.

THE PACK FROM HELL

One question I was asked time and again on the walk was 'What the **** have you got in that rucksack?' At the time my main reply was 'Too bloody much!', but now that the blisters have healed and my shoulders are responding to treatment, I can at last provide an answer:

One thermal T-shirt
Two Teflon-coated long-sleeved shirts
One lightweight fleece jacket
One pair lightweight walking trousers
One pair trousers with zip-off legs
Four pairs silk boxer shorts
Two pairs thin hiking socks
Two pairs thick wool socks
Woolly hat
Gore-Tex jacket
Waterproof trousers
Gore-Tex lined boots
Moccasins

Mobile phone
Charger for phone
2 small torches
Spare batteries and bulbs
Compact camera
Films galore
Walkman FM radio

Sleeping-bag
Lightweight one-man tent
Trowel and toilet paper
MSR multi-fuel stove
Fuel bottle
Two Trangia pans (one jettisoned in Luxembourg)
Trangia kettle (jettisoned in Luxembourg)
Tea (jettisoned in Luxembourg)
Mug (jettisoned in Luxembourg, replaced on the Camino)
Two spoons
Three lighters
Candle
1-litre aluminium water-bottle
2 2-litre plastic water-bags
Food for up to four days

First aid kit
Sewing kit
Wash-kit and Per-Tex travel towel
Writing paper
Pens
Address book
Maps and guide books (bought on the way and posted
    home)
French and Spanish dictionaries, Spanish grammar
Novels (bought on the way and posted home)

Trombone
2 collecting boxes (emptied into prearranged bank accounts
    at every opportunity)

One day's food generally consisted of bread and cheese or
fruit-cake for breakfast, at 11 a.m., 1 p.m. and 3 p.m.; 100 g
of chocolate and handfuls of dried fruit during the day; at least
two pieces of fresh fruit; 250 g dry weight of pasta, a packet
of soup for sauce, followed by 200 g of chocolate and more

fruit for tea. Kendal Mint Cake and tubes of concentrated milk provided energy in emergencies. Wild boar pâté and local wine were optional extras.

I lost just over three pounds during the walk. It's not a diet which is likely to catch on.

INDEX